The Science of Sherlock Holmes

From Baskerville Hall to the Valley of Fear, the Real Forensics Behind the Great Detective's Greatest Cases

E. J. WAGNER

BICENTENNIAL
1807
WILEY
2007
BICENTENNIAL

John Wiley & Sons, Inc.

Published by John Wiley & Sons, Inc., Hoboken, New Jersey
Published simultaneously in Canada

Wiley Bicentennial Logo: Richard J. Pacifico

Illustration credits: Pages 111–114 from *Engravings Explaining the Anatomy of the Bones, Muscles, and Joints* by John Bell (London, 1794); page 115 from *Report of the Case of John W. Webster: Indicted for the Murder of George Parkman* by George Bemis (Boston, 1850); page 116 from *How to Read Character: A New Illustrated Hand-Book of Phrenology for Students and Examiners with a Descriptive Chart* by Samuel R. Wells (New York, 1873); page 117 (top) from *The Identification Facilities of the FBI* by John Edgar Hoover (Washington, D.C., 1941); page 117 (bottom) by Ira Bradley and Company for *Warren's Household Physician: For Physicians, Families, Mariners, Miners; Being a Brief Description, in Plain Language of Diseases of Men, Women, and Children* by Ira Warren and A. E. Small (Boston, 1891); page 118 from the Catalog of Medical and Surgical Works appended to *A Manual of Medical Jurisprudence and Toxicology* by Henry C. Chapman (Philadelphia, 1893).

For general information about our other products and services, please contact our Customer Care Department within the United States at (800) 762-2974, outside the United States at (317) 572-3993 or fax (317) 572-4002.

Wiley also publishes its books in a variety of electronic formats. Some content that appears in print may not be available in electronic books. For more information about Wiley products, visit our web site at www.wiley.com.

Library of Congress Cataloging-in-Publication Data:

Wagner, E. J.
    The science of Sherlock Holmes : from Baskerville Hall to the Valley of Fear, the real forensics behind the great detective's greatest cases / E. J. Wagner.
        p. cm.
    Includes bibliographical references and index.
    ISBN: 978-0-470-12823-7 (paper)
    ISBN: 978-0-471-64879-6 (cloth)
    1. Forensic sciences—History. 2. Criminal investigation—History. 3. Holmes, Sherlock (Fictitious character) I. Title.
HV8073.W34 2006
363.25—dc22   2005022236

Printed in the United States of America

10 9 8 7 6 5 4 3 2 1

To Bill, my beloved husband and tech support

Contents

Illustrations follow page 110

Preface

I first met Sherlock Holmes on Mosholu Parkway in the Bronx during the 1950s. At the time I was suffering through the torments of junior high school, my misery relieved only by the combined English and social studies class taught by a singularly humane teacher named Benjamin Weinstein.

It was Mr. Weinstein's engaging habit to invite his students to bring lunch to the park when the weather permitted. We would perch on logs and on the grass while he entertained us by reading aloud from work with which he felt we should be familiar. I always went.

He read with a fine but gentle authority. He did no funny voices. He did not perform strained pantomimes. He just provided a conduit that allowed the author to speak to us.

He read tales from Mark Twain and tales from Damon Runyon. Toward the end of autumn, when it was growing cold and most of the leaves had fallen, he opened an unfamiliar book that had a dark blue cover and read:

> On glancing over my notes of the seventy odd cases in which I have during the last eight years studied the methods of my friend Sherlock Holmes, I find many tragic, some comic, a large number merely strange, but none commonplace; for, working as he did rather for the love of his art than for the acquirement of wealth, he refused to

associate himself with any investigation which did not tend towards the unusual, and even the fantastic.

It was the opening of "The Adventure of the Speckled Band." The next day I was at the library to obtain the collected works.

There's been a great deal written about the intense appeal of the Sherlock Holmes tales. I suspect it lies largely in the contrast between the emotional excitement of wild adventure and the reassuring intellectual control represented by Holmes. As I write this in 2005, when superstition threatens to seduce the civilized world with its dangerous embrace and science is dismissed in some quarters as merely an amoral discipline that humanity is free to abandon, a literary hero who possesses both intellect and a sense of ethics is particularly compelling.

Sherlock Holmes may have been fictional, but what we learn from him is very real. He tells us that science provides not simplistic answers but a rigorous method of formulating questions that may lead to answers. The figure of Holmes stands for human reason, tempered with a gift for friendship. (He may claim to be merely a brain, but he betrays an intense emotional core when he says to the villain in "The Adventure of the Three Garridebs," "If you had killed Watson, you would not have got out of this room alive.") Holmes has an incisive mind, a warm heart, and an artistic dimension—he skillfully plays the violin. No wonder I and so many others are entranced.

Over the years I acquired rather more copies of the Canon than was sensible, and from time to time I would indulge myself, read a bit, and wonder if there was a way of incorporating my weakness for Holmes with my job of lecturing on the history of crime and forensic science. I did present a program called "The Science of Sherlock Holmes: True Cases Solved by Conan Doyle," but that was about the author rather than the Great Detective. I kept toying with ideas, but basic sloth made it difficult to decide how to combine Holmes with criminal history.

And then one cold February afternoon while I was waiting for a loaf of bread to rise, I received an e-mail asking if I would be interested in writing a book that would use the Great Detective's adventures as a jumping-off point to discuss forensic science during the Victorian age. There could be chapters on anatomy, toxicology, blood chemistry, and a variety of other very complicated things. I could see at once that this endeavor would involve a prodigious amount of work.

It would mean contacting old friends who were specialists on fingerprinting, trace evidence, poisoning, and a number of other esoteric subjects and begging them for information. It would require detailed reading of old autopsy reports, crumbling newspapers, and lecture notes. It would mean convincing my husband that he would be delighted to spend weeks scanning fragile old pictures, formatting my messy typing, and compiling a bibliography that promised to be sizable. (My secretarial skills are sadly lacking.)

It would mean spending many hours poring over ancient medical tomes, dusty trial transcripts, and yellowing letters and papers, tracking down the details of crimes centuries old, isolated in my workroom with only hundreds of antiquarian books and Dr. Watson, our black Labrador Retriever, for company.

So of course I said yes.

Acknowledgments

Profound thanks to Mark Beneke, Ph.D., for details on insects; Robert A. Forde, for background on both the British legal system and the pronunciation of British names; Ernest D. Hamm, who can trace anything; Lee Jackson, for insight into Victorian life; Professor Erwin T. Jakab, for translations from the French; Professor Gernot Kocher, for information about Hans Gross; Sigmund Menchel, M.D., former chief medical examiner of Suffolk County, for much-needed help in analysis of the drowning at Tisza-Eszlar, as well as many other cases; James J. Maune, Esq., and William Nix, for information on the law; Andre A. Moenssens, Douglas Stripp Professor of Law Emeritus, University of Missouri at Kansas City, for background on legal photography; Stephen S. Power, my editor at John Wiley & Sons, for his patience and sensitivity and a really good idea; Marcia Samuels, for amazingly precise and considerate copyediting, and William R. Wagner, for both emotional and technical support. Without them this book would not exist. Any mistakes are mine.

I am deeply grateful to the members of the forensic world who over the years have, with great generosity, in different ways, helped me to learn. They include Jack Ballantyne, Ph.D.; Robert Baumann; Vincent Crispino, retired director of the Suffolk County Crime Laboratory; Leo Dal Cortivo, Ph.D., retired director of laboratories of the Suffolk County Office of the Medical Examiner; Joseph Davis, M.D., chief emeritus, Miami–Dade

County Medical Examiner Department; Robert Golden; Charles Hirsch, M.D., former chief medical examiner of Suffolk County, currently chief medical examiner of New York City; Jeffrey Luber; and the late Sidney B. Weinberg, M.D., former chief medical examiner of Suffolk County, all of whom I met through the Suffolk County Office of the Medical Examiner, an organization that has been a continuing source of support and information. Other forensic scientists who helped me learn include Michael Baden, M.D., chief forensic pathologist for the New York State Police; the late Theodore Ehrenreich, M.D., consultant in clinical pathology to the New York Office of the Medical Examiner; Zeno Geradts, forensic scientist at the Netherlands Forensic Institute; the late Milton Helpern, M.D., chief medical examiner of New York City; and Peter D. Martin, retired deputy director of the Metropolitan Police Forensic Science Laboratory, United Kingdom (Scotland Yard).

I am also grateful to the Museum of Long Island Natural Sciences at Stony Brook University, which as sponsor of the annual Forensic Forum has aided and abetted my efforts.

CHAPTER 1

Dialogue with the Dead

"You can take him to the mortuary now."
—Sherlock Holmes in *A Study in Scarlet*

Lᴏɴᴅᴏɴ ɪɴ 1887. Cobblestones and narrow, twisting streets. Hansom cabs driven on urgent errands, rumbling past public houses bursting with noise and smoke. Bearded men wearing capes, carrying walking sticks with silver heads. Vast museums holding jumbled curiosities, visited by veiled ladies draped in furs and discreetly scented with lavender—ladies whose rigid carriage somehow implies they expect to be embraced rarely and reverently by their husbands but firmly and constantly by their corsets.

Street women florid with gin. Homeless and diseased, laden with every garment they own, agitated by lice, they move heavily, heading to the public house, the doss-house, the workhouse, the river . . .

And the river is the slow-moving Thames. It penetrates the city, its water brown in response to the strong current stirring the bottom mud, its flow the only power carrying flatboats that convey the desperately needed black coal. The banks of the river swarm with mudlarks, young boys who scavenge for anything salvageable—wood, coal, coins—their reward often cholera from the raw sewage that churns through the great river.

The city teems with street vendors, drivers, horses, pickpockets, chimney sweeps, and nursemaids, the exalted and the wretched. It is home to the elegant parks and to the noisome slaughterhouses, to the tenements and to the majestic houses, all of them wrapped in swaths of thick fog and illuminated by gaslight.

It is home as well to the great hospitals, St. Mary's, Guy's, St. Bart's, and their lecture halls and laboratories, where sometimes macabre research is undertaken, hidden from public view by drawn blinds. In the first Sherlock Holmes story, the novel *A Study in Scarlet*, we are taken behind those blinds and watch as Stamford, an old acquaintance of Watson, leads him toward the laboratory where the most famous friendship in detective fiction will soon be forged:

> [W]e turned down a narrow lane and passed through a small side-door, which opened into a wing of the great hospital. It was familiar ground to me, and I needed no guiding as we ascended the bleak stone staircase and made our way down the long corridor with its vista of whitewashed wall and dun-colored doors. Near the farther end a low arched passage branched away from it and led to the chemical laboratory.
>
> This was a lofty chamber, lined and littered with countless bottles. Broad, low tables were scattered about, which bristled with retorts, test-tubes, and little Bunsen lamps, with their blue flickering flames. There was only one student in the room, who was bending over a distant table absorbed in his work.

Stamford has already warned Watson of his future roommate's many eccentricities, which include Holmes's beating of dissecting room cadavers with sticks in order to study postmortem bruising and his frequent dabbling in poison:

> "Holmes is a little too scientific for my tastes [Stamford tells Watson]—it approaches to cold-bloodedness. I could imagine his giving a friend a little pinch of the latest vegetable alkaloid, not out of malevolence, you understand, but simply out of a spirit of inquiry in order to have an accurate idea of the effects."

And Holmes, when they finally meet, doesn't disappoint in this respect:

> "Dr. Watson, Mr. Sherlock Holmes," said Stamford, introducing us.
>
> "How are you?" he said cordially, gripping my hand with a strength for which I should hardly have given him credit. "You have been in Afghanistan, I perceive."
>
> "How on earth did you know that?" I asked in astonishment.
>
> "Never mind," said he, chuckling to himself. "The question now is about hæmoglobin."

Watson is a medical man, comfortable with dissecting rooms and their pungent odors. He is also well traveled and well read, and he is probably familiar with the enormous advances that were being made in the new world of forensic medicine, many the result of experiments done on corpses, so he finds Holmes's interests congenial. They are thus well matched to share a series of adventures in a Victorian world that becomes their laboratory for applying science to criminal investigation.

In 1887, forensic science was largely a function of the medical profession and was most frequently referred to as "Medical Jurisprudence" or "Legal Medicine." An accurate understanding of fingerprint and trace evidence was still in the future, but a few adventurous physicians versed in anatomy, pharmacy, and microscopy were beginning to use their skills in the study of unexplained sudden death.

At first, this new field grew most vigorously on the European continent. Across the channel from England, there had been an old, if not entirely respectable, tradition of anatomical exploration, and in past centuries innovative artist-anatomists such as Andreas Vesalius and Leonardo had been known to liberate bodies from the dead houses and the gallows to study and draw them. Vesalius had to answer to the Inquisition, and Leonardo could not publish his anatomical studies within his lifetime. But gradually, the established Church withdrew its opposition to dissection, and more students were drawn to the subject.

At the beginning of the eighteenth century, the great Italian physician Giovanni Battista Morgagni began to change the focus of anatomical dissection, not only searching for an understanding of the structure of the human body, but also trying to match the changes in the cadaver to the clinical symptoms of disease reported before death. From there it was a short step to the idea of dissecting bodies to look for changes caused by criminal acts.

By 1794, the famous Scottish anatomist and surgeon John Bell was insisting on the primacy of dissection in the study of medicine and anatomy, writing in his *Engravings Explaining the Anatomy of the Bones, Muscles, and Joints*, "Anatomy is to be learnt only by dissection. Dissection is the first and last business of the student." Bell's engravings of dissection are extraordinary, both detailed and instructive, but they gave no guidance on obtaining subjects.

In nineteenth-century France and Germany, subjects for dissection were easily available for research, as unexplained deaths were automatically referred to the police for examination. Working conditions were forbidding, the mortuaries being poorly ventilated, malodorous, and churning with infectious matter. The scent of the charnel house clung to doctors' clothes, to their hair, to their skin. There was inevitably a certain social disdain for their specialty.

In spite of these impediments, the work was fascinating, and in Paris, two physicians, Paul Brouardel and Ambrose Tardieu, were busily studying the signs of suffocation and hanging on cadavers. Tardieu published a paper titled "La Pendaison, la strangulation, et la suffocation," in which he described the tiny spots of blood that may be found at the heart and under the pleura in the corpses of people who have been quickly suffocated; these spots are still known today as "Tardieu spots." In 1897, Brouardel's book, *La Pendaison, la strangulation, la suffocation, la submersion*, described the marks left on the neck by hanging and the damage to the hyoid bone caused by manual strangulation.

In Lyon, Dr. Alexandre Lacassagne's detailed examination of the dead resulted in a new understanding of the physical changes that take place with the end of life. He made notes on rigor mortis, the way in which the muscles stiffen, becoming first evident in the jaw a few hours after death, then spreading downward, and finally retreating in the same order in which it appears.

He described livor mortis, the discoloration of death, which occurs as the circulation ceases, allowing the blood to settle. He observed algor mortis, the cooling of the body, and the rate at which it reaches the temperature of its surroundings.

Lacassagne saw all these as useful tools in estimating the time of death. But he also noted many possible exceptions. The temperature of the surroundings, the circumstances of death, the age and physical condition of the deceased—all could affect the appearance of these signs. He warned against too-rapid conclusions and impressed upon his students his dictum: "One must learn to doubt." And the pathologist Charles Meymott Tidy concurred, saying, "There is a scientific certainty which only the coward treats as uncertainty, and there is an uncertainty which only the boldness of ignorance ignores."

In the fervor of discovery, new methods of dissection were evolving and were the subjects of much controversy. In Vienna, Karl Rokitansky, who obtained his subjects from hospital deaths and autopsied two cadavers a day, every day, for forty-five years, taught his students a postmortem technique he had developed. The internal organs were exposed and then dissected and examined in situ (in place; that is, in the body).

This technique was modified by Gohn, who introduced the method of removing the organs in blocks related to their function. A version of this technique is most often seen today in medical school dissections.

Maurice Letulle favored the en masse version, in which the contents of the chest and abdominal cavities were removed as a whole. Rudolf Virchow, working in Berlin, advocated his own method, in which the organs were removed and examined separately. It is this technique that is most often used in forensic autopsies at the present time. This more delicate procedure is preferred by many pathologists, as they feel it is less likely to lose small traces of medical evidence.

New discoveries simmered on the continent, but in the British Isles things were very different. The English had always relied on a system in which suspect deaths were referred to the Coroner, or Crowner, a political official who was not required to have any scientific or medical training. He might, if he thought a case warranted it, obtain an opinion from a physician, but that physician was not necessarily skilled in forensic work. Until the late nineteenth century, there was not even a registry for deaths, and many cases that cried out for investigation were simply left in the hands of next of kin.

The treatment of human remains had long been a sensitive issue in England. A mixture of religious practices, superstition, and emotional regard for the deceased made the thought of allowing the dissection of human beings abhorrent.

Historically, dissection had been performed in England either to explore anatomy or to humiliate the subject of the procedure. It was seen as a disgrace. For centuries, the bodies of executed criminals had been left in the hands of the executioners, who displayed the decaying corpses on gibbets and sometimes eviscerated them before attentive crowds as an added punishment.

Scotland pioneered in the study of surgery, but the medical schools there labored under the burden of finding adequate subjects. Under English law, a few bodies of the executed were given to the surgeons as teaching material each year. There were never enough. The needs of medical schools were filled by bodies illicitly obtained from recent burials.

The wealthy dead were offered some degree of protection by armed guards provided by their relatives. Iron grids known as "mort safes" were laid at large expense on new graves as an additional precaution. Elaborate arrangements of flowers and pebbles were used on burial plots to make it harder for grave robbers to do their work unnoticed. But often the skills of the "sack 'em up men" prevailed. The corpses of the poor, whose relatives could ill afford such precautions, were at even greater risk. Public opinion was further enraged by the ghastly crimes of Burke and Hare, the depraved, if enterprising, entrepreneurs who murdered sixteen people and sold the corpses to surgeons, thus avoiding the labor of disinterment.

The English public was deeply ambivalent, and similar sentiments were prevalent in America. On the one hand, if an internal organ urgently needed treatment, it was reassuring if the surgeon had an accurate idea of where it might be located. On the other hand, no one wanted the remains of their dear ones to provide the example.

There was great resentment over the surgeons' business dealings with grave robbers, and since forensic autopsies and dissections were similar, there was little public support for forensic medicine. This began to change in the mid-nineteenth century when Alfred Swaine Taylor, a young British pathologist who had trained in Paris, was appointed to teach forensic medicine in London. He brought with him a new perspective on examining violent death and presented his ideas in a carefully reasoned text full of detailed examples. Taylor's seminal work on pathology and toxicology, the first in the English language, had enormous influence on criminal investigation in the days of Holmes and Watson.

Consider Watson's vivid description, in *A Study in Scarlet*, of Holmes examining not only the corpse but everything at the crime scene: "[H]is nimble fingers were flying here, there, and everywhere, feeling, pressing, unbuttoning, examining." It is clearly an echo of Taylor's exhortation in the 1873 edition of *A Manual of Medical Jurisprudence*:

> The first duty of a medical jurist is to cultivate a faculty of minute observation. . . .
>
> A medical man, when he sees a dead body, should notice everything. He should observe everything which could throw a light on the production of wounds or other injuries found upon it. It should not be left to a policeman to say whether there were any marks of blood on the dress or on the hands of the deceased, or on the furniture of the room. The dress of the deceased as well as the body should always be closely examined on the spot by the medical man.

There being no forensic medical specialist at the scene, Holmes simply fills the role himself. He does depart from Taylor's precepts in accepting Lestrade's opinion that there is no wound on the body, but then, Holmes follows no man slavishly. He takes what he likes from the new science and improvises the rest.

In "The Resident Patient," we see Dr. Watson dabbling in forensic medicine by giving an opinion on time of death based on the amount of rigor established in a hanged man. True, he doesn't consider possible variables, but he is aware of the concept.

Many of the texts on medical jurisprudence were an odd mixture of fact and myth, and perhaps Watson relies too heavily on them. In *A Study in Scarlet*, he offers this description of a corpse: "On his rigid face there stood an expression of horror, and as it seemed to me, of hatred, such as I have never seen upon human features." Except in the very rare case of cadaveric spasm, or instant rigor, the muscles, including those of the face, relax at the moment of death. What were sometimes interpreted as expressions of horror or fear were the result of physical change or injury caused by a weapon, a caustic substance, or an animal or insect, or the discoloration caused by suffocation, lividity, or the onset of decay. Many doctors saw and observed, but they did not yet fully understand.

And what of the dissecting rooms themselves, in which we are told Holmes spent so much time? What mysteries did they hold?

Bodies used for dissection were usually drained of blood and injected with preservatives so that the specimens could be reused. Holmes notes this in "The Cardboard Box" when he dismisses the theory that the severed ears sent to an elderly lady are relics of a dissecting room. He also makes the point that the ears are packed in salt—not something, he believes, that would occur to a medical student. (The mention of severed ears must have sent a shiver through Londoners when the story was published in 1893, resonating as it did with a letter sent to authorities during a string of sadistic murders a few years before. That note had threatened, "Next job I do I'll clip the lady's ear off and send it to the police officers just for jolly." It had been signed "Jack the Ripper.")

Between anatomy demonstrations, the bodies were stored in cadaver boxes—chambers in which they were hung from hooks. The corpses were carted back and forth as needed by *dieners* (mortuary assistants).

The tables used for dissection were flat and had neither drains nor rims, so fluids ran onto the floor, which was usually covered with sawdust so that it could be easily swept clean. Natural light was preferred, as the interior lighting available—oil lamps, candles, and gaslight—distorted color. In the interest of evading the prying eyes of the public, hospitals were often built around interior courtyards, and dissecting rooms faced the courtyards rather than the street. Windows were sometimes coated with soap or tallow to provide privacy.

Occasionally there were hiding places adjacent to dissecting rooms in case a doubtfully acquired cadaver needed concealment from overly enthusiastic investigators. Large fireplaces often served this purpose. A questioned body would be lifted by a hoist into the chimney and a fire lit below. It's true the corpse would smoke slightly, but it would still be perfectly serviceable when retrieved. This technique was particularly popular in New England. When not so warmed, the rooms were cold and reeked of preservatives. In the more progressive places, carbolic acid was added to the stench.

The demonstrators in anatomy and their students wore hats and aprons but otherwise had no protective gear and worked with bare hands.

The first step in the dissection was to remove identifying characteristics from the subject to make sure no frantic relative who had noticed an empty grave could claim ownership of the corpse. Clothing, if any, was discarded. The law defined purloining corpses as a misdemeanor, but stealing clothes was a felony, for which there was a severe penalty.

Usually the subjects—particularly if they were stolen—arrived naked, in sacks or barrels. If they had been brought from a distance, they were packed in alcohol and often discreetly labeled as "pork" or "beef." The corpses of children were referred to as "smalls."

The body was arranged on its back, its head raised on a block of wood to make the neck easily accessible. The initial incision was made from the chin down, over the throat, across the chest, around the navel, to the pubis. Sometimes the bodies were propped up by ropes to demonstrate the way the limbs extended in life.

Without the powerful electric rotating saws of the present day, dissection was physically arduous. The skull was opened with knife, saw, and chisel. The various organs, muscles, arteries, and veins were removed, inspected, and studied as systems. Drawings and notes were made, and those parts still usable were replaced in the body, which was then sewn up by the *diener* and returned to the cadaver box.

The system of the medicolegal autopsy evolved from dissection but had several important differences. In a suspicious death, the victim's identifying traits were carefully noted and retained by drawing or photography. The clothing was not stripped and discarded but examined and kept for evidence. Preservatives or any chemicals that might confuse the pathologist's sense of smell were discouraged. (Many anatomists, willing to sacrifice olfactory information, smoked prodigiously during autopsies, claiming it was for reasons of hygiene.)

The body was opened with the classic incision from chin to pubis but only after careful external examination. Wounds and their direction and depth were recorded. Since blood was not drained and replaced with chemicals, it oozed and dripped, carrying with it the threat of disease. Unexpected broken bits of bone could injure the most careful investigator, who had to work with bare hands thrust deep inside gaping incisions.

The mortuaries stank of decay, of fecal matter and vomitus. They boiled with danger, but physicians and *dieners* did their work with the same determination as the dissectors. As swarms of flies bore buzzing witness, they coaxed the last sad secrets from the murdered dead.

The anatomist, in demonstrating a dissection, had asked his subject, "How are you made?" The pathologist now asked the corpse on his autopsy table, "How did you die?" The answers were not always clear. It seemed sometimes that for every two steps forward, there was one taken backward, and that forensic medicine, if poorly applied, could be the cause of dangerous mistakes.

In the seventeenth century, a doctor in Czechoslovakia named Johann Schreyer devised a test he believed would prove whether a child had been born alive. Basing his test on earlier work by the Danish physician Caspar Bartholin, who wrote that air present in the lungs of a dead infant indicated a live birth, Schreyer threw the lungs of allegedly stillborn infants into basins of water. If they floated, Schreyer said, this would prove the child had been born alive.

For many years, this was the standard test. Many distraught mothers were accused of infanticide on the strength of it before it was observed that putrefaction in the lung tissue could also cause the lungs to float. Schreyer's procedure underwent a number of adjustments over the next two hundred years before it became truly useful, and even then it was considered only an indication, not absolute proof, of live birth.

The new science was slowly emerging from a mass of myth and misunderstood observations. It had been demonstrated repeatedly that the hair and nails do not continue to grow after death but that they appear to do so due to the contraction of the skin and underlying muscles. As recently as 1882, however, a pathology text by Charles Meymott Tidy reported, erroneously, that both hair and nails increase in length after death.

Dr. Tidy happily recounted that knowledge of this "fact" had protected a group of medical students from conviction in a body-stealing case. The relatives of a recently deceased retarded boy had discovered his grave empty. They identified a dissected corpse at the anatomy school as the child's by its extraordinarily long fingernails. At trial, a medical "expert" explained that the nails, which were so long that they curved around the tips of the fingers and toes and extended along the palms of the hands and the soles of the feet, had grown that way postmortem. The charges were dismissed, and the medical students were free to continue digging for knowledge.

In the same year that Tidy published his text, a complex forensic case was causing intense sensation in Central Europe. In the small Hungarian village of Tisza-Eszlar, a fourteen-year-old Catholic domestic servant named Esther Solymossy disappeared while on an errand for her mistress. It was early spring, the season of Easter and Passover, and it was not long before the ancient and terrible folk belief in Jewish ritual murder was resurrected in the town. Jews, it was whispered, killed Christian children to obtain their blood with which to make Passover matzos. Obviously, the Jews had stolen Esther for this ghastly purpose.

Several Jewish children were taken into custody for questioning. Threatened and beaten, one "confessed" that he had seen Esther taken captive in the synagogue by some of the Jewish elders, and, through a keyhole, had witnessed her throat being cut and her blood being caught in a pot. But the child was unable to say where Esther's remains were hidden.

A number of Jews were arrested, although there was no objective evidence against them. They were interrogated and tortured until several of them signed confessions. But they made no statement as to the location of the corpse. Extensive searches for the remains were fruitless. As summer approached, the medieval serpent of anti-Semitism uncoiled further, and violence against the Jewish community raged through the town. Jews were beaten, and their property was ransacked, burned, and stolen. And still no sign of Esther.

But then, in the nearby town of Tisda-Dada, the body of a young woman was recovered from the river. The corpse was wearing a dress similar to the one Esther was wearing when she vanished. The length of the body was consistent with that of the missing girl. No other woman had been reported missing in the area. Several of the townspeople insisted that this was indeed the body of Esther Solymossy.

But the throat of the woman from the river was untouched. And the body was intact. Esther had been missing for months. Surely, if she had been in the river so long, decay would have made its ugly inroads. Esther's mother viewed the corpse and furiously denied that it was her daughter.

Three medical men, entirely unburdened by any training or experience in forensic pathology, were given the job of determining the identity of the girl from the river and the cause of her death. They contemplated a very pale female body, with soft, unstained nails on both hands and feet. The genitalia were expansively swollen. The intestines and internal organs were well preserved. The body seemed devoid of blood.

Based on these observations, the doctors solemnly reported

their conclusions: The dead girl was at least eighteen years old and possibly a bit older. She was of privileged background. Although she was unused to physical labor, the enlarged genitals indicated that she was very accustomed to sexual intercourse. The cause of death was anemia. She could not have been dead more than ten days. In short, this was clearly not the body of Esther Solymossy, who had been fourteen, and who habitually walked barefoot and was tanned from walking bareheaded in the sun.

This was a great relief to the town fathers. They reasoned that since the body in question was determined not to be that of Esther, there was no reason to examine the discrepancies between the corpse and the confessions, and therefore the pillaging and destruction of Jewish property could be allowed to proceed in traditional fashion. The accused Jewish elders remained in prison, and the pathetic remains of the girl from the river were buried.

But the case caught the attention of journalists and became the subject of intense argument throughout Europe. A group of lawyers from Budapest, well educated and knowledgeable about the new world of forensic pathology and skeptical of the concept of blood as an ingredient in matzo, offered to appear for the defense. They demanded that the body be exhumed so that it might be examined by three doctors experienced in legal medicine. This met resistance by Bary, the examining magistrate, who was a great believer in the myth of ritual murder. The state prosecutor, however, supported the idea, as he was uneasy with the sparse evidence and nursed an interest in justice.

In the icy cold of December, the river body was removed from its resting place, and Professors Johannes Belki, Schenthauer, and Michalkovics of Budapest performed a second autopsy. Their findings differed strikingly from those of the local doctors.

The experienced Budapest group insisted the body was that of a female not more than fifteen, as shown by the immaturity of her bones. Her swollen genitalia resulted from long immersion in water rather than from sexual relations, and her extreme whiteness was due to the outer skin having been stripped off by the water, leaving only the pale corium, the inner layer of skin, through which the blood had oozed.

The unusually clean fingernails and toenails, they pointed out, were not the nails at all but the nail beds, the outer portions having been pulled off by the river current. Further, since the intense cold of the water had kept the body from decay, it was quite possible that she had been in her gelid grave for three months. The clothes on the corpse and the other physical details were a match for those of the missing girl. The professors from Budapest concluded that this was indeed the body of Esther Solymossy and that the undamaged throat made it clear that the "confessions" were invented. Thus exonerated, the accused Jews were freed to take up the burden of their lives.

The new technique of forensic autopsy had commanded justice. It was a beginning. There would be many twists in the path—superstitions and prejudices to overcome, scientific truths yet to be discovered. But the use of autopsy in the pursuit of justice had been established. The idea that a murder victim must be meticulously examined in the context of the crime, that science had an essential part to play in the legal system, was becoming accepted.

It was the first great building block of the science of Sherlock Holmes.

WHATEVER REMAINS

> *"How often have I said to you that when you have eliminated the impossible, whatever remains, however improbable, must be the truth?"*
> —Sherlock Holmes in *The Sign of Four*

- Physicians who acquired infections from subjects they autopsied could transmit disease to their living patients. A classic example of this occurred in 1847, when the Hungarian physician Ignaz Semmelweis became greatly distressed by the high rate of puerperal fever and maternal death in the Viennese hospital in which he worked. Observing that women delivered by doctors were much more commonly infected than those attended only by midwives, Semmelweis began to suspect that the physicians were inadvertently carrying disease to their patients. His suspicion became conviction when his mentor, Dr. Jacobus Kolletscha, acquired a fatal infection similar to puerperal fever after receiving a minor cut during an autopsy. Semmelweis then insisted that physicians scrub with chloride of lime before examining the living, and the death rate fell dramatically. Many of the doctors, feeling pricked in their amour propre, never forgave him. Semmelweis died in an insane asylum.

- Autopsies were made much less physically strenuous by the development of the oscillating surgical saw. It was first patented by Dr. Homer Stryker, an orthopedist, in 1947, and so is commonly referred to in autopsy suites as the "Stryker saw."

- It is not only disease that threatens the forensic pathologist and his team. Shooting deaths caused by explosive bullets are a hazard for the unwary mortuary worker. When such projectiles have failed to explode in the victim, they may do so during the postmortem, and they must be handled with long-handled instruments and great care.

- The term *diener* comes from the German and literally means servant. The term "mortuary assistant" is preferred today, *diener* being seen as patronizing. However, seen in the context of "servant to anatomical science," it seems both more acceptable and is more accurate historically. In many medical examiners' offices, the assistants are highly trained—skilled, if unsung—anatomists. They are often former army medics.

CHAPTER 2

Beastly Tales and Black Dogs

"Mr. Holmes, they were the footprints of a gigantic hound!"
—Dr. Mortimer in *The Hound of the Baskervilles*

IN ARTHUR CONAN DOYLE's novel *The Hound of the Baskervilles*, Sherlock Holmes ensures the triumph of fact and science over fantasy and superstition. Many of Holmes's real-life counterparts in the British Isles, striving to do the same, found it a rough road. Long before crime was the subject of scientific study, the physical evidence of mysterious events was observed and discussed but was interpreted only through the murky lens of superstition and folklore. Tales of witchcraft, ghosts, werewolves, and vampires were not merely entertainment for a cold winter's night, they were attempts to explain occurrences that filled people with terror.

After all, superstition hallowed by the centuries can be not only seductive but also, in a gifted storyteller's hands, quite lucrative. Certainly Conan Doyle was to find it so.

In 1901, the author visited the north coast of Norfolk,

England, with his friend, Bertram Fletcher Robinson, a young journalist whom Conan Doyle had met on a sea voyage from South Africa. (Robinson was affectionately known to his friends as "Bobbles.") Robinson entertained his famous companion with tales of the grim folklore of his native Devon, dwelling on the legend of the Great Black Dog that was said to haunt the region. So fascinated was Conan Doyle by the image that he conceived of the idea for a new story, to be called "The Hound of the Baskervilles," and although he finally wrote it on his own, his first intention was to collaborate with Robinson on the project.

With this story in mind, the two traveled to Dartmoor, Robinson's home. It was a land of moors and mires, bogs and Bronze Age ruins. Dartmoor Prison was not far away, giving rise to rumors of dangerous escaped prisoners lurking in the desolate countryside. All this was intriguing background, but it was the Black Dog that provided Conan Doyle with the essential literary shudder.

The Black Dog has many names in Britain: Padfoot, Hooter, Barghest, Old Shuck, Galleytrot, the Shug, Hairy Jack, and Gurt Dog, among others. Not limited to Devon, Black Dog stories are told in all parts of the British Isles. In the old tales the dog is usually a "fetch" or a psychopomp—that is, a presence whose purpose is to warn of approaching disaster or to accompany a human to the afterworld. It is often described as having flaming eyes and slavering, foaming jaws, and being of enormous size.

It is this fearsome legendary creature that Conan Doyle evokes in *The Hound of the Baskervilles*. "A hound it was," he writes, "an enormous coal-black hound, but not such a hound as mortal eyes have ever seen." And in this tale, of course, perhaps the best known of the Sherlock Holmes series, the fearsome hound is believed to bring death to the Baskervilles who meet it. As Mortimer recounts the Baskerville saga to Holmes and Watson in their rooms at Baker Street,

"[S]tanding over Hugo, and plucking at his throat, there stood a foul thing, a great, black beast, shaped like a hound, yet larger than any hound that ever mortal eye has rested upon. . . . [A]s they looked the thing tore the throat out of Hugo Baskerville, on which, as it turned its blazing eyes and dripping jaws upon them, the three shrieked with fear and rode for dear life, still screaming, across the moor. One, it is said, died that very night of what he had seen, and the other twain were but broken men for the rest of their days.

"Such is the tale, my sons, of the coming of the hound which is said to have plagued the family so sorely ever since."

This was intensely dramatic storytelling. Conan Doyle made full use of the mythic background, and while he freely changed the details of geography to suit his story, the time he spent wandering through Dartmoor is evident. Just as there was a prison near the Robinson home, so there was in the Baskerville environs. "Then fourteen miles away the great convict prison of Princetown. Between and around these scattered points extends the desolate, lifeless moor. This, then, is the stage upon which tragedy has been played."

And just as there were Bronze Age ruins in Devon, so they appear on the fictional moor of the Baskervilles, as Stapleton explains to Watson:

"Yes, it's rather an uncanny place altogether. Look at the hillside yonder. What do you make of those?"

The whole steep slope was covered with gray circular rings of stone, a score of them at least.

"What are they? Sheep-pens?"

"No, they are the homes of our worthy ancestors. Prehistoric man lived thickly on the moor, and as no one in particular has lived there since, we find all his little arrangements exactly as he left them. These are his wigwams with the roofs off. You can even see his hearth and his couch if you have the curiosity to go inside."

"But it is quite a town. When was it inhabited?"

"Neolithic man—no date."

"What did he do?"

"He grazed his cattle on these slopes, and he learned to dig for tin when the bronze sword began to supersede the stone axe. Look at the great trench in the opposite hill. That is his mark."

The Hound of the Baskervilles was an enormous success, not least because of its eerie resonance with ancient folklore. But the very prevalence of superstitions such as Black Dog tales sometimes proved a hindrance to the investigation of very real crimes. One such instance, a particularly bloody murder, took place in 1945 but had its unsavory beginnings in Warwickshire, England, in 1885.

Two years before Sherlock Holmes made his first appearance in literature, a fourteen-year-old farm boy named Charles Walton walked in the gathering twilight toward his home in the small English village of Lower Quinton. As he reached a crossroads, he was disturbed to see an extraordinarily large black dog seated in the path, staring at him. He had seen the same dog on several other evenings. It wore no collar and, as far as Charles knew, belonged to none of the villagers.

Charles was well schooled in the local lore regarding mysterious black dogs as harbingers of misfortune, and he shivered. As he later recounted the incident, the dog walked beside him for some time, making no sound. As the last light faded, it seemed to Charles that the dog changed shape, until it appeared to become a woman wearing a black cloak. The lady paused and then slowly drew back her hood and turned toward the boy, who observed with horror that her cloaked dark figure was without a head.

Charles ran the rest of the way home frantic with fear, only to learn upon his arrival that his sister, who that morning had been in apparent health, had just died. The tale was told often in the village and was believed to be the reason that Charles disliked dogs forever after, although he had a peculiar affinity for other animals and was believed by many to converse with them in a strange language.

The story was recalled with shudders sixty years later when Charles Walton, then a rheumatic old man of seventy-four, was found dead close to the spot where he had claimed to see the spectral dog. Evidently he had been taken by surprise at his job of trimming his neighbor's hedges, and his throat had been cut with his own billhook. His body was pinned to the ground with his pitchfork, and a cross had been deeply carved in his chest. His blood soaked the ground.

Whispers about witchcraft immediately spread. The location of the murder scene, in the shadow cast by Meon Hill, was near the Neolithic circle of stones called the Whispering Knights. Tradition claimed it was a gathering place for witches. Meon Hill itself was said to have been created by the devil in an angry passion because an abbey had been built nearby. It was claimed that the phantom hounds of a Celtic king sometimes raced there in the light of a full moon.

The grotesque nature of Charles Walton's wounds and the way in which his body was pinned to the ground and exsanguinated recalled the ancient method of killing a witch to prevent it from rising from the dead. It was well remembered in the village that in 1875 a local woman named Ann Turner had been similarly butchered with a hayfork by a young man called John Hayward, who was firmly convinced that she had bewitched him.

But by 1945, when Charles Walton was murdered, the matter was investigated not only by the local constable but also by Detective-Superintendent Robert Fabian, the best Scotland Yard had to offer, and the corpse was autopsied by pathologist J. M. Webster. Every attempt was made to examine the Walton case in the objective light of forensic science. Forensic science, however, still had to contend with tradition and tease grim fact from frightful fancy.

Lower Quinton is part of Warwickshire, which lies in the midlands of England. It is Tolkien country, where you may easily picture hobbits and other magical beings scurrying beneath the earth. It is in the very heart of Shakespeare's country, rich with farmland, gently rolling hills, hedgerows, and the half-timbered thatch-roofed cottages that have stood since the Tudors ruled Britain. It is also rich in a history of ancient beliefs about magic and witchcraft. The atmosphere was heavy with these strange concerns and myths when Robert Fabian of Scotland Yard arrived in Lower Quinton to investigate the murder of old Charles Walton. Even in 1945, at the end of the Second World War, the villagers were reticent, unwilling to talk freely to the detective.

At the crime scene, the body was pinned to the ground with such force that it took the combined efforts of two police officers to free it. Walton's throat was cut so deeply that his head was partially severed. The weapon was left buried in the wound. Walton's walking stick, covered with blood, was found at the scene. "His injuries were hideous," Fabian wrote later in his memoirs. "It looked like the kind of killing Druids might have done in ghastly ceremony at full moon."

Alec Spooner, the Superintendent of the Warwickshire constabulary, told Fabian of a book of local folklore that recounted the tale of Charles Walton as a young lad and his encounter with the black dog. Fabian was unimpressed.

The full investigative resources available at the time were put to use. Fabian had brought one of the nine brown leather "murder bags" innovated by Scotland Yard. Each was packed with everything thought to be needed at a murder scene at the time: rubber gloves, handcuffs, bottles for samples, screwdriver, magnifying glass. Plaster was used to make casts of the many boot marks at the scene. A Royal Air Force plane flew overhead, taking photographs of the corpse and the surrounding area. In the fields, men with mine detectors slowly swept the area, looking for an old tin watch missing from the dead man's pocket. The postmortem examination had disclosed no dog hairs on the corpse.

It was noted that a prisoner-of-war camp stood not far from the crime scene, and one of the prisoners had been seen trying to scrub blood from his jacket. Although he claimed it was the blood of a rabbit he had poached (security at the camp was evidently somewhat casual), he was promptly detained, and the Birmingham Laboratory was asked to determine the source of the blood.

Fabian looked forward to closing the case and dispatching the whispers of witchcraft and black dogs. Working at top speed, the laboratory announced that the blood on the jacket was that of . . . a rabbit.

Fabian worked on. He and his men took four thousand statements, most from unwilling villagers. They sent twenty-nine samples of clothing and hair to the laboratory, to no result. During the investigation, Fabian reported that he saw a black dog that ran out of sight down Meon Hill. A farm lad came along just then and Fabian asked him, "Looking for that dog, son? A black dog?" The boy turned pale and ran.

Shortly afterward, a black dog was found dead, hanging from a tree. The people of Lower Quinton became even less willing to discuss the murder. "Cottage doors were shut in our faces," Fabian wrote. "Even the most innocent witnesses were unable to meet our eyes . . . some became ill after we spoke to them."

Who would kill an old man with his own tools? Who would pin him to the earth with a pitchfork? What reason could there be, unless it was bizarre ritual, to pin a witch to the ground?

The crime was never officially solved. The old tin watch turned up in 1960 in what had been Charles Walton's garden. It bore no useful prints.

Before he died, Fabian was said to have confided that he suspected the villager who found the body had killed Walton because he owed the old man money. The villager's fingerprints had been on the weapon, but he had explained this by saying he tried to remove the hook from the body. Fabian theorized that the ritual aspects of the scene had been deliberately arranged to terrify the townspeople into silence about any suspicions they might have had.

Fabian believed this because he felt he had eliminated the impossible, and he saw the staged crime scene as the one possibility left. But even using the impeccable logic of the Great Detective, Fabian couldn't get past the persistent fear caused by tales of haunting black dogs, so he couldn't prove his theory.

Which brings us to the question of why tales of spectral black dogs were so prevalent and so widely believed well into twentieth-century Britain. It is sometimes argued that the prevalence of black Labrador Retrievers, a breed common in Britain and often allowed to roam the countryside, provided the source for Black Dog stories. But St. John's Dogs, the progenitors of black Labradors, were first imported to England from Newfoundland in the early 1800s, and Black Dog tales may be traced back further than the twelfth century.

It seems more likely that the ubiquity of the tales is due to a mixture of truly ancient folklore: that of the Nordic tradition, with its myth of the great wolf Fenris, who if freed from his chains will bring about the end of the world; and that of the occupying Romans, who brought with them traces of all the nations they had previously conquered and whose myths they had assimilated. These myths inevitably connected the Black Dog with death and its rites. Notable among these were the customs of the ancient Greeks, who told tales of the hell-hound Cerberus, who guarded the kingdom of the dead, and of the Egyptians, whose elaborate concern with the afterlife and the preservation of human remains rested heavily on the figure of the black dog–headed god Anubis. According to legend, it was Anubis who brought the art of embalming and mummification to the Egyptians.

According to Egyptian mythology, Osiris was the child of the sun god Ra and was both brother and husband to the goddess Isis. Osiris was much loved by the people but greatly resented and envied by his evil brother, Set. Set murdered Osiris by trickery, locking him into an ornately carved chest and throwing it into the Nile. When Isis succeeded in recovering her husband's body, Set wrested it from her and hacked the corpse into fourteen pieces, scattering them throughout the land of Egypt. Isis persevered, gathering up all the bloody shreds of her husband except the phallus, which had been thrown into the Nile and devoured by the fish Oxyrhynchus, a species of long-nosed sturgeon.

Anubis, the god of embalming, always represented as having the head of a black dog or a doglike jackal, came to the aid of the goddess. He helped her to restore the corpse and guarded her as she fashioned an artificial penis for the body. Isis, who is usually represented with winged arms, fluttered them over Osiris, restoring his life force so that he might take his proper place as the god of the afterworld.

In this tale we find many seeds of ancient British folklore, including the ubiquitous Black Dog, its association with death, and the view of the dead body as somehow magical. "Mummy" was a common ingredient in potions and medicines in Britain, as well as on the continent, and a lucrative commerce existed from the Middle Ages on in the importation of the dried dead. (Much of the "mummy" was manufactured by clever entrepreneurs with an eye for both money and the macabre. It was possible to buy powdered mummy in a New York City pharmacy as recently as 1955 for twenty-five dollars an ounce.)

The common folk belief in Britain that animal "familiars"— usually black cats, dogs, or sometimes hares—were given to witches by the devil to carry out evil deeds shows traces of Egyptian-Roman lore. Animal body parts figured heavily in recipes for complex elixirs, as did human body fragments.

The notion that body parts of the dead had connections to witchcraft and black magic was firmly held well past the Victorian age. Rope that had hanged a man was prized for its supposed healing qualities, and the application of the hand of a hanged man to a wen, or skin blemish, was supposed to cure it. It was partly because of the connection with black magic that dissection of the human body was originally held in disrepute. The great fear was that the parts might be put to dangerous uses.

For many centuries it was a religious precept that the human body contained the "luz" bone—a particular bone from which the entire body of a dead individual would be resurrected at the Day of Judgment. There was no agreement as to where this part lay, although a sizable group of religious experts claimed that the coccyx—the bone at the base of the spine—was the appropriate spot.

This ingrained fear of the dead as dangerous, and the fact that animal predators such as dogs attracted by the scent could often be found near gallows or shallow graves, fed the Black Dog stories and provided them with lasting power. Arthur Conan Doyle made such striking use of the Black Dog tales in *The Hound of the Baskervilles* that in spite of Sherlock Holmes's steely logic in confronting the beast, the fearsome image continues to haunt:

> "[I]t was a huge creature, luminous, ghastly, and spectral. I have cross-examined these men, one of them a hard-headed countryman, one a farrier, and one a moorland farmer, who all tell the same story of this dreadful apparition, exactly corresponding to the hell-hound of the legend. I assure you that there is a reign of terror in the district, and that it is a hardy man who will cross the moor at night."

The mysterious qualities of dogs made for fascinating fiction, but in the real world of crime investigation their abilities took longer to find a purpose. Conan Doyle has Sherlock Holmes make use of them in several stories, such as "The Adventure of the Missing Three Quarter," in which the hound Pompey has evidently been taught to track drags or lures scented with aniseed. (This was often done by sportsmen—either to train young dogs to follow a scent, or to have the excitement of the chase without the cruelty of the kill.) Holmes uses the scent to track the solution to the mystery.

In "The Adventure of Shoscombe Old Place," the family spaniel's ability to tell mistress from stranger provides Holmes with the vital clue, and he announces to Watson, "Dogs don't make mistakes." Maybe not, but their handlers often do, as was made very apparent during the search for the serial killer known as Jack the Ripper in 1888. Two highly touted English bloodhounds, Barnaby and Burgo, were brought to Regent's Park, very near Sherlock Holmes's Baker Street address in London, to practice tracking before being placed on the killer's trail. The first trial runs were successful, but disaster followed when they were allowed off their leads and seemed to disappear. There is some disagreement as to where the dogs went—whether they were lost or simply had been returned to their kennel without the authorities being told. What is certain is that the *Times* of London printed an item asking anyone with information about the dogs' whereabouts to inform Scotland Yard at once.

When it became known that Burgo and Barnaby had been located, they and their handlers were the subject of many clever remarks. But the odd fact is that while the public believed them to be roaming free in London, there were no Ripper murders, and the crimes began again only after it was announced that the dogs were back and restrained in their kennels. Perhaps an atavistic belief in the mysterious powers of dogs stayed the Ripper's hand for a bit. But that was all the help the dogs supplied, for Burgo and Barnaby, lacking the specialized training needed for police work, never found helpful evidence in the case of Jack the Ripper.

In "The Adventure of the Creeping Man," Sherlock Holmes announces, "I have serious thoughts of writing a small monograph upon the uses of dogs in the work of the detective." If only he had, Scotland Yard might have made excellent use of it in the 1888 "autumn of terror."

Dogs as well as assorted other animals were also the subjects of a number of other early criminal investigations. A great preoccupation during the Victorian age was the charge of bestiality, and the presence of animal hair was considered important evidence of this crime. The English pathologist Alfred Swaine Taylor wrote in the late 1800s, "Trials for sodomy and bestiality are very frequent, and conviction of men and boys have taken place for unnatural connection with cows, mares, and other female animals. It is punishable by penal servitude for life." (As recently as 1950, the Scottish pathologist John Glaister included in his text the tale of a man "who was apprehended after having been seen to have unnatural intercourse with a duck," leaving us to wonder precisely what natural intercourse with a duck would involve.)

An amazing amount of police laboratory time and money was spent collecting evidence in bestiality cases, which might have more appropriately fallen to the province of the ASPCA. But in the process some useful information about hair and fur comparisons was acquired. A primary issue was the difficulty in firmly establishing the difference between human and animal hair.

During the middle of the nineteenth century, some work had been done on differentiating between horsehair and human hair, and in 1869, a German researcher named Emile Pfaff was credited with a paper on a similar subject. It was noted that animal hair generally had cuticle cells that were larger and not as regular as those in humans. Taylor made many references in his text to identifying animal hairs on weapons as well as on clothing.

"If a hair submitted for examination be not human, from what animal has it been derived?" asked pathologist Charles Meymott Tidy in his 1882 *Legal Medicine*. And to provide an answer to his own question, he wrote that he "found it convenient [just as Holmes might have done] to keep a series of hairs of different animals ready mounted, for purposes of comparison."

As forensic techniques have improved, animals have provided important information about crime scenes. In 2003, Reuters reported that a white-crested cockatoo, found dead at the scene of his master's murder, held vital evidence of the murderer. The bird's beak was found to be wet with the blood of the assailant, whom the valiant bird had attacked (reminding us of Holmes's remark in *The Hound of the Baskervilles*: "The devil's agents may be of flesh and blood, may they not?"), and the DNA extracted from the bloody beak was sufficient to ensure a life sentence for the killer.

But no matter how strong the science, we still cannot forget the image of Old Shuck, the Gurt Dog, the Padfoot, Hooter, Barghest, Galleytrot, the Shug, Hairy Jack—the Great Black Dog, waiting at the crossroads in the fading light to meet an unfortunate traveler and guide him to a fatal appointment.

Whatever remains

- It was traditional in Egyptian mummification rites that the first embalmer to incise the corpse, known as the "cutter," was ritually cursed and chased away from the embalming table by the other attendants. The remainder of the embalming process was carried out by the "salter," who was depicted wearing the black dog–mask of Anubis. This ambivalence toward opening the human body foreshadowed the resistance to human dissection that limited anatomical exploration for centuries.

- To protect against witches, British villagers often buried "witch bottles" near their front door steps. The bottles contained urine, pins and needles, and other odds and ends, and were believed to keep witches at bay. The custom was imported to New England.

- In 1944, during the Second World War, Helen Duncan was tried at the Old Bailey (London's historic criminal court) on charges of witchcraft, under a law that had not been applied for more than a century. Helen, who had been born in 1887, held regular séances, and a few of her predictions were so accurate that some in the War Office became seriously concerned that she would somehow discern and reveal the date of the forthcoming landing at Normandy. She was found guilty under the Witchcraft Act of 1735 and sentenced to nine months' incarceration at Holloway Prison.

The Witchcraft Act was not repealed until 1951.

CHAPTER 3

A Fly in the Ointment

*"From a drop of water a logician could infer the
possibility of an Atlantic or a Niagara without having
seen or heard of one or the other."*

—Sherlock Holmes in *A Study in Scarlet*

Unusual animals and insects fly and creep and slither
through a number of Sherlock Holmes stories. The snake coils in
"The Adventure of the Speckled Band," the jellyfish lies in wait in
"The Adventure of the Lion's Mane," and the haunting hound
terrifies the peasants in *The Hound of the Baskervilles*. But the
bizarre animals are not there just to frighten—they are foils for
scientific inquiry. Conan Doyle repeatedly describes these creatures as being pursued by eccentric amateur naturalists who are
eager to capture and classify them and their habitats.

Conan Doyle often used odd bits of scientific atmosphere to
dramatic advantage. In "The Adventure of the Three Garridebs,"
he describes the surroundings of a gentleman scientist:

The general effect, however, was amiable, though eccentric.
The room was as curious as its occupant. It looked like

a small museum. It was both broad and deep, with cupboards and cabinets all round, crowded with specimens, geological and anatomical. Cases of butterflies and moths flanked each side of the entrance. A large table in the center was littered with all sorts of debris, while the tall brass tube of a powerful microscope bristled up among them.

There were many such intense students of science in the days of the Holmes stories. The nineteenth century was a period of enormous interest in exploring the natural world. Conan Doyle, along with many of his contemporaries, frequented lectures on the subject and was fascinated by the theories of Charles Darwin and his followers.

In *The Hound of the Baskervilles*, Stapleton, the naturalist, is described on the moor incautiously ignoring the dangers of the treacherous terrain: "[A] small fly or moth had fluttered across our path, and in an instant Stapleton was rushing with extraordinary energy and speed in pursuit of it."

Stapleton, we are told, believes the insect to be a "Cyclopides." This specimen is not found on English moors, so his passionate haste is understandable. The Baskerville moor, as Conan Doyle described it, is extraordinary in another way, as it harbors a number of orchids within its wild and forbidding landscape.

The mention of an orchid and a moth in the same story must have reminded many of the original readers of the hound tale of the strange prediction Charles Darwin had made thirty-eight years before. Darwin firmly believed that insects and plants coevolved and were interdependent. On examining an unusual orchid from Madagascar called the star or Christmas orchid (*Angraecum sesquipedale*), which possesses a nectar spur almost twelve inches long, Darwin postulated that somewhere in Madagascar there must exist a moth with a proboscis, or noselike part, that is almost a foot long to allow it to reach the bottom of the nectar spur and so pollinate the orchid. He published this idea in 1862, in his work

"On the Various Contrivances by Which British and Foreign Orchids Are Fertilized by Insects," in which he states:

> [I]n Madagascar there must be moths with the proboscis capable of extension to a length of between ten and eleven inches! . . .
>
> The pollinia would not be withdrawn until some huge moth, with a wonderfully long proboscis, tried to drain the last drop. If such great moths were to become extinct in Madagascar, assuredly the Angraecum would become extinct.

Charles Darwin died in 1882, still believing in the existence of the extraordinary moth, although it had never been found. His theory was considered by many an amusing fancy, but the creative, confident reasoning from a small bit of evidence was typically Sherlockian.

Sherlock Holmes, Conan Doyle tells us, demanded acute observation, accurate data, and careful method. This was precisely the view of the dedicated amateur naturalists of the period. The collection, study, and classification of insects and plants, and the systematic reasoning based on the information so gathered had great implications for evolving forensic science.

Naturalists observed that there were millions of species of insects. They were ubiquitous as well. Many too tiny to notice, they still left traces of themselves in the form of larvae and exudates as they invaded homes, populated gardens, and intruded even into medical consulting rooms, laboratories, and hospitals. They were found on the carcasses of animals and on the corpses of humans. Clearly, these creatures were often present at the scene of violent crime. Could science find a way to make these silent witnesses give testimony?

Although this was a new concept in most of Europe, it had actually been put to use in China as far back as A.D. 1235. A death investigator named Sung T'zu, the author of the earliest known work on forensic investigation (the title of which is usually translated as *The Washing Away of Wrongs*), described a case in a small village in which a man was slashed to death. The shape and depth of the fatal injury indicated that it had been inflicted by a farmer's sickle. When questioned, the villagers denied all knowledge of the crime.

The investigator demanded that all of the townspeople bring their sickles to the central square and lay them on the ground. The tools all appeared to be clean. But tiny flies gathered, hovered hungrily, and then, buzzing with appetite, landed on one blade. They were evidently attracted by the minute traces of blood and tissue that scented the instrument. The owner of the weapon confessed.

In the West until the seventeenth century, insect activity had been observed but misinterpreted. It was known for centuries that many insects had hallucinogenic or poisonous effects if ingested. They were often ingredients in elaborate recipes for magical potions that were meant to seduce or to kill. In rural England, a tradition persisted that if a family member died, the bees on the property must be informed, or they would leave the hives in anger and deprive the bereaved of their honey. It was firmly believed that flies and maggots as well as bees and beetles generated spontaneously from decaying flesh. (This, of course, was an ancient idea, represented in the Bible by the tale of Samson finding the carcass of a lion he had slain filled with bees and honey.)

The first experiment on record to examine the validity of this theory was performed in 1668 by a physician and poet from Arezzo, Italy, named Francesco Redi. He had observed that meat that butchers and hunters had covered had fewer maggots than meat that was displayed unwrapped.

Redi filled three jars with putrid meat. He left one open, covered the mouth of the second with gauze fabric, and covered the third jar tightly. After several days, Redi found that the flesh in the open jar was covered with maggots. The jar covered with gauze had attracted flies, but the meat was without maggot activity. The covered jar had been untouched. Redi concluded that maggots were immature flies and that flies laid eggs on decaying meat.

The realization that some insects breed in decaying flesh and that they totally change form as they mature was a new idea. If it could be determined exactly how each type of insect colonized the dead, and if the length of time it took to do so could be accurately predicted, it might prove a valuable tool in establishing time of death in a homicide.

Although the concept was brilliant, it was difficult to put to prompt practical use. Many different sorts of insects are attracted to cadavers, and each species has its own breeding habits. Further, as insects are cold-blooded, their reproductive and feeding behaviors are strongly affected by ambient temperature.

Some insects are particularly difficult to identify, because they imitate the appearance of others. The *Syrphidae*, or common hover flies, are a prime example. They often appear in the coloring of honeybees or wasps. Although they are largely found in contaminated water, they also target dead flesh. All of these variables made accurate classification of insects of the dead, including their larvae and pupae, very complex.

For many years after Redi's experiment, the study of insects in relation to criminal investigation remained largely academic. In 1850, a case in France made innovative use of this natural science. Laborers making repairs in a house of rental flats noticed that a few bricks behind a fireplace were improperly fitted. When the bricks were removed, the tiny corpse of what appeared to be a newborn child was disclosed. The body was mummified, evidently due to the dry heat to which it had been exposed. Insects of various kinds had made their home in the nooks and crannies of the corpse.

It was not infrequent for workmen to find this sort of piteous remnant in the walls and cellars of ancient houses. Terrified young women had been known to make use of the sturdy, thick construction to hide the sad souvenirs of illicit passion. But was this case a murder, or only the irregular disposal of a child born dead?

The police posed a number of questions to the medical inves-tigators. Was the child full term at birth? Had it been stillborn? If born alive, how old was it at death? What was the cause of death? If it was a homicide, who was most likely responsible? The prob-lem was complicated by the fact that four different tenants had lived in the apartment in the previous three years.

Dr. M. Bergeret of the Hôpital Civil d'Arbois was asked for his opinion, as he had done a number of studies on the changes that occurred in long-buried cadavers. Bergeret approached the problem with the classic techniques of legal medicine. He dis-sected the body, measured the bones, and minutely examined the desiccated tissues.

He concluded that the child had been full term and had been born alive. But in order to determine how long the baby's body had lain in its brick-lined tomb, Bergeret turned to the natural science of entomology, the study of insects. Carefully observing and classifying the moths, mites, and pupae that infested the corpse, he felt certain that the body had been in the wall for at least two years.

This removed suspicion from the most recent tenants and cast it instead on a young woman who had lived in the flat in the sum-mer of 1848. The neighbors and the landlady, Madame Saillard, believed that the woman had been pregnant, but the child had never been seen. Although the woman was arrested and brought to trial, she was not convicted. Suspicious circumstances notwith-standing, Bergeret was unable to establish that the manner of death was homicide.

When Bergeret wrote his report of the case in 1855, he stressed both the small amount of knowledge available at the time about the effects of insects on the dead and the need for additional research. Still, he had demonstrated that entomological evidence could be useful to help determine postmortem interval, one of the most difficult problems in legal medicine.

In 1878, Brouardel was faced with a similar case and found guidance in Bergeret's work. The mummified newborn corpse that Brouardel autopsied was a nesting place for a number of arthropods. Brouardel asked an army veterinarian, Pierre Megnin, and a professor of the Natural History Museum in Paris to consult.

They identified butterfly larvae, the skin and feces of mites, and moth larvae. There were millions of mites present, both living and dead. Considering these factors, as well as the remnants of plant life on the body and the number of generations of insects present, the scientists agreed that the cadaver had been placed at the scene between five and seven months before it was discovered.

The information they gained by observing the flora and fauna of the dead was carefully preserved. They assumed it would be of use in the future. Just as Sherlock Holmes would have demanded, they collected data. As the data accumulated, the connection strengthened between the natural sciences and legal medicine. Megnin continued his research with the intention of writing definitive works on the subject, which he finally accomplished in *Fauna of the Tombs*, published in 1887 and *Fauna of the Cadavers*, published in 1894.

To further understanding of the effects that plant and insect life have on long-buried corpses, large-scale exhumations were carried out during the nineteenth century in France and Germany under the direction of medicolegal doctors. Researchers also exposed the corpses of animals to observe the postmortem changes caused by various insects under a variety of weather conditions. They observed that some beetles carried tiny mites on their bodies, thus allowing the mites access to cadavers. Roaches and other large insects walked through blood and other body fluids and could deposit them some distance from the death scene. Insects were often responsible for postmortem or perimortem injuries. The knowledge prevented a number of judicial disasters.

In Frankfurt, Germany, in 1889, a nine-month-old baby from an impoverished family died. At autopsy, which was performed three days later, injuries to the face were noted. In spite of the child's history of illness, the wounds made the police suspect the father of feeding the child sulfuric acid. (At the time, this was a common method of disposing of inconvenient children.) Entomologists, however, demonstrated that the injuries were due to the bites of roaches, and the bereaved father was released from prison after several weeks of incarceration.

A similar case was reported in Germany in 1899, when a woman was suspected of causing the death of her child because of a pattern of abrasions on the exterior of the child's body. The frantic mother insisted that she was innocent of any crime and that she had seen the body of her child covered with a blanket of roaches when she had returned from choosing a casket. The physician examining the case put bits of human tissue in glass vessels filled with roaches. The resultant damage caused by the insects proved that the injuries found on the child could be caused in this way, and the wretched mother was spared prosecution.

These cases and the importance of insects and plants in legal investigation were much discussed in central European scientific circles at the time. Conan Doyle spent months in Berlin and Vienna in 1890. Given his medical background, he was most likely well aware of this growing research.

Interest in the subject spread rapidly. Research was done in Canada by Wyatt Johnston and Geoffrey Villeneuve and in the United States by Murray Motter. The differences in climate and animal life in various geographical areas made it difficult to usefully share information, but the methods of observation were similar. Bit by bit, the importance of the insect world became evident.

While scientists in laboratories were struggling to understand the interrelationships of carrion beetles, flesh flies, ants, roaches, and mites, an extraordinary discovery was announced in England. It was 1903, only a year after the publication of *The Hound of the Baskervilles*, the novel that included the vivid description of the passionate collector of butterflies, Stapleton, and of orchids growing wild on the mysterious moor.

Walter Rothschild, who was a scion of the famous family of financiers and a dedicated naturalist, and his curator, Karl Jordon, described a fabulous moth that possessed an eleven-inch-long proboscis—long enough to pollinate the mysterious star orchid. The moth had been discovered in Madagascar, just as Darwin had speculated forty years before. Commonly called the hawk moth, it was officially named *Xanthophan morgani praedicta* in honor of Darwin's prediction. This was proof that Sherlockian scientific reasoning was a spectacular success.

In "The Adventure of the Lion's Mane," Sherlock Holmes describes his retirement as isolated but implies it is full of scientific curiosity when he says, "My house is lonely. I, my old housekeeper, and my bees have the estate all to ourselves." In the story "His Last Bow," Conan Doyle tells us further that during his retirement, Holmes has composed his magnum opus: "Practical Handbook of Bee Culture, with Some Observations upon the Segregation of the Queen."

If an investigator with Holmes's interests had truly written this monograph, it would certainly have included some information on the *Syrphidae*, the hover flies that masquerade as bees and visit the dead. Clearly this would have been more than the casual amusement of a gentleman; it would have been a careful study contributing vital data to forensic science.

WHATEVER REMAINS

- Many humble and tiny creatures continue to contribute to forensic investigation. In 2004, the *Journal of Forensic Science* reported that human DNA profiles could be obtained from maggots that had fed on a cadaver, even after a postmortem interval of sixteen weeks—raising the possibility that even if a victim's body had been destroyed, its identity might be established by the maggots left behind.

- Because maggots devour diseased or decaying flesh, they have proved useful in cleansing wounds in situations where antibiotics are unavailable or their use is inadvisable. The diseased flesh is exposed to flies; the flies deposit eggs in the wound; the injury is bandaged; and the maggots are allowed to remove the damaged tissue. The main difficulty is the provenance of the flies. Their living habits are unsavory, and one can never be sure of where they have been.

- Leeches, which belong to a phylum of segmented worm, have always played a part in primitive medicine, which found them useful in order to bleed patients. Certain leeches, such as the helpful *Hirudo medicinalis*, are now enjoying a renaissance as part of the healing arts. They aid in maintaining circulation in surgically reattached parts.

CHAPTER 4

Proving Poison

"How about poison?"
—Sherlock Holmes in "The Adventure
of the Speckled Band"

SHERLOCK HOLMES contemplates poison a good deal. A scientific thinker of his era was bound to do so, as the nineteenth century was a time of seminal discoveries in the detection of venomous substances.

At Dr. Watson's first meeting with Sherlock Holmes in the laboratory at St. Bart's Hospital, Holmes's hands are covered with bits of sticking plaster, the Victorian precursor to Band-Aids. "I have to be careful, for I dabble with poisons a good deal," Holmes explains. As a medical man, Watson absorbs this bit of information with equanimity, knowing that experiments in chemistry inevitably involve contact with dangerous materials. Watson does not realize that this mention of poison is a foreshadowing of fascinating problems that he will share with Holmes when the pair investigate cases such as "The Adventure of the Speckled Band," "The Adventure of the Devil's Foot," and *A Study in Scarlet*.

These tales of Conan Doyle are clearly informed by the ambivalent fascination the public felt for poisoners and their crimes. Great throngs of Victorians, full of passionate attention, regularly attended celebrated trials for poisoning as though going to the theater. It excited interest that many of the accused were disarmingly attractive, educated women. As Holmes notes in *The Sign of Four*, "I assure you that the most winning woman I ever knew was hanged for poisoning three little children for their insurance-money."

Women had access to the sickroom and the kitchen. Well-born, educated women were believed to be implicitly trustworthy. In the nineteenth century, many stood in the dock only because recent advances in toxicology made it possible to detect delicate but sinister handiwork.

Among the ladies whose trials attracted intense interest and overflow crowds were: Madeleine Smith, the cool and controlled young woman of Glasgow who was accused in 1857 of poisoning her lover by serving him cocoa accented with arsenic (during her trial, the courtroom scene was drawn for a newspaper by the artist Charles Doyle, father of Arthur Conan Doyle; the jury delivered the singularly Scottish verdict of "Not proven"); Florence Bravo, who was suspected of killing her difficult husband, Charles, by placing the heavy metal poison antimony in his burgundy (the jury at the 1876 inquest found that although Charles had been murdered, "there is insufficient evidence to fix the guilt upon any person or persons"); and Adelaide Bartlett, whose beauty and dignified bearing drew sympathy when she was tried at the Old Bailey in 1886 on charges of dispatching her husband with chloroform (the verdict was "Not guilty").

In 1889, Florence Maybrick was not so fortunate, as she was convicted on shaky evidence of the arsenic murder of her drug-taking, abusive husband, James. A large part of her conviction rested on the fact that Mr. Justice Fitzjames Stephen, who presided over her trial, was slithering toward senility and allowed copious amounts of extraneous testimony to be admitted. He also delivered a rambling but most unfavorable summation.

The English public was outraged by what was seen as an unfair verdict. The government compromised by commuting Florence's death sentence to life imprisonment. She was released in 1904 and promptly wrote a book entitled *My Fifteen Lost Years*. It sold very well.

Observing the trial of a woman whose life hung in the balance was titillating, but actually convicting her was avoided. As a rule, convictions were hard to achieve. Reasonable doubt was easily raised, as the times were awash in lethal substances. Mercury was used in the manufacture of hats. Small doses of arsenic and similar substances were often taken as tonics. Women used arsenic to whiten their complexions and belladonna to enlarge the pupils of their eyes. The laws were lax, and poisons of all kinds were readily available for purchase "to rid the home of vermin."

At the beginning of *A Study in Scarlet*, Watson has just returned from Afghanistan and is perhaps unaware of the details of the contemporary cases that fascinated England. But as an educated physician, he undoubtedly knows something of the sinister history of poisoning and the problems that subtle homicides presented to both the judicial system and the medical profession.

In ancient times, poisoning was both obsessively feared and ferociously punished. The first poisons noted historically were venomous animal substances, usually derived from reptiles or amphibians. *Venin de crapaud*, or toad venom, was a favorite. These poisons were often tested on prisoners or slaves, and if proved effective, they were used to coat weapons. Animal poisons are a familiar concept to Holmes, and he is quick to suspect their presence in a number of stories, including "The Adventure of the Speckled Band":

> "The idea of a snake instantly occurred to me, and when I coupled it with my knowledge that the doctor was furnished with a supply of creatures from India, I felt that I was probably on the right track. The idea of using a form of poison, which could not possibly be discovered by any

chemical test was just such a one as would occur to a clever and ruthless man who had had an Eastern training. The rapidity with which such a poison would take effect would also, from his point of view, be an advantage. It would be a sharp-eyed coroner, indeed, who could distinguish the two little dark punctures."

Holmes's thought was prescient. Several twentieth-century poison cases were solved when a medical examiner's painstaking external exam disclosed the mark of a hypodermic needle. Among these was the unusual death of Elizabeth Barlow of Thornbury Crescent, in Bradford, England.

On a May evening in 1957, Elizabeth's husband, Kenneth, a nurse who worked at a nearby hospital, had called a local doctor to see her, saying that she was very weak and had collapsed in the bathtub. The doctor discovered Elizabeth's dead body lying on its side in an empty tub. She had vomited. The bereaved husband explained that she had complained of feeling ill and had decided to take a bath. He had fallen asleep waiting for her to return to bed. When he awakened, he discovered her still in the tub, her head submerged in water. He had tried to lift her, but found that even given his nursing skills she was too heavy for him. Therefore, he had drained the tub and tried to resuscitate her where she lay, clearly to no avail. The doctor called the police.

Detective Sergeant Naylor, who responded, was immediately struck by the fact that Kenneth Barlow's pajamas were absolutely dry. There were no signs of splashed water anywhere in the bathroom.

The attention of forensic pathologist David Price was requested. Dr. Price at once noticed that water still clung to the crook of the dead woman's arm, which raised additional questions about Kenneth's claim of vigorous efforts to save her. The body was brought to the Harrowgate mortuary, and the postmortem was performed at once.

External examination showed no unusual marks on the corpse's heavily freckled skin. Internal examination revealed an early pregnancy but no clear cause of death. Price, wielding a magnifying glass, went over the body slowly and methodically a second time. After two painstaking hours, he was rewarded by the discovery of two sets of tiny hypodermic marks on the buttocks. But the toxicology screen had been negative. What could have been injected into this young woman?

The police, questioning Kenneth's coworkers, had discovered that his nursing job involved injecting insulin. It was known that Elizabeth was not a diabetic, and therefore injecting her with a large dose of insulin would result in fatal hypoglycemic shock. There was no precedent for murder by insulin, no accepted test.

Price sectioned out the hypodermic marks. He and A. S. Curry, the toxicologist, injected a group of mice with insulin and a second group with a slurry made from the sectioned tissue. Both groups of mice developed identical symptoms and died. The tests were repeated several times with the same results.

Kenneth Barlow was found guilty of poisoning his wife and sentenced to life in prison. In the interest of fair play, the jury had not been told of another discovery by the police: that his first wife had died of similar symptoms a few years before. It had been accepted as a natural death. If that woman's body had been examined with Sherlockian care and each bit of skin peered at through a magnifying glass, tiny marks might well have been found— marks like those of a snake's bite. If a "sharp-eyed coroner" had distinguished "two little dark punctures" in that case, Elizabeth Barlow might not have married the snake named Kenneth.

Although reptiles and the odd amphibian were the most common sources of poison in the ancient world, plant poisons were also known. Hemlock, oleander, monkshood, hellebore, opium, and various unsavory varieties of mushrooms took their toll on unsuspecting victims.

Arsenic was known, but its distinctive taste limited its use as part of the poisoner's arsenal until about A.D. 800, when an Arab researcher named Jabir ibn Hayyam refined it into a white powder with little taste, which was easily hidden in food or drink.

With grim humor, people referred to arsenic as "inheritance pow-der," as unhappy families were believed to make efficient use of it. Although it was often a suspected cause of death, its presence could not be clearly demonstrated in a court of law.

During the Middle Ages, the pervasive fear of poisoning led to complex but ineffective antidotes and superstitious methods of detection. It was believed that black spots appearing on a corpse denoted the presence of poison, thus confusing natural signs of putrefaction or disease with evidence of homicide.

Supposed universal antidotes included dried powdered mummy, "unicorn horn" (this was usually the relic of an unfortu-nate rhinoceros), and theriac, a concoction that consisted of thirty to sixty ingredients, depending on the recipe of the apothecary mixing it. It was useless to the patient, although most helpful to the financial situation of the consultant.

Usnea, made of moss scraped from the skull of a dead man, preferably that of an executed criminal, was a favorite "cure." There was also a brisk business in bezoar stones. These are accretions usu-ally formed in the intestines or gallbladders of animals, and they were bought at enormous cost by many credulous heads of state.

Ambroise Paré, a sixteenth-century surgeon possessed of sci-entific skepticism and a spirit of inquiry worthy of Sherlock Holmes, insisted bezoars were without value and was determined to prove the point. As a medical adviser to Charles IX of France, he was in a good position to do so. He chose for his experiment a palace cook who had been accused of stealing some silver and was therefore languishing in prison while he awaited execution. Paré proposed to feed the cook a poison and then administer part of the king's prize bezoar stone as antidote. The prisoner would be granted a pardon if he survived.

Eager for a chance at life, the cook agreed to the trial. Within an hour, in spite of the bezoar stone, the cook was in agony, crawl-ing on all fours, vomiting, purging, and bleeding from every orifice. Paré's attempts to assuage his suffering were of no avail, and the hapless man expired after seven hours of torment. Charles destroyed the bezoar stone as a result, although there were some at court who believed that Paré had proven not that bezoars were worthless but only that Charles's bezoar was a counterfeit.

Paré's use of human beings in poison experiments in the sixteenth century was not unique, and fear of such activities was deeply embedded in folklore. Catherine de Medici was popularly believed to have brought poison recipes along with her dowry when she wedded the French king. It was whispered that she sent baskets of poisoned food to the poor and then ordered her servants to visit the recipients the next day and inquire about their health. This procedure, people claimed, allowed her to add to the body of scientific knowledge while conveniently reducing the number of impoverished citizens in France.

The image of the murderous woman tied neatly in with the fear of witchcraft and magic. In the seventeenth century, an inventive lady called Teofania di Adamo sold a clear fluid to the ladies of Rome and Naples labeled "Manna of St. Nicholas of Bari." It was officially known as a cosmetic, but a tiny amount was said to cause a rapid death that featured a natural appearance. It became known as "Aqua Tofana." Difficult husbands began to experience fatal digestive complaints.

When at last official suspicion focused on Teofania, she sought refuge in a convent, from which she was eventually expelled. Under intense questioning, she confessed to more than six hundred murders and was promptly strangled. Her daughter, Giulia, is believed to have carried on the family business. Following as well in her treacherous footsteps was a French woman, Madame de Brinvilliers, who separated a number of relatives and lovers from life before she was caught and executed.

Both Aqua Tofana and Madame de Brinvilliers are mentioned by Watson in *A Study in Scarlet* when he sardonically sums up a newspaper article:

> After alluding airily to the Vehmgericht, aqua tofana, Carbonari, the Marchioness de Brinvilliers, the Darwinian

theory, the principles of Malthus, and the Ratcliff High-
way murders, the article concluded by admonishing the
government and advocating a closer watch over foreigners
in England.

Until the early nineteenth century, convictions for poisoning
depended on circumstantial evidence and confessions elicited by
torture. When Mary Blandy was tried and hanged for poisoning
her father in 1752, the medical evidence against her was merely
that the white powder she was seen putting in her father's food
looked like arsenic and that the deceased's intestinal tract was irritated.

By 1814, it was clear that progress was being made, largely
due to the efforts of Mathieu Joseph Bonaventure Orfila, who was
born on the Spanish island of Minorca in 1787. A brilliant student
of medicine and chemistry, he left Spain for Paris at the age of
eighteen to continue his studies. In the course of his research, he
discovered that many of the primitive tests for poisons and their
antidotes were worthless, and he embarked on new experiments
that he designed himself.

Orfila's first publication, *Treatise on Poison*, established the new
science of toxicology as a vital part of medical jurisprudence. He
demonstrated the effects of arsenic and other poisons on the
intestinal tract by experimenting on dogs and developed new
methods of recovering arsenic from animal tissue.

Building on Orfila's work, a chemist from the British Isles,
James Marsh, invented the first test for heavy metal poisoning
that produced results vivid enough to convince a jury. The device
was simple. A glass tube shaped like a U, with one open end and
a pointed nozzle at the other end, was made. Zinc was suspended
in the pointed end; in the other end, the suspect fluid was mixed
with acid. When the liquid and the zinc met, if arsenic was at all
present, arsine gas emerged from the nozzle. A flame was held to
the gas until it ignited, and an icy piece of porcelain was placed
near the flame. A black, shiny deposit called an arsenic mirror

would form on the china. It was a mirror that could reflect a murder. The Marsh method was capable of finding even minute quantities of arsenic as well as antimony. It was dramatic enough to impress a courtroom.

It produced the crucial evidence at the 1840 trial of Marie Capelle Lafarge, who was accused of eliminating an ill-mannered husband with arsenic-laden cake. Born in 1816 to parents who, it was rumored, had blood ties to the French nobility, Marie was orphaned as an adolescent and raised in Paris by an aunt and uncle. Sent to expensive schools, she made friends among the wellborn, but as she had only a modest dowry, she was not considered an attractive marriage prospect.

Her foster parents, grimly determined to have her settled, secretly approached a matrimonial agency to locate a candidate for her hand. They found one in Charles Lafarge and presented him to Marie as a family acquaintance. The fact that he was a widower was not mentioned. Marie was told only that he owned profitable ironworks and a magnificent château called Le Glandier in the provinces. Although repelled by Charles, whose manners and appearance were unfortunate, she was dazzled by detailed drawings of his exquisite château. Passionately encouraged by her aunt, Marie married Charles and traveled with him to his home.

She was shocked to discover that Le Glandier was actually a festering pile of crumbling stone—cold, gray, grim, and forbidding. Worse, it was inhabited by Charles's mother, who was also cold, gray, grim, and forbidding. A few other relatives and hangers-on lived on the premises, including Anna Brun, who had drawn the imaginative pictures of the mythical Le Glandier, and who seemed to have a romantic interest in Charles and resented his marriage. Armies of resident rodents roamed freely through the rooms, competing for sustenance with the assorted poultry that nested, clucking comfortably, in the kitchen. Marie, in hysterics, locked herself in her room.

She eventually emerged, only to discover over the next few weeks that Charles's business was bankrupt, that he was a widower who had spent his deceased wife's fortune, and that he evidently had married Marie for her dowry, which, while modest by Paris standards, had marvelous appeal in the provinces. Marie appeared to adjust to this situation calmly and busily went about improving the household. She ordered new curtains, joined a library, cooked complicated dishes involving truffles, and, no doubt in the interests of hygiene, wrote to the local doctor, "I am overrun with rats. Will you trust me with a little arsenic?"

She seemed to have acquired affection for Charles. When he went to Paris on business, she arranged for cake to be sent to him. Unfortunately, he became seriously ill after a small bite and returned to Le Glandier so that his new wife could nurse him. She was attentive, bringing him all sorts of soothing drinks and soups. Still, he worsened. Anna Brun claimed she had seen Marie stirring a white powder that she carried in a small malachite box into Charles's food and drink. Anna discreetly gathered samples of the food and hid them.

After two weeks of increasing agony, Charles died. Anna produced the samples she had hidden. The local doctors tested them and the contents of the malachite box with the primitive method of exposing them to heat. They gave off a strong smell of garlic and turned yellow. On this basis, the doctors declared that they contained arsenic. Tests on the dead man's stomach contents gave similar results, so Marie was charged with the murder of her husband.

Her aunt, no doubt worried about the family reputation, as the case was widely covered in the press, hired, at enormous expense, Maître Paillet, a lawyer of great reputation and skill, to defend Marie. He immediately attacked the tests as inadequate. As a friend of Orfila, Paillet was aware of recent advances in poison detection, and at Orfila's suggestion, he insisted that the new Marsh test be performed. Apothecaries from Limoges were instructed by the court to do so. Unwilling to admit their inexperience, they attempted the procedure and finally reported that no arsenic could be detected by the Marsh test. Marie's many supporters were jubilant.

The prosecutor countered by insisting that the famous Orfila himself be asked to repeat the Marsh test. The defense was forced to agree. Orfila arrived from Paris and tested the specimens in full view of the local experimenters, working all through the night. The following afternoon, he testified to a hushed courtroom that he had found arsenic in all of the samples. He explained that the Marsh test was delicate and required administration by an expert.

Marie Lafarge was found guilty and was sentenced to death, which was reduced to life imprisonment at hard labor; the hard labor was subsequently eliminated. She served ten years in a suite of cells, writing her memoirs and corresponding with sympathetic supporters, among them the writer Alexandre Dumas (*père*). She was released by Napoleon III and died of tuberculosis shortly after her release, claiming her innocence to the end.

If Marie's attorney had rested his case less on the Marsh test and more on the fact that the physical evidence had been collected by Anna Brun, a clearly prejudiced party with a motive of her own, the result might have been different.

Whatever the legal issues, the Lafarge case made clear the fact that toxicology was complex and required skill and experience as well as theoretical knowledge. It also opened the door for the great poison trials of the Victorian era.

By 1842, a simpler method of testing for arsenic had been developed by Hugo Reinsch of Germany. The new science of toxicology seemed sure to grow in importance. And then came a devastating setback, when Dr. Thomas Smethurst was tried at the Old Bailey for the arsenic murder of Isabella Bankes.

"When a doctor does go wrong he is the first of criminals. He has nerve and he has knowledge," says Sherlock Holmes in "The Adventure of the Speckled Band." And his observation is borne out by the number of Victorian and Edwardian poisoners with medical training. Pritchard, Cream, Palmer, Warder, Waite, and Crippen—all murderous doctors whose names conjure nightmares.

But the Smethurst case was unique. It was not simply a matter of a rogue physician poisoning a trusting soul. It was as well the case of an eminent medical expert whose careless error damaged the public's trust in the accuracy of scientific testimony.

In 1858, when Dr. Smethurst was in his fifties and his wife was almost twenty years older, they arrived by carriage at the London suburb of Bayswater and rented lodgings in a boardinghouse. Smethurst specialized in hydrotherapy, a Victorian medical therapy that involved the forceful application of water to every possible orifice in the human body. He told the landlady that he was considering opening a practice in Bayswater and wished to familiarize himself with the area.

Isabella Bankes, a fellow tenant, was forty-two, possessed of a bit of charm, a moderate amount of money, and a medical history of occasional digestive complaints. She was happy to confide her problems to a doctor. He seemed delighted to discuss her symptoms. As their clearly intimate chats grew lengthy, the landlady grew uneasy, in spite of the fact that Mrs. Smethurst seemed to view the matter with an odd detachment.

Finally, the indignant landlady asked Miss Bankes to leave. She did, but accompanied by Dr. Smethurst. They were married in a religious although bigamous ceremony at Battersea Church and then moved to Richmond to enjoy domestic bliss.

It was not to be. Shortly after the "wedding," Isabella became ill, suffering from violent diarrhea and vomiting. When a few days of treatment by her "husband" did not help, a local practitioner, Dr. Julius, was sent for. The patient was given chalk to drink in an effort to control her symptoms, but she grew worse. Another opinion was sought. And another. The illness intensified. A lawyer was called, and Isabella signed a will, leaving all of her money to "my sincere and beloved friend, Thomas Smethurst."

Dr. Julius and his partner, suspecting an irritant poison, removed the contents of Isabella's chamber pot and took it to the laboratory of Alfred Swaine Taylor, the eminent pathologist who also practiced toxicology. He undertook to examine the specimen using the elegantly simple Reinsch method.

The suspect material was mixed with hydrochloric acid and heated. A copper mesh was then inserted in the solution. If arsenic was present, it would appear as a dark gray coating on the copper. Taylor reported that the test on Isabella's specimen was positive for arsenic.

Smethurst was usually the person who had given food and drink to Isabella, and he rarely left her side. In view of these suspicious circumstances, he was arrested. He tearfully told the examining magistrates that his wife's illness made it a hardship for him to be separated from her and that she was in sore need of his care. He was promptly released.

Isabella Bankes died the next day.

Smethurst was charged with murder. The trial, in July 1859, attracted great attention as one that would hang almost completely on scientific evidence. The medical testimony was unexpected. At autopsy, the deceased woman was found to be five to seven weeks pregnant. Her intestines appeared to be greatly inflamed, consistent with arsenic poisoning. But an attempt to demonstrate arsenic in her internal organs was unsuccessful. How was it possible for arsenic to be clearly present before death and disappear after it?

Further experiments yielded a distressing fact. When Taylor initially carried out the Reinsch procedure, he had not considered testing the copper mesh before inserting it into the slurry of acid and fecal matter. The copper, which had been used many times before, had been contaminated with arsenic. Dr. Taylor had fatally damaged the experiment with his own reagent.

Several expert witnesses for the defense argued that the cause of death was a form of dysentery, aggravated by a first pregnancy in a lady of mature years, but the judge's summation was damning. After forty minutes of deliberation, a verdict of guilty was delivered and a death sentence decreed.

There was an immediate outcry from the medical community, which argued that the scientific facts did not justify the verdict. A lengthy and emotional plea for mercy was made to Queen

Victoria by the first and only legal Mrs. Smethurst, who had evidently awakened from her torpor. The home secretary gathered the facts, considered them carefully, and overturned the verdict.

As Dr. Smethurst left the jail a free man, he was immediately rearrested on charges of bigamy and sentenced to a year in prison. Thus, with one stroke the government met the highest ethical standards of Anglo-Saxon jurisprudence and at the same time fulfilled the deepest needs of British middle-class morality.

When he was finally released from prison, Dr. Smethurst (clearly a man ahead of his time) sued for Miss Bankes's estate. He won the case, pocketed the money, and disappeared from public view, some say in the cheerful company of Mrs. Smethurst. The lay public as well as the scientific community reacted with grave mistrust of "expert" witnesses, and the entire field of medical jurisprudence was viewed as tainted for years.

Arthur Conan Doyle was born in the same year as the Smethurst trial. Decades later, when he was a medical student, the reverberations were still being felt. Joseph Bell, the physician who was Conan Doyle's teacher, mentor, and model for the character of Sherlock Holmes, was deeply ambivalent about the forensic world and is said to have hidden his participation in a number of cases. Conan Doyle had met Bell in 1876 and was enormously impressed by the older man's incisive personality and deductive powers.

As a medical student, Doyle must have been a close observer of the Chantrelle case of 1878, which some historians believe Dr. Bell took part in solving. Eugene Marie Chantrelle was an immigrant from France to Edinburgh, Scotland. He had spent some time in medical school in Nantes, France, but did not complete his degree. In Scotland, he taught French with reasonable success. He formed a romantic relationship with a student, Elizabeth Dyer, and married her when she was just sixteen. A child was born to them two months later.

The marriage was unhappy. Chantrelle tormented Elizabeth by frequently jesting in public that his medical knowledge would allow him to poison her without a trace. After ten years of wretched matrimony, in October 1877, he insured her life, over her objections, for one thousand pounds. The policy was unusual—it would pay only if Elizabeth died by accident.

On January 2, 1878, a maid entered the bedroom of Elizabeth Chantrelle to find the lady deeply unconscious. Some vomited pieces of fruit stained the bedclothes. There was a strong smell of gas. Amazingly, there had been an accident.

A Dr. Carmichael, who had never treated the patient before, was called. After a brief examination, he sent a note to Dr. Henry Littlejohn, who was both police surgeon and toxicologist. (He was also a colleague and frequent collaborator of Dr. Joseph Bell.) The note read, "Dear Sir, if you would like to see a case of coal gas poisoning, please come."

Littlejohn's immediate impression was that the symptoms were more in keeping with narcotic poisoning than gas exposure. He collected the vomited matter and had Elizabeth sent to the hospital, where the unfortunate woman expired.

The postmortem revealed no narcotics in the corpse but a lethal quantity of opium in the vomited material. This was not unusual. It was known that opium could escape detection in animal tissues if the deceased lived long enough for it to have passed through the system.

Upon examining the premises, the gas company found a broken gas bracket and determined it had been deliberately damaged.

It took a jury only one hour and ten minutes to find Eugene Marie Chantrelle guilty of murder. Three weeks later, he was hanged.

The Chantrelle case attracted great attention. Many felt that toxicology had redeemed itself as a weapon in the interest of justice. But although a number of researchers believe that Littlejohn consulted with Joseph Bell on the case, Bell's name does not appear on the official documents. He is known to have suppressed knowledge of his involvement in a number of forensic cases, evidently fearing that it might damage his reputation as a gentleman.

The Smethurst affair had cast a long shadow. Along with problems of trust, toxicologists had to battle the very complex nature of their calling and the fact that every advance seemed to be followed by a setback.

Heavy metal poisons such as arsenic and antimony could now be found even in small quantities in human tissue. Determining how they got there was another matter. Arsenic, for instance, is common in the environment. It is found in rocks, in soil, and, until the late twentieth century, in synthetic materials such as paint and wallpaper. Arsenic is naturally found in small amounts in the living human body. An excellent preservative, it was often an ingredient in embalming fluid. Experimental burying and exhumation of corpses disclosed that bodies could absorb arsenic after death, thus raising the ghastly possibility that convictions based purely on the presence of arsenic might have been in error.

Recovering plant alkaloid poison from dead tissue had long been a major problem, as the alkaloid left no detectable traces. Orfila, considered the father of toxicology, thought it might be hopeless.

In 1851, a Belgian chemist named Jean Servais Stas devised a complex method for extracting the potent poison nicotine from human remains to solve a murder. Grinding the corpse's organs to a pulpy mass, Stas then combined them with alcohol and acid, which separated the alkaline poison from the tissue. Building on his work, chemists all over the world developed reagents to test for various alkaloids.

It seemed the problem was solved. But research on the bodies of people known to have died of natural causes disclosed that certain alkaloids form in the body after death. These cadaveric alkaloids could appear dangerously similar to plant poisons. The stage was set for decades of conflicting expert testimony.

As the nineteenth century wore on, scientists published their findings at a rapid pace, newspapers were full of accounts of sensational crimes, and the public's taste for suspense fiction grew. Although some lugubrious commentators warned that access to such material would give criminals new and dangerous ideas and make crime harder to combat, calmer heads found this unlikely—most of the fiction published was wildly inaccurate and the tabloid press even more fanciful. But it is true that poisoning cases grew in complexity as new and dangerous drugs became available.

In New York City in 1891, a young medical student named Carlyle Harris had been secretly married to Helen Potts, a residential pupil at the Comstock School for Young Ladies, for almost a year. The other girls at Comstock were told that he was Helen's fiancé. Harris claimed that the marriage had to remain secret for fear his family would not continue to support his studies if he married while still at school.

Helen's mother began to insist on disclosure. Not surprisingly, Helen developed insomnia, for which Harris prescribed six low-dose capsules of quinine and morphine. (In those halcyon days, medical students were allowed to prescribe.) This was a common sedative at the time, and it was made to order by McIntyre & Son, a respected New York pharmacy.

Harris picked up the capsules and gave only four of them to Helen. She was directed to take one capsule a night. She did so for three uneventful nights. On the fourth evening, she awoke in a delirium, breathing with great difficulty, her pupils clearly contracted. The school doctor's frantic efforts to save her were to no avail.

Harris produced the two capsules he had held back, which upon examination proved to contain only a benign dose of morphine. Helen was buried, but so many questions were raised by the newspapers that she was exhumed. The New York toxicologist Rudolph Witthaus found morphine in all of the girl's organs but no quinine. The implication was that the last capsule she took contained only pure morphine. Given the size of the capsules, it would have been an overdose. The pharmacy insisted that it could account for all the drugs it dispensed and that there was no mistake on the pharmacy's part.

Harris was arrested and charged with murder. The investigators concluded that Harris had filled one of the four capsules Helen had been given with a lethal dose of morphine, which he could easily obtain at the medical school. He had kept two capsules to enable him to show that they were harmless in case Helen took the fatal one last. Harris was convicted and executed in 1893.

It was a plot intricate enough to have been influenced by a Sherlock Holmes story. It is interesting to note that *A Study in Scarlet*, the first novel in which the Great Detective appeared, had been published in the United States by J. B. Lippincott in 1890, just a year before the Harris case. The book attracted more attention and much greater popularity in America than it had in its native Britain, and it was widely discussed. It includes a famous scene in which the character Jefferson Hope describes how he plotted to kill his victim, saying:

> "One day the professor was lecturing on poisons, and he showed his students some alkaloid, as he called it, which he had extracted from some South American arrow poison, and which was so powerful that the least grain meant instant death. I spotted the bottle in which this preparation was kept, and when they were all gone, I helped myself to a little of it. I was a fairly good dispenser, so I worked this alkaloid into small, soluble pills, and each pill I put in a box with a similar pill made without the poison."

The name of the poison isn't given, but the method of deployment is. Did Carlyle Harris read *A Study in Scarlet* and see in it a way out of his difficulties? It's equally possible that one of the investigators read the novel and realized how the murder of Helen Potts had been accomplished.

As Sherlock Holmes remarked in "The Adventure of the Dancing Men," "What one man can invent, another can discover."

Whatever remains

- The hypodermic syringe was developed in 1853 by Charles Pravez and Alexander Wood, working simultaneously but separately. Its minuscule punctures have served as important clues in a number of historic medical murders.

- In 1965, Dr. Carmela Coppolino died of a homicidal injection of the anesthetic succinylcholine. Her husband, Dr. Carl Coppolino, was convicted of the crime.

- In 1975, Dr. Charles Friedgood was found guilty of killing his wife by injection of Demerol. It is of dubious comfort to note that homicides of this nature are often performed by well-trained health care professionals in the privacy of their own homes.

- The summation offered by Justice Fitzjames Stephen in the 1889 trial of Florence Maybrick lasted two full days and was riddled with errors of fact. By long tradition, judges of the period were rarely censored and were allowed enormous control over juries. During the early Victorian era, an undecided British jury could be locked up without fire, food, or light until it reached a verdict. No doubt as a result of this draconian rule, juries were rarely hung, and the accused often was. By the more enlightened 1870s, a sequestered jury was allowed refreshments and warmth as long as it paid the bill for them. At the whim of the judge, trial sessions often stretched for many hours with no break for the call of nature. Judges were thoughtfully provided with vases discreetly hidden behind the high bench, but the unfortunate jury was not so privileged.

- There were two famous medical forensic experts named Littlejohn, father and son. They were both knighted, and both taught at the Medical School at Edinburgh. The father, Sir Henry Duncan Littlejohn, had the official title of Professor of Medical Jurisprudence. His son, Sir Henry

Harvey Littlejohn, was appointed Professor of Forensic Medicine. The similarity of names has led to frequent confusion among historians. One surmises similar confusion among the Littlejohn family and social circle, as the younger Littlejohn was informally referred to as "Harvey."

CHAPTER 5

Disguise and the Detective

*"Some touch of the artist wells up within me, and
calls insistently for a well staged performance."*
—Sherlock Holmes in *The Valley of Fear*

THINGS ARE SELDOM what they seem / Skim milk masquerades
as cream," Gilbert and Sullivan warned in *H.M.S. Pinafore*, the
witty, popular operetta that tickled the English stage in 1878.
Nowhere was this observation more appropriate than in the world
of Holmes and Watson based at 221B Baker Street.

Sherlock Holmes is a supreme master of disguise and the
dramatic arts, frequently demonstrating his skill as he gathers
information in the pursuit of justice. He is adept at makeup, clever
at costume, and gifted at altering his movements. Watson
describes his friend's ability at extraordinary metamorphosis in "A
Scandal in Bohemia":

> It was close upon four before the door opened, and a
> drunken looking groom, ill-kempt and side-whiskered,
> with an inflamed face and disreputable clothes, walked

into the room. Accustomed as I was to my friend's amazing powers in the use of disguises, I had to look three times before I was certain that it was indeed he.

Not only can Holmes change his physical appearance, Watson continues in the same tale, but he also has the ability to submerge his unique personality in that of the role he adopts:

> It was not merely that Holmes changed his costume. His expression, his manner, his very soul seemed to vary with every fresh part that he assumed.

This style clearly places the Great Detective in the vanguard of theatrical expression. During the nineteenth century and the early years of the twentieth century, the supremely artificial, declamatory style of acting was by far the dominant one in Europe. In the tradition of the famous French actress Sarah Bernhardt, stage gestures were sweeping. Histrionic poses were struck and held for as long as thirty seconds. Lines were recited sonorously and rhythmically rather than naturally. Makeup was elaborate and highly artificial. Much of this overly emphatic technique originally developed because of the inadequate lighting and poor acoustics that existed in early theaters, but it continued in vogue simply because both actors and audiences were accustomed to it.

The idea of a player completely immersing himself in a role, speaking his lines simply and naturally, creating the illusion of spontaneity, as Holmes is credited with doing, was a novel one in conservative Britain. Some of the credit for it must go to Bernhardt's great Italian rival, Eleanora Duse, who refused to wear stage makeup and whose natural delivery charmed her audiences and inspired a new realism in theater.

But the impetus for an acting style so natural that it was believable at intimate quarters can be traced even further back, to late eighteenth-century France. The teeming world of thieves, informers, whores, and cutthroats that swarmed in the shadow of the guillotine gave rise to a clever progenitor of both disguise artists and forensic reasoning: Eugène François Vidocq (also known as François Eugène Vidocq).

In considering Vidocq's life, it is difficult to separate fact from fiction. Details of his adventurous career are cloaked in legend and garnished with myth. Most historians give his birth year as 1775, although some express a preference for 1773. Either way, it was within a year of the coronation of Louis XVI, the French king who was fated to lose his head in 1793 amid the turmoil of revolution.

There is general agreement that Vidocq was born the son of a baker in Arras, France, and that he was an obstreperous child who blithely stole from his parents. As a youth, he reportedly ran away with a troupe of actors and learned much of the dramatic art from them. The written records show that he then joined the military, although the reasons for this are in dispute. He managed to fight on both sides of the war between France and Austria, changing uniforms and identities with ease. He was a frequent dueler, brawler, and womanizer.

In the late eighteenth century, the country was convulsed by the convergence of the Reign of Terror and the French involvement in foreign wars. The constant presence in the streets of mobs of people bent on attending the ritual of the guillotine and regiments of soldiers marching to battle provided convenient cover for both escaped convicts and deserters.

Although it is usually Paris that we think of as the residence of "Madame la guillotine," it was not only there that the dread machine entertained an avid populace. The larger provinces had been provided with their very own engines of death, although the chief executioner, M. Sanson, complained bitterly that these were of inferior quality.

Equipping the provinces was a complicated business, as the machines needed to be accompanied by a large assortment of important accessories. These included leather-lined wicker baskets, fetters, sawdust, brooms for the inevitable cleaning up, and hatchets or axes in case of unfortunate mechanical failure.

In his *Memoirs*, Vidocq described returning to Arras, the town of his birth, during a sick leave from his current military employers. Dressed as a civilian, he found himself caught up in a crowd that filled the narrow, winding streets, marching toward the fish market.

In the center of the market stood the hideously efficient machine. Strapped to the bloodstained bascule, the wooden see-saw plank of the device, was an elderly man who had been condemned as an "aristocrat." Joseph Lebon, the notoriously cruel proconsul, stood on a balcony directing the proceedings. An orchestra was playing. The trumpets, Vidocq noted, were particularly loud. Lebon, who was smiling and wearing a stylish hat with a tricolor ribbon, kept time with his foot. The two half-moon-shaped parts of the wooden lunette, or collar, were already fastened about the old man's neck.

Lebon ordered a clerk, who was evidently drunk, to read a long and irrelevant bulletin about a military engagement, while the old man teetered on the plank. At the end of each paragraph, the musicians played a loud chord. At last, evidently tiring of the game, Lebon gave the signal, and the executioner pressed the *declic*, or lever, the blade fell, the head rolled into the waiting basket, and the enthusiastic crowd shouted, "*Vive la république!*"

Vidocq reports being sickened. He tells us that in the weeks that followed, he saw people in the grip of madness, hastily denouncing their neighbors before their neighbors could denounce them. He particularly noted one unfortunate, a M. de Vieux-Pont, who had his head confiscated merely because his pet parrot squawked something that sounded vaguely like "*Vive le roi.*" The parrot was adopted by proconsul Joseph Lebon's wife, who promised to undertake the fortunate avian's reeducation.

In spite of his stated disgust for Lebon, Vidocq later gratefully accepted his help in escaping the attentions of the guillotine when an accusation by a rival placed him in danger. Lebon, it seems, felt warmly toward Vidocq's mother.

Vidocq spent the ensuing few years dancing on the edge of the

law. Arrested and jailed on numerous occasions on charges rang-
ing from disturbing the peace to smuggling to deserting, he made
a habit of escape, using complex disguises to do so. According to
his *Memoirs*, he appeared at various times as a Jewish merchant, a
naval officer, and a nun, the chaotic social conditions and the poor
record keeping of the time providing convenient cover.

Comparative calm returned as Napoleon acquired increasing
political power. He crowned himself emperor in 1804. The new
government planted spies in a determined effort to apprehend
criminals. Vidocq was caught in the net. Finding himself facing a
particularly long sentence in the notorious galleys, he offered his
services to the police as an informer and a spy. The offer was
accepted, and Vidocq, this time with the complicity of the authorities, "escaped" from prison once more. Thus provided with a
cover story bound to impress the denizens of the underworld and
to win their trust, he took on the role of undercover operative.

From the beginning of his new career in 1811, Vidocq made
good use of both his underworld connections and his ability at disguise. A great believer in data and records, he compiled detailed
reports of the modus operandi of the criminals he investigated, an
innovation at the time. He noted their physical characteristics and
their associates. Like Sherlock Holmes, he valued system. Vidocq
also hired and trained as his assistants a number of former convicts,
planting them in prisons to acquire information. The operation he
formed was so successful that the French government expanded it.
It became known as the Brigade de la Sûreté and would eventually
develop into a world-famous security force.

In time, Vidocq's position became known in the underworld,
and he had to place even greater reliance on his skill with disguise.
As his notoriety grew, he gained the fascinated friendship of some
of France's greatest novelists, among them Honoré de Balzac,
Alexandre Dumas (*père*), and Victor Hugo. When Vidocq's highly
popular if somewhat lurid *Memoirs* were published in 1828, it was
whispered that his heavily embroidered adventures were influenced by the work of these literary lions. The mixture of styles in

the book makes it likely that it was a compilation by a committee. What is certain is that Vidocq's literary friends made frequent use of his knowledge and personality as components of their work. Alexandre Dumas's *Count of Monte Cristo*, Victor Hugo's *Les Misérables*, and Honoré de Balzac's *Comédie Humaine* all revolve around disguise, dramatic escapes, and the tracing of criminals.

Balzac in particular questioned Vidocq in detail about his use of disguise. Vidocq's view was that developing a role began with careful observation. A subject's ways of walking, gesturing, and eating were tools of the trade. "Observe he whom you would become, then adopt his manner." A costume must be complete, down to the underclothes. "If you would play a peasant, there must be dirt under the nails." Vidocq suggested that undercover operatives carry a number of different-colored scarves and hats so that they could change their appearance rapidly, a simple but effective technique still used by plainclothes detectives today.

When it was necessary for him to take an aristocratic role, Vidocq was also prepared, as he notes in his *Memoirs*, to win the confidence of a female witness:

> I soon determined on the disguise which was best adapted for my purpose. It was apparent that I must assume the guise of a very respectable gentleman, and consequently, by means of some false wrinkles, a pig-tail, snowy-white ruffles, a large gold-headed cane, a three-cornered hat, buckles, breeches and coat to match,—I was metamorphosed into one of those good sexagenarian citizens, whom all old ladies admire.

Vidocq occasionally used walnut stain to darken his face, made fake blisters out of wax, and imitated facial blemishes with glued coffee grains. We can hear echoes of these practices in "The Dying Detective," when Sherlock Holmes explains to Watson his technique of appearing deathly ill:

"Three days of absolute fast does not improve one's beauty, Watson. For the rest, there is nothing which a sponge may not cure. With vaseline upon one's forehead, belladonna in one's eyes, rouge over the cheekbones, and crusts of beeswax round one's lips, a very satisfying effect can be produced."

Vidocq's picaresque adventures included the creation of the first private detective agency, Le Bureau des Renseignements, during a hiatus in his government work, and he has been credited with encouraging early studies in fingerprinting, ballistics, and crime scene analysis. But it is for his genius at disguise that he is best remembered.

In 1845, Vidocq, whose *Memoirs* in English translation had been the talk of London, arrived there to open an exhibit of his memorabilia. The *Times* of London, reviewing the presentation, remarked on the detective's extraordinary flexibility. Although in his seventies, he appeared a vigorous twenty years younger. He stood five feet ten inches, the paper wrote, but could change his stature and make himself smaller by flexing his knees under his coat, walking about with casual ease. According to other observers, he was only five feet six inches but could make himself look taller. The one thing certain about Eugène François Vidocq was that nothing was certain. He aged as he had lived, a chameleon.

Another dashing figure of the period gifted at dissembling and changing his appearance was Richard Burton, explorer, swordsman, linguist, scholar, collector of erotica, and general irritant to the proper British middle class. Forced to leave his studies at Oxford due to all-around bad behavior, he managed on his own to acquire fluency in twenty-five languages, among them Arabic, and an even larger number of dialects.

Fascinated by Arab culture, Burton was determined to enter the Muslim holy cities of Mecca and Medina, which were forbidden to non-Muslims on pain of death. Always willing to flirt with the supreme penalty, he disguised himself as a Muslim pilgrim from Afghanistan, further darkening his naturally olive skin and dressing the part, down to the undergarments, just as Vidocq would have done. Burton accomplished his mission in 1855, and, returning safely, published his account of it, *Pilgrimage to Medina and Mecca*, to the astonished applause of British intellectuals.

Conan Doyle mentions Burton's great appeal to women in his story "The Lost World," and he was certainly aware of Burton's exploits. Perhaps Conan Doyle was further intrigued by the explorer's trip to study the Mormons of Utah in 1860. Burton's book on the subject, *The City of the Saints*, may well have provided some of the inspiration for the section of *A Study in Scarlet* that takes place in Utah. Certainly, the Victorian public was intrigued by Burton and his dashing adventures and disguises.

Disquise, useful to detectives, intrepid explorers, and the dishonest, was the subject of "The Man with the Twisted Lip," in which Neville St. Clair confesses to Holmes:

> "When an actor I had, of course, learned all the secrets of making up, and had been famous in the green-room for my skill. I took advantage now of my attainments. I painted my face, and to make myself as pitiable as possible I made a good scar and fixed one side of my lip in a twist by the aid of a small slip of flesh-colored plaster."

As clever criminals turned disguise to their own advantage, it took imaginative detective work to see through it. Just such talent was found in Detective Henry Goddard. In 1864, he was practicing as a private operative in London when he received an unusual assignment from the Gresham Life Assurance Company. A notice of the death of Edward James Farren, actuary and secretary of the company, had appeared in the *Times* of London. Shocked that they had received no direct information from the Farren family that their employee was either ill or dead, the directors asked Goddard to investigate.

They had chosen their representative well. Goddard was a former member of the Bow Street Runners, the organization that was a forerunner of the London Metropolitan Police. He was intelligent, well organized, and intuitive. Learning that Farren had been traveling alone on the continent, that Farren's wife had received news of her husband's death only from a stranger's letter, and that there were certain peculiar discrepancies in the assurance company's accounts, Goddard suspected fraud. Farren, he believed, had faked his own death to escape with the missing funds and to allow his wife to collect a death benefit.

Farren was known to have a deformed foot and to walk with a severe limp. Reasoning that if Farren hoped to escape notice the limp would have to be hidden, Goddard visited Mr. Walsh, an anatomical boot-maker who he believed had the skills that might have been useful to the missing man. Walsh easily remembered constructing special footgear for Farren, who had promised him fifty pounds if he could make a boot that would hide his disability.

As Farren's heel was about three inches higher than was natural, Walsh had cut a piece of cork to fill the space. To keep this firmly situated, he made a thin slipper to place over the cork and another outer boot to cover the whole thing. A piece of steel was slipped through both boot and cork and held in place by two lengths of iron worn under the trousers on either side of the shortened leg. The complex arrangement was braced with straps. The result was that Farren could walk with only a slight unevenness of gait.

Suspecting that Farren was still in London, Goddard questioned hotel employees until he found one who remembered a man of Farren's description who had a very slight limp. This man had ordered traveling trunks of the sort used for long journeys to be delivered to the hotel and had left with them for Liverpool, which was the port from which ships left for Australia as well as for America. Goddard discovered that the suspect was using the name J. Williams and had left behind a discarded note indicating he had paid the shipping line 144 pounds, an amount sufficient for passage to Australia. Goddard assumed that's where Farren was headed and set out to follow him.

Farren had a head start of seventy days. The way to Australia was arduous and Goddard was sixty-four years old, but he was also grimly determined. He pursued his quarry from Liverpool to Marseilles, to Sicily, to Egypt (where he stopped to pay his respects to the Sphinx, which, he noted in his memoirs, was "of colossal Magnitude"). He encountered mosquitoes in murderous numbers, traveled by donkey, was carried piggyback by Arabs, and at last arrived by ship in Australia.

He began by visiting the spots frequented by English tourists. Knowing that Farren was an ardent music lover, Goddard attended the opera, where he spotted someone who he believed fit the missing man's description. He followed the subject to Scott's Hotel and saw him enter.

The next day, Goddard approached the hotel's owner, Mr. Scott, and explained the problem. Waiting until Farren/Williams was out for the day, Scott accompanied Goddard to the suspect's room. In the closet, they discovered several pairs of boots made by Walsh.

Like the prince seeking Cinderella, Goddard had brought with him all the way from London a copy of the boot that Walsh had made for Farren. It corresponded exactly with the boots in the closet. The boots had holes in their sides to accommodate the rivets that held the prosthesis. The very disguise that allowed Farren to leave London unnoticed served to identify him now.

Goddard noted in his *Memoirs of a Bow Street Runner* that his trip home was pleasant and that his bill to the assurance company "amounted to a goodly sum. It was paid, and most liberally."

There is no public record of any punishment or penalty inflicted on Mr. Farren. It may have been that the Gresham Life Assurance Company preferred to dispose of the matter with genteel discretion, as Sherlock Holmes and the police were to do in "The Man with the Twisted Lip."

Disguise among criminals was a serious enough matter for

Hans Gross, the famous Austrian legal expert, to address the subject at length in his great work *Criminal Investigation*, which was first published in the late nineteenth century and has had a lasting influence on forensic science. He noted that generally "a novice commits a crime and then disguises himself; an expert criminal disguises himself before the offence."

Gross describes a case of bank robbery in which the teller insisted that the thief was very short. The suspect apprehended with the stolen money was quite tall. It seems the robber had worn a long coat and that, like Vidocq, he possessed the ability of walking easily with his knees bent.

Gross warns investigators to be wary of descriptions of scars, limps, and other deformities, as criminals often adopt these to carry out crimes only to discard them afterward. And in a case reminiscent of the false beggar in "The Man with the Twisted Lip," Gross writes of a man who asked for charity because of blindness, a condition he simulated by inserting drops of erserine in each eye, which caused the pupils to contract severely and gave the eyes a damaged appearance.

Gross suggests testing for pretended deafness by dropping a heavy object just behind the subject. A truly deaf person, he writes, will react because he feels the vibration in the floor. A malingerer will not respond, as he thinks that that will be convincing.

Gross's book was translated into English by 1907, but although it was widely read by scientists, it was evidently ignored by one medical practitioner who would have benefited from the chapter on seeing through disguises. His name was Hawley Harvey Crippen (although his wife insisted on addressing him as "Peter"), and in 1910, his home at 39 Hilltop Crescent became the scene of domestic disaster.

Dr. Crippen, a very small man with a large mustache and thick glasses, was an American who had acquired somewhat dubious medical credentials in his native land before taking up residence in London. He worked for both a patent medicine firm and a dental practice, with no great professional success.

The large and demanding wife with whom he unhappily lived was known as Belle Elmore. Previously she had called herself Cora Turner. Mrs. Crippen, who harbored theatrical aspirations, evidently felt that the name with which she had been graced at birth, Kunigunde Mackamotzski, lacked a certain je ne sais quoi.

As Mrs. Crippen indulged in expensive clothes and jewelry, finances were strained in the Crippen ménage. To make ends meet, they took in occasional boarders, whom Mrs. Crippen intimately entertained.

Dr. Crippen was responsible for most of the ensuing housekeeping chores. After a long day of mixing complicated but useless elixirs and pulling occasional teeth, he came home to a dark basement kitchen grimly redolent of meals long past and was required to tidy up.

He was temporarily distracted from the difficult situation by Ethel Le Neve, a young typist in his employ with whom he had formed a romantic attachment. But when Belle announced she planned to remove her savings from their joint account, tension grew.

On January 31, 1910, the Crippens, who had no boarders at the time, entertained a couple named Martinetti as dinner guests. The visitors said later that it was a very jolly evening. They left at one-thirty in the morning, waving farewell to Belle as she stood under the gas lamp near the front door. They were never to see her again.

Ten days before, Dr. Crippen had ordered and received five grains of hyoscine, a potent narcotic, from the chemists Lewis and Burrows. A few days after the dinner with the Martinettis, Crippen pawned most of his wife's jewelry. He informed their friends that his wife had gone to California. He later told them that Belle had been stricken with a sudden illness and had died in America.

Ethel was seen with Crippen wearing a brooch that had belonged to Belle. The Crippens' friends, suspicious, reported the matter to the police.

Chief Inspector Walter Dew interviewed Dr. Crippen at

home. Crippen confessed that he had been lying—his wife had left him for another man, and he had been too humiliated to admit it. He made no objection to the inspector's searching the house. Sympathetic to the clearly distressed little man, Dew made a casual inspection that produced nothing suspicious.

A few days later, Dew returned to check on some minor details and learned that Crippen and Ethel had disappeared. A thorough search of the house was ordered. In the coal cellar beneath some loose bricks lay a mass of putrid human flesh and hair. The limbs and head were missing, as were the bones.

One of the medical experts who examined the remains, Bernard Spilsbury (who was just making a name for himself in the forensic world), identified a mark on the skin as a surgical scar, which corresponded to surgery that Belle was known to have undergone. A large amount of hyoscine was recovered from the tissue. The location of Belle seemed clear. The question now was, where were Crippen and Ethel?

A vessel named the *Montrose* was slowly making its way from Europe to Canada. Its captain was Harry Kendall, a meticulously observant gentleman with an interest in detective stories. He was curious about two passengers named Robinson—a father and his son. The elder had a pale patch above his lip, as though a mustache had recently resided there. Faint marks on either side of his nose seemed to indicate the recent presence of glasses.

Young Master Robinson, who was said to be sixteen, seemed to have a very high-pitched voice. His walk appeared odd. Kendall observed them closely. The young boy's suit fitted poorly—it was split up the back and held together by safety pins. The elder man was most solicitous of the younger, cracking nuts for the boy at dinner.

Kendall had a copy of the newspaper that was published the day the *Montrose* sailed. It featured a story on the Crippen murder and a large photo of Crippen and Ethel. Kendall noticed that "Mr. Robinson" reacted slowly to his name if called from behind.

The captain reached the obvious conclusion. His ship was one of the few that boasted a wireless, and he made use of it. He sent a message detailing his observations. Scotland Yard dispatched Inspector Dew on the *Laurentian*, a faster ship than the *Montrose*. The chase across the Atlantic was featured every day in the papers, although the "Robinsons" were blissfully unaware of it. Often, according to Kendall, the elder suspect would sit on deck, look up at the wireless antenna aloft, and say, "What a wonderful invention it is!"

Before the *Montrose* reached the dock at Quebec, she was approached by a pilot boat and boarded by its crew. One of them was actually Inspector Dew. He was disguised as a harbor pilot.

The inspector greeted "Mr. Robinson" on the deck, saying cordially, "Good morning, Dr. Crippen. . . . Do you remember me?"

Crippen was returned to London, where he was found guilty of the murder of his wife. The jury deliberated for twenty-seven minutes. He was hanged at Pentonville Prison on November 23, 1910. Ethel was acquitted and lived an apparently uneventful long life.

Hawley Harvey Crippen was the most hapless of criminals. Not only did he have to contend with Captain Kendall, who possessed both Sherlockian acuity and a wireless, but Dr. Crippen couldn't help betraying the classic sign of the novice criminal when he clumsily disguised himself after the fact.

There are times, as Sherlock Holmes observed while identifying the poorly disguised villain in "A Case of Identity," when "There is no possible getting out of it. . . . It is quite too transparent."

WHATEVER REMAINS

- Dr. James Barry was a brilliant and much-respected Victorian-era physician who had obtained a diploma as Doctor of Medicine from Edinburgh when only fifteen years of age, and who served with distinction in the British army in such exotic locations as St. Helena, the Ionian islands, Malta, and the West Indies. Easily angered, the touchy doctor had fought a duel with a fellow officer. Upon retiring from the military, Dr. Barry was appointed to the prestigious civilian post of inspector of hospitals. When James Barry died at the age of eighty in 1865, a postmortem examination disclosed the fact that the doctor was a woman. She had lived her entire adult life in disguise. Since inheritance rights, access to professional training, and voting rights often hinged on gender, there was ample motivation for such dissembling, and a number of similar cases appear in the medical texts of the period.

- George McWatters, originally from the British Isles, was a member of the New York Metropolitan Police. In his memoirs of 1871, he described searching for a swindler who was believed to be missing a finger joint. He located the suspect, who had hidden his deformity for years by use of a cleverly made wax finger joined to his hand by a large and valuable ring. McWatters kept the wax finger as a souvenir. The ring, alas, disappeared.

- In the Sherlock Holmes story "Silver Blaze," a racehorse is disguised to hide its identity. In 2003, a Chicago-area veterinarian tried to hide the appearance of a stolen dark gray gelding named San Diego by spraying the animal's white legs and facial blaze with caustic black paint. The horse's face was blistered as a result. The vet was charged with grand theft and burglary. The unfortunate horse was left with scars.

- During World War II, a secret apartment in London was maintained by the office of the Special Operations Executive. Within it, operatives created false documents and designed elaborate disguises for use by British undercover agents. The apartment was located at number 64 Baker Street.

CHAPTER 6

The Crime Scene
by Gaslight

*"Nothing has been touched up to now. . . . I'll answer for that.
You see it all exactly as I found it."*

—Cecil Baker in *The Valley of Fear*

Wʜᴇɴ ᴇxᴀᴍɪɴɪɴɢ the scene of a crime, Sherlock Holmes
exhibits an amazing intensity of concentration and passion for
detail. In the first Holmes story published, *A Study in Scarlet*,
Watson describes Holmes's approach:

> [H]e whipped a tape measure and a large round magnify-
> ing glass from his pocket. With these two implements he
> trotted noiselessly about the room, sometimes stopping,
> occasionally kneeling, and once lying flat upon his face. So
> engrossed was he with his occupation that he appeared to
> have forgotten our presence, for he chattered away to
> himself under his breath the whole time, keeping up a run-
> ning fire of exclamations, groans, whistles, and little cries
> suggestive of encouragement and of hope. As I watched
> him I was irresistibly reminded of a pureblooded, well-

trained foxhound, as it dashes backward and forward through the covert, whining in its eagerness, until it comes across the lost scent. For twenty minutes or more he continued his researches, measuring with the most exact care the distance between marks.

At just about the same time Conan Doyle was writing those words in England, across the sea in Vienna, Hans Gross, the brilliant professor of criminology, was composing the standards for investigating what he called "the Scene of the Offence."

"The first duty of the investigator," he wrote in his *Handbuch für Untersuchungsrichter* (Manual for Examining Magistrates), published in English as *Criminal Investigation*, is to "observe absolute calm." Further, it is vital to remember one inviolable rule: "Never alter the position of, lift, or touch any object before it has been described in a detailed written record."

Like Holmes, Gross believed you must have strictly accurate and complete data before reaching a conclusion. To this end, he required that at a crime scene, the investigator keep in mind that anything and everything may be of importance. He stressed that absolutely nothing is too small to have a bearing on the case.

Gross insisted that the position of objects at the scene be preserved until sketched or, if possible, photographed. Footprints should be covered with boxes to preserve them. The exact distance between objects at the scene, the furniture, doors, windows, and so forth, must be noted in writing and by diagrams. Dr. Gross devoted pages to describing the care needed to transport evidence from the crime scene to the laboratory. Anything that needed to be changed in any way, such as floorboards that needed to be cut for removal, had to be drawn or photographed before they were altered. Body parts or fluids were to be placed in separate containers free of preservatives and clearly labeled.

There were strict rules as well for the handling of evidence once it arrived at the laboratory or mortuary. If essential parts of the crime scene had been moved to a scientific setting, great care was to be exercised to keep them from contamination.

Even negative facts were important, Gross wrote. If, for instance, blood was present at a murder scene, but a washbasin at the location was free of bloody water, that fact must be included in the detective's notes, as it indicates that the assailant may have left the scene with blood still marking his hands. What did not happen is every bit as important as what did.

This stress on the value of negative facts quickly calls to mind the famous moment in "Silver Blaze" when the Great Detective is asked:

> "Is there any point to which you would wish to draw my attention?"
>
> "To the curious incident of the dog in the night-time."
>
> "The dog did nothing in the night-time."
>
> "That was the curious incident," remarked Sherlock Holmes.

But the concern for careful analysis at a crime scene did not originate with either the factual Gross or the fictional Sherlock. Fifty years before, Eugène François Vidocq, writing about the early days of the Sûreté in his *Memoirs*, described his investigation of a crime scene:

> The most minute exactitude had been observed in removing the body. Nothing had been neglected which might lead to the discovery of the assassins. Accurate impressions were taken of the footmarks; buttons, fragments of paper dyed in blood were carefully collected: on one of these pieces which appeared to have been hastily torn off to wipe the blade of a knife found at no great distance from it, were observed some written characters. . . . [A] second morsel was picked up which presented every appearance of being part of an address. . . . The following words were deciphered;—*A Monsieur Rao— Marchand de vins bar,— Roche—*.

The body of the victim, whose name was Fontaine, was removed for examination to the hospital. The physicians and Vidocq were amazed to discover that although the victim bore twenty-eight stab wounds, he was still alive. Exhausted from loss of blood, he was nevertheless able to haltingly report that there had been two attackers with whom he had struggled, and that he was certain he had wounded one of them in the leg. They had made off with his moneybag.

Vidocq noted that he carefully studied the torn bits of paper found at the scene and concluded that the writing on them was a name and an address. "*Rao*" he thought might be the beginning of "*Raoul*." "*Marchand de vins*" indicated a wine merchant, and the rest of the words fit the address of such an establishment not too far away. Vidocq postulated that the full phrase had been "*Marchand de vins, Barrière Rochechouart*." He sent undercover operatives to study the place.

They reported that two men, one with a limp from what seemed to be a recent injury, were seen several times at the wine merchant's shop. They had been spending freely. One of the men was known as Raoul.

A search of the premises disclosed recently washed clothes with traces of what appeared to be blood. The lame man's wound corresponded to the description of the injury the victim said he inflicted on the assailant. Vigorously questioned by Vidocq, the suspects confessed.

This story has appeared in a number of versions of Vidocq's *Memoirs*. The details vary and are very likely embroidered. But it is certain that the details of the crime scene, the description of the paper fragment, and the deciphering of the words upon it were available in the English translation of the *Memoirs* sold in London by 1859. We cannot be certain that Conan Doyle was familiar with Vidocq's story, but it is intriguingly reminiscent of the written clue that appears at the crime scene described by Watson in *A Study in Scarlet*:

[T]he paper had fallen away in parts. In this particular cor-
ner of the room a large piece had peeled off, leaving a
yellow square of coarse plastering. Across this bare space
there was scrawled in blood-red letters a single word—

RACHE

Sherlock Holmes examines this clue carefully with his magnifying glass, "going over every letter of it with the most minute
exactness." In Conan Doyle's tale as well as in Vidocq's, painstaking consideration of a mysterious word is a vital step to the
solution.

Clearly, by the late nineteenth century, the need for a systematic approach to a crime scene had been expressed in academic
papers and in literature. But that was theory. In practice, a less rigorous approach often prevailed.

In the late summer and early fall of 1888 (just a year after
the first publication of *A Study in Scarlet*), a series of hideous
mutilation-murders of prostitutes gripped Londoners in a state of
titillated horror. Prostitutes had been found murdered in London
before, of course, but not in so bloody a fashion. In addition, lit-
eracy was increasingly common, creating a wide readership for
the penny dreadfuls that happily published and embellished the
gory and terrifying details that riveted public attention.

A number of probably fraudulent letters were sent to the
police boasting of the crimes and flaunting the signature "Jack the
Ripper." News of these added to the panic.

Among historians there is disagreement as to exactly how
many women were victims of the Ripper, but most concur that the
five who were killed between August 31 and November 8 of 1888
within the same half-mile in the slum of Whitechapel were the
prey of that killer.

The first four corpses, all with throats cut, were found
outdoors in public areas. The flayed cadaver of the last victim,
Mary Jane Kelly, was found on the bed of her small room. An
assortment of her body parts were scattered about the chamber.

All of the victims were killed in the dark hours of early morning.

The exterior settings, and the dim light by which the bodies were first discovered, would have made containment and examination of the scenes difficult even if all the police involved had been highly trained. It is clear that although there were a number of dedicated investigators attached to the Ripper cases, lack of funding and training for support staff meant that the evidence was often treated with an impressive lack of scientific organization.

Many of the original documents of the Ripper inquest have been lost, but a number of newspapers, including the *Times* of London and the *Daily Telegraph*, printed detailed accounts of the testimony. Since the stories agree in all but an occasional choice of words, we are safe in accepting the accuracy of their reports. These bear witness to an often chaotic investigation.

In the case of Mary Ann (Polly) Nichols, usually counted as the Ripper's first victim, the corpse, having been superficially examined at the scene by a physician, was moved to the mortuary. One investigator, Detective-Sergeant Enright, being deposed, stated that the mortuary workers had stripped the body:

> The Coroner [the government official whose job it was to lead the inquest] asked, "Had they any authority to strip the body?"
>
> Enright: "No, sir; I gave them no instructions to strip it. In fact, I told them to leave it as it was."
>
> The Coroner: "I don't object to their stripping the body, but we ought to have evidence about the clothes."

As the inquest continued, it became apparent that no logical method had been applied in moving the corpse or in collecting the clothes and other physical evidence. The "mortuary attendants" were totally untrained inmates of the workhouse, that Victorian repository for indigent souls who were forced into all manner of repellent work in exchange for bare sustenance. With no idea of proper procedure, they had made no notes, labeled no evidence, and had only vague recollections of what they had done, as we see from the following exchange between the coroner and the "keeper" of the mortuary:

> Question: "Had you been told not to touch it? [the body]"
> Answer: "No."
> Question: "Did you see the Inspector?"
> Answer: "I can't say."
> Question: "Was he present?"
> Answer: "I can't say." . . .
> Question: "You cannot describe where the blood was?"
> Answer: "No, sir; I cannot."

The coroner evaluated the testimony for the jury: "It appears the mortuary-keeper is subject to fits, and neither his memory nor statements are reliable."

The coroner was at pains to state publicly that the mortuary and its keeper were inadequate. "The mortuary is not fitted for post mortem examination. It is only a shed. There is no adequate convenience [washing facilities] . . . as a matter of fact there is no public mortuary from the City of London up to Bow."

The coroner, still trying for a coherent approach, said to one of the investigating officers, an Inspector Helson, "I hope the police will supply me with a plan [a crime scene drawing]. In the country, in cases of importance, I always have one."

Helson informed him, "We shall have one at the adjourned hearing."

The coroner gloomily replied, "By that time we should hardly need one."

In the case of Elizabeth Stride, one of two women murdered on September 30, 1888, the coroner, questioning the constable who responded to the scene, received less than precise results:

> Question: "Was there anything to prevent a man escaping while you were examining the body?"

Answer: "Several people were inside and outside the gates, and I think that they would be sure to observe a man who had marks of blood. . . ."

Question: "But supposing he had no marks of blood?"

Answer: "It was quite possible, of course for a person to escape while I was examining the corpse."

Catherine Eddoes, the second victim on September 30, was found dead at Mitre Square, but a piece of her bloodstained apron was discovered not far away on Goulston Street. Above the apron was a wall that bore a graffito in chalk. It read, "The Juwes are the men that will not be blamed for nothing."

Sir Charles Warren, in charge of the Metropolitan Police, insisted that the slogan be removed immediately for fear it would foment anti-Jewish riots. Evidently, the thought of covering the word "Juwes" until a photograph could be taken did not strike him as helpful, and another piece of evidence was lost.

If the investigation of the Ripper murders had been carried out with the rigorous methods advocated by Vidocq, Gross, and their fictional descendant, Sherlock Holmes, the killer might have been identified. But witnesses wandered through the crime scene, evidence was mishandled, and facilities for postmortem examination were primitive. As Sherlock Holmes remarked in *A Study in Scarlet*, "If a herd of buffaloes had passed along, there could not be a greater mess."

The series of murders ended with the killing of Mary Jane Kelly on November 8, 1888. There had been a great deal of investigation and vigorous, ghoulish speculation, but no solution to the crimes. Jack the Ripper has provided fodder for many literary efforts—some factual, some fictional, and some fraudulent. In spite of imaginative claims to the contrary, the case remains unsolved.

The debacle of the Ripper investigation demonstrated that the procedure at the crime scene and the proper securing of physical evidence were of enormous importance. No matter how adept a pathologist, how clever a detective, their usefulness would always be determined by the skill and integrity of the professionals at the scene.

In spite of this famous example, crime scenes continued to be casually mishandled. In 1903, a series of animal mutilations in the English rural district of Great Wyrley appalled the public. Over the course of half a year, horses and cattle were found dead with long, shallow wounds in their abdomens. The cuts were not deep enough to penetrate major organs, so the animals slowly exsanguinated. The mutilations all occurred in the darkness of night.

Suspicion fell on a young solicitor named George Edalji, largely because he was a dark-skinned man of Asian descent and therefore was resented by the highly insular community. In spite of the fact that Edalji was a member of the Anglican Church (indeed, his father was the local vicar), many of the townspeople believed the crimes were part of a bizarre, primitive religious ritual. After roughly fifteen animals were found dead, the police were pressured to act, and the house in which Edalji lived with his parents was searched. Anything that might be suspected of being evidence—razors with brown stains, a shirt belonging to the suspect, his mud-stained boots—was seized. The items were not carefully sealed or labeled.

In short order, the police announced that the shirt was found to be covered with horsehairs that matched those of a recently deceased pony and that blood was found on a shirt. The mud on Edalji's boots was still wet. Several threatening letters had been sent to the Edalji family. The police insisted they had been written by the suspect himself. A handwriting "expert" concurred, in spite of the fact that witnesses swore Edalji was sitting in their view when the letters were pushed under the door. Edalji was tried and sentenced to seven years of prison at hard labor.

Many journalists were uneasy about the accuracy of the investigation and kept the case alive on the editorial pages. In 1906, without explanation by the court and after the slightly built prisoner had spent three grim years hacking at rocks, Edalji was released. As his conviction was allowed to stand, he could not practice his profession. He filled time by working as a clerk and writing an article about his experience.

Arthur Conan Doyle's famous Sherlock Holmes tale "Silver Blaze," which was published in 1892, had hinged on the attempted nighttime mutilation of a racehorse on an open moor. Perhaps that is one reason that a story about the Edalji case originally caught Conan Doyle's eye. But his attention was held by the ethical issues involved.

Appalled by what he considered an obvious case of injustice and racial prejudice, Conan Doyle carefully went over the evidence. He visited the crime scene. Even after three years, the truth was obvious. The horsehair had been transferred to the shirt because the police had wrapped the shirt in a piece of horsehide from the dead animal. The razor stains were rust. The blood on the shirt consisted of three tiny drops—clearly an animal severely cut would have bled a great deal more. The mud on Edalji's boots did not match the mud in the field where the pony died. The handwriting "expert" had given grossly inaccurate testimony in a previous case that had led to the incarceration of a completely innocent man.

Finally, Conan Doyle, who had been trained as an ophthalmologist, examined Edalji. He found him to be severely myopic, so much so that it would have been impossible for him to have located a pony in the dark, let alone to have sliced the animal's abdomen.

Conan Doyle published a lengthy pamphlet on the case, which led to the partial exoneration of the beleaguered solicitor. The charge of animal mutilation was dismissed, but the charge of having written the letters stood. There are cynical souls who believe this was due to the influence of Sir Albert de Rutzen, one of the three members of the commission deciding the matter. By an uncanny coincidence, he was the cousin of the chief constable of the Great Wyrley Police. Conan Doyle remarked that he was never able to think back on this case without anger.

The crime scenes in the Edalji case were largely exterior, involving fields, grass, and varieties of soil. Interpreting them properly required a good knowledge of natural science. Interior crime scenes presented a different set of difficulties and often required an understanding of architecture and interior decoration.

One problem of interior crime scene investigation addressed by both Sherlock Holmes and Dr. Hans Gross was determining whether one had, in fact, located the entire crime scene. The existence of secret rooms, trap doors, and hidden evidence needed to be considered.

Gross insisted that absolutely everything needed to be examined, and he mentioned some of the peculiar hiding places in which evidence had been found: a birdcage, a clock, a prayer book, even a pot of boiling soup that was found to contain missing gold pieces. Walls must be tapped on to uncover a hollow sound, which might indicate a cavity.

Floors were a problem, as they were hard to remove entirely. Gross suggested examining the nails holding the floorboards. He noted that these would show signs of rust if they had been there for a long time. If the wood around the nails showed signs of bruising, it was an indication that something had been hidden there. In the case of an earthen floor, water was to be poured over it; the place where bubbles appear and where the water filters through rapidly indicates an area where the floor has been recently disturbed.

In the nineteenth century, secret passageways and hidden rooms were a more frequent part of private houses than they are today. As there was no central heating, homes of the period were constructed with thick walls to provide insulation. These accommodated discreet space for hollows in which to store things. Even modest middle-class households made their homes accessible to a wide variety of hired help—chimneys needed to be swept, laundry to be washed. It was comforting to be able to hide valuables from strangers. In some very old houses, elaborately disguised rooms, often referred to as "priest's holes," had been constructed to hide fugitive adherents of out-of-favor religions.

All of these architectural oddities provided happy inspiration for criminals, detectives, and writers of fiction. In "The Adventure of the Speckled Band," Holmes, carefully inspecting the victim's room, quickly focuses on an inconsistent detail that indicates that the crime scene must include the neighboring room:

> "Very strange!" muttered Holmes, pulling at the rope. "There are one or two very singular points about this room. For example, what a fool a builder must be to open a ventilator into another room, when, with the same trouble, he might have communicated with the outside air!"

And, of course, the ventilator was used by a murderous serpent.

Harry Söderman, the famous Swedish forensic scientist, writing his memoirs in the twentieth century, described a crime scene with a similar zoological detail. In New York City during the 1930s, police were certain that a merchant was selling small packages of opium from his apartment, but they had no idea where he stored the drug. The merchant had a pet ferret of which he seemed very fond, as it sat on his lap and fed from his hand.

The detectives stationed themselves outside the apartment and watched through the window. They saw what they believed to be a customer arrive and give money to the merchant, who whispered to the ferret. The animal promptly disappeared under the sink, returning a few seconds later with a packet in his mouth. The ferret was rewarded with a bit of raw meat. As the customer left with the packet, he was stopped and searched. The packet he carried contained opium.

A complete examination of the premises disclosed an opening below the sink that was too small for human access. The police enlarged it and found thirty-nine packets of opium neatly lined up. Evidently, Söderman surmised, they had been arranged by the tidy but felonious ferret.

Sherlock Holmes locates hidden rooms by careful measurement as well as by observing inconsistent design. In "The Adventure of the Norwood Builder," knowing that the scheming villain is a builder, Holmes suspects that the man has altered his house to provide a hiding place and thus is able to determine the man's whereabouts: "When I paced one corridor and found it six feet shorter than the corresponding one below, it was pretty clear where he was."

In "The Adventure of the Golden Pince-Nez," Holmes locates a hidden assailant by a combination of attention to detail and a knowledge of the frequent use of bookcases to conceal hidden rooms:

> "I examined the room narrowly for anything in the shape of a hiding-place. The carpet seemed continuous and firmly nailed, so I dismissed the idea of a trap-door. There might well be a recess behind the books. As you are aware, such devices are common in old libraries. I observed that books were piled on the floor at all other points, but that one bookcase was left clear. This, then, might be the door."

And, of course, it is indeed the door.

It is a pity that Sherlock Holmes's techniques were not promptly utilized in 1992 when Katie Beers, just short of her tenth birthday, disappeared on December 28 in Bay Shore, Long Island, while on an outing with John Esposito, a family friend. Police had immediate suspicions of the middle-aged Esposito, but he denied all knowledge of where the child might be. A search of his home disclosed nothing that seemed unusual.

He was followed constantly and interrogated repeatedly. Finally, on January 13, 1993, pressured by questioning beyond his endurance, Esposito confessed that he had kidnapped Katie and had been holding her captive. He directed the police to the place where he had hidden her. She was found, fortunately still alive, in the grim, secret room that Esposito had constructed under his house. As in "The Adventure of the Golden Pince-Nez," the entrance to it was concealed behind a bookcase.

Much like the title character in "The Adventure of the Norwood Builder," John Esposito was a contractor. Those who searched for Katie, unlike the clever chap in Conan Doyle's *The Sign of Four*, had not "worked out all the cubic space of the house, and made measurements everywhere, so that not one inch should be unaccounted for."

Hans Gross wrote in his *Criminal Investigation* regarding the proper examination of a crime scene:

> In no other duty are power of observation, logical reasoning, and keeping the purpose in view so clearly revealed; and nowhere else can more striking examples of disorder, feebleness of observation, vagueness, and hesitation be found.

"You know my method. It is founded upon the observation of trifles," Holmes said in "The Boscombe Valley Mystery." As Gross would have agreed, it is the observation of "trifles" at a crime scene that is the heart of forensic science.

WHATEVER REMAINS

- In 1916, at Berkley, California, Dr. Albert Schneider, a chemist, eager to gather and retain every possible scrap of evidence from a crime scene, realized that the household vacuum cleaner, which had been patented in 1901, was the perfect device for collecting dust particles. He published a paper explaining his method in the journal *Police Microscopy*.

- Animals, wild or domesticated, roaming loose at a crime scene often devour or otherwise disarrange vital evidence. When O. J. Simpson's estranged wife, Nicole, and her friend, Ron Goldman, were stabbed to death in June 1994, a large dog was present at the scene. The canine witness, an Akita, was briefly evaluated by a K9 handler but was returned to the Simpson family by the police. As veterinarians and distressed owners will attest, dogs sometimes swallow large and surprising objects, including knives. The Simpson Akita was not x-rayed, nor was his fecal matter collected or examined. This may have been a mistake, as the murder weapon remains unaccounted for.

• When a victim's body has been moved from the homicide location, the crime scene to be investigated includes the disposal spot, as well as the route and vehicle used to reach it.

CHAPTER 7

A Picture of Guilt

"You are aware that no two thumb-marks are alike?"
—Inspector Lestrade in "The Adventure of
the Norwood Builder"

SHERLOCK HOLMES dedicates much of his time to identifying the perpetrators of complex crimes. Sometimes, as in *The Valley of Fear*, he must uncover the identity of the victim as well. Holmes, of course, could accomplish this with practiced panache. As he remarks in *A Study in Scarlet*, referring to a Gallic fictional detective (who was no doubt modeled by his creator, the French novelist Emile Gaboriau, after the famous Vidocq):

> "Lecoq was a miserable bungler; he had only one thing to recommend him, and that was his energy. That book made me positively ill. The question was how to identify an unknown prisoner. I could have done it in twenty-four hours. Lecoq took six months or so. It might be made a textbook for detectives to teach them what to avoid."

Sherlock Holmes, of course, had the easy confidence of a man who not only possessed very special talents but who also practiced detection with the adroit help of Conan Doyle. In the more plebian real world, accurate identification of individuals had always been a recalcitrant conundrum that complicated criminal investigation, and it wasn't until the nineteenth century that scientific solutions to this problem began to be utilized. But as the field developed, the Sherlock Holmes stories provided effective advertisement for the new ideas.

Since multiple convictions evoked greater penalties and in some cases death sentences, the authorities were at pains to determine the criminal history of prisoners. The earliest method of identifying criminals was by physically marking them. Mutilation by court order was a lucrative sideline of executioners on the European continent, who charged extra for branding, nose cutting, and the occasional amputation.

Branding was abandoned in France under the revolution (with the guillotine so busy, there may have been a shortage of enough surviving subjects to wear the brand), but the penalty was revived later. It was finally abolished in 1832. The Swedish criminalist Harry Söderman noted in his memoirs that in France prisoners not sentenced to death were marked *TF* for "*travaux forcés*" (hard labor); a *V* stood for "*voleur*" or thief, with a second *V* added for a second conviction. A life sentence was indicated by the letter *P*, which stood for the ominous "*en perpétuité*."

In Russia, well into the mid-nineteenth century, the faces of prisoners were commonly branded—one large letter burned upon the forehead, accompanied by one on each cheek.

While one would expect convicts to hide their identities, some, perhaps driven by a need to flirt with disaster, would mark themselves with painfully acquired tattoos. These too provided a convenient source of identification for the authorities. Both the nineteenth-century pathologist Alexandre Lacassagne and the Italian criminologist and anthropologist Cesare Lombroso collected notes on the variety of tattoos favored by criminals. In his paper

"The Savage Origin of Tattooing," published in the April 1896 edition of *Popular Science Monthly*, Lombroso wrote of an assassin named Malassen who had ultimately followed a second career path as an executioner. Malassen flaunted a red and black guillotine on his chest, accessorized by an inscription in red letters: "*J'ai mal commencé, je finirai mal. C'est la fin qui m'attend*" (I began evil, I shall end evil. That is the end that awaits me). His right arm, with which he had dispatched a number of his criminal former colleagues, bore the legend "*Mort à la chiourme*" (Death to the convict).

Lombroso also quoted from Lacassagne's collection of other such spirited messages. They ranged from the self-pitying "Son of misfortune," "Born under an evil star," "The present torments me; the future frightens me," and "No chance" to the threatening "Death to unfaithful women!" and "Vengeance!" to the cheerfully patriotic and gustatory "*Vive la France* and fried potatoes!"

Lombroso, firmly convinced that tattooing was a sign of atavism, criminality, and insensitivity to pain, was appalled to discover his theory somewhat shaken by a fad for tattooing among the upper classes in Victorian London, embraced especially by the ladies. Even Lady Randolph Churchill (the former Jenny Jerome and the mother of Winston) wore a delicately designed snake encircling her wrist. (She hid it discreetly under a bracelet on formal occasions.)

Lombroso might have been shocked, but Sherlock Holmes, as an expert on tattoos, would have found Lady Churchill's ornament intriguing and would no doubt have been able to determine at a glance the origin of the design. He demonstrates his knowledge in "The Red Headed League" when he says to a client:

> "The fish that you have tattooed immediately above your right wrist could only have been done in China. I have made a small study of tattoo marks and have even contributed to the literature of the subject. That trick of staining the fishes' scales of a delicate pink is quite peculiar to China."

A good knowledge of tattoos and scars was most useful to a Victorian-era detective. The English police of the period maintained a tattoo index that listed designs popular among criminals. The forensic pathologist Charles Meymott Tidy devoted pages in his 1882 textbook, *Legal Medicine*, to the formation and appearance of "Cicatrices [scars] and Tattoo Marks" and included exhaustive instructions on how to differentiate between them. Clearly, Conan Doyle was well aware of the issue, as he has the local doctor observe in *The Valley of Fear*:

> The dead man's right arm was thrust out from his dressing gown, and exposed as high as the elbow. About halfway up the forearm was a curious brown design, a triangle inside a circle, standing out in vivid relief upon the lard-colored skin.
>
> "It's not tattooed," said the doctor, peering through his glasses. "I never saw anything like it. The man has been branded at some time as they brand cattle."

Both scars and tattoos figured heavily as evidence in the famous identity case of the Tichborne Claimant in 1866, which had riveted England and much of the rest of the world for eight years. Holmes, whose knowledge of old cases is described as prodigious, would certainly have been familiar with it.

Sir Roger Tichborne, the unmarried heir to a baronetcy and the vast Tichborne estate, was twenty-five years old when he was reported lost at sea off the coast of Brazil in 1854. His French mother, who had raised him in her native land and language until he was sixteen, refused to accept his loss.

In 1866, a man from Wagga Wagga, Australia, who had been living under the name of Castro, claimed to be the lost heir. He explained that having made his way to Australia after surviving the sea disaster, he determined to make a success on his own before returning to England. Unable to succeed, he had been too embarrassed to contact his relations, but seeing an advertisement for his whereabouts on behalf of his dear mother, he'd been full of remorse and desired to travel to Europe to establish his identity. He needed passage money for himself. And his wife. And his children. Lady Tichborne sent it at once. The Castro family set sail for Europe.

When last seen, Roger Tichborne had been very thin and possessed a narrow, gracile frame. He was, of course, fluent in French, which had been his first language. The man who presented himself was enormously obese and spoke no French at all, explaining that he had somehow forgotten it during his sojourn in Australia. The given names of Lady Tichborne (Henriette Félicité), whom he claimed as his mother, had also unfortunately slipped his mind. (Happily, he did recall the name of the family dog.) Full of hopeful anticipation, Lady Tichborne insisted on seeing the gentleman for herself.

Carefully surveying the bulky body and heavily jowled face of the Claimant, she joyfully proclaimed that he was indeed her son, proving that the eye sometimes sees only what the heart desires. She proceeded to grant him an allowance of a thousand pounds a year.

The lady may have chosen to ignore the physical differences between her lost son and the Claimant, but it was impossible for many other members of the family to agree. The physical factors included extensive tattoo marks that had been inscribed on Roger's arm. These were remembered, described in detail, and sketched by a number of friends and relations. There were no tattoos on the Claimant. The Claimant had a birthmark on his side, but there had been no such mark on Roger, who had been bled many times for a variety of illnesses, as was common in that era. These procedures had left scars. They were not present on the Claimant.

There were a number of other inconsistencies, not the least of which was that Roger's eyes had been blue and the Claimant's were brown. The noses and the ears of the two men were of different shapes. The Claimant was taller by an inch. You might think these facts would have given Lady Tichborne pause, but she remained adamant that her son had miraculously been restored to her and with mulish stubbornness continued to maintain that position until her sudden death of heart failure in 1868.

With her demise, the Claimant's allowance stopped and his legal troubles began. The many other members of the Tichborne family who had refused to accept the gentleman from Wagga Wagga as the heir to the estate were obdurate. As a result, the English judicial system was called upon to settle the issue. This was much to the advantage of many members of the legal profession, whose exchequers grew plump on the proceedings. A vast amount of newsprint was spent on the case, much of it hyperbole. The public, unwilling to be restrained by lack of accurate information, took passionate sides.

There were debates in Parliament. Benjamin Disraeli, the prime minister, although convinced that the Claimant was an imposter, allowed petitions on his behalf to be read in Commons in the interests of fairness and keeping the peace. After four years and two well-attended trials (even the prince and princess of Wales made an appearance), the Claimant was found guilty of imposture and sentenced to fourteen years of penal servitude. He served ten years of his sentence, leaving prison a sadder, wiser, and much thinner man. The case stood as a testament to the unreasoning force of wishful thinking, the unreliability of eyewitness testimony, and the serious need for a scientific method of objectively establishing physical identification.

Across the channel, the French had followed the Tichborne case with interest. Since the formation of the Sûreté, the identification system in Paris had depended largely on the extraordinary memory of Eugène François Vidocq. The huge number of files that he had developed were of limited use without him. Dossiers were listed under the name of the criminal, and a criminal typically used many names. Vidocq was able to recall enormous numbers of aliases and could tap into his proficient system of police spies to keep abreast of name changes, but his less adroit successors were lost.

The advantages afforded by photography were quickly appreci-
ated, and "mug" shots by daguerreotype, the complex photographic
process first introduced by Louis Jacques Daguerre in 1839, were
used by police in Belgium as early as 1843. But daguerreotypes
were extremely expensive and required skill and considerable time
to produce. As a result, they were not often used by police.

Even by the middle of the nineteenth century, by which time
photographic methods were simplified, the process was still cum-
bersome. Slow lenses required identification photographs to be
made in sunlight, and the exposure time could be as long as
twenty minutes. The unhappy subject was often strapped in a
chair to limit movement.

As lenses became faster and photography cheaper, police
made greater use of the technology. In Paris, Gustave Macé, head
of the detective division, decided to require photographs of all
criminals. The photographic files grew, filling cabinets and boxes
and lining corridors but providing little useful information. Not
only was there no clear method of organizing them, there was no
standardized method of taking them.

All the photographs were taken full face and at whatever distance seemed convenient at the time. Light came from whichever
side the photographer fancied at the moment. Hair was allowed to
cover ears, and facial hair often obscured features. The files and the
pictures in them continued to be classified by the criminal's name.

And then, in 1882, it all changed, thanks to a twenty-six-year-
old neurasthenic clerk in the Paris Police named Alphonse
Bertillon. It is possible that Bertillon possessed some social
graces, but if so, he was amazingly discreet about them. He
rarely spoke, and when he did, his voice held no expression. He
was bad-tempered and avoided people. He suffered from an
intricate variety of digestive complaints, constant headaches,
and frequent nosebleeds. He was narrow-minded and obsessive.

Although he was the son of the famous physician and anthropologist Louis Adolphe Bertillon and had been raised in a highly
intellectual atmosphere appreciative of science, he had managed

to be thrown out of a number of excellent schools for poor grades. He had been unable to keep a job. His employment at the police department was due entirely to his father's influence. But this misanthropic soul managed to accomplish what no one else had: he invented a workable system of identification.

Sherlock Holmes remarks in *The Hound of the Baskervilles*, "The world is full of obvious things which nobody by any chance ever observes." It was Bertillon who first observed the obvious need for a scientific method of identifying criminals. He recalled discussions in his father's house about the theory of the Belgian statistician Lambert Adolphe Jacques Quetelet, who in 1840 had suggested that there were no two people in the world who were exactly the same size in all their measurements.

Bertillon reasoned from this that if multiple measurements were taken of individuals and classified according to type, locating records would be easier and the chance of confusing subjects unlikely. In 1879, after a few months as a clerk, during which he had done some preliminary research, he wrote a report to offer his ideas to his superiors. The report managed to be both pedantic and complex and was dismissed as a presumptuous jest. The senior Bertillon, who realized that his difficult son's theory was a brilliant application of science to criminal investigation, tried to intervene, but the police administration, demonstrating an impressive flair for avoiding creativity, refused to even consider the matter. There it rested until 1882 when the administration, intensely pressured by influential friends of Dr. Bertillon, gave in. The persistent clerk was given two assistants and some funds to further research his system.

After considerable study, he designed a procedure he named anthropometry. It required at least eleven bodily measurements that were believed to be unchangeable after the age of twenty. These included: the total length of the arms when outstretched; height both sitting and standing; the length of the head; the width of the head; the width of the cheek; and the lengths of the right ear, left foot, left little finger, left middle finger, and each arm from elbow to outstretched middle finger. Each measurement was to be made three times and the mean chosen for the record.

Alphonse suggested that all photographs be taken from the same angle and lit the same way, and that profile views be included. He also invented the *portrait parlé*, or "speaking picture," to accompany the photographs. This required the recording of eye color, hair color, and complexion, shape of the head, stoutness, posture, voice, accent, scars or marks, and usual style of dress. The complete version of the *portrait parlé* required hundreds of exact bits of information, and detectives resisted its demands. Eventually, it was simplified into the "Wanted" descriptions familiar to us today.

It was not a perfect system. It was time-consuming. It required training to implement and a severe eye for detail if measurements were to be made with complete accuracy. But it was a vast improvement. Bertillon had created some order out of chaos, and his new system became an established part of police procedure in France. Reading about it in Austria, Hans Gross at once began to adapt the system in his country.

It became the general standard in much of the industrialized world, although some countries used different numbers of required measurements. Even England, never comfortable with French leadership, was considering bertillonage.

The sour, introverted Bertillon was a success. He was given the title of director of the Police Identification Service. He was awarded a staff and a new office. He became world famous.

By 1893, Conan Doyle, in his story "The Naval Treaty," had Watson say, in describing traveling with Sherlock Holmes, "His conversation, I remember, was about the Bertillon system of measurements, and he expressed his enthusiastic admiration of the French savant." Sherlock Holmes admired Bertillon! What greater accolade could be hoped for?

But a tiny worm was wiggling within Bertillon's apple. In 1880, while Bertillon was impatiently waiting for a chance to prove his theories, a Scottish medical missionary in Japan named Henry Faulds wrote a letter to the journal *Nature*. It was published on October 28 of that year and was titled "On the Skin-furrows of the Hand." It was a very moderate statement of a concept that would cause a revolution in criminal investigation. Faulds's letter began:

> In looking over some specimens of "prehistoric" pottery found in Japan I was led, about a year ago, to give some attention to the character of certain finger-marks which had been made on them while the clay was still soft. Unfortunately all of those which happened to come into my possession were too vague and ill-defined to be of much use, but a comparison of such finger-tip impressions made in recent pottery led me to observe the characters of the skin-furrows in human fingers generally. From these I passed to the study of the finger-tips of monkeys, and found at once that they presented very close analogies to those of human beings.

"An ordinary botanical lens is of great service in bringing out these minor peculiarities," Faulds wrote (reminding us inevitably of Sherlock Holmes and his magnifying lens). He continued:

> Where the loops occur the innermost lines may simply break off and end abruptly; they may end in self-returning loops, or, again, they may go on without breaks after turning round upon themselves. Some lines also join or branch like junctions in a railway map. All these varieties, how-ever, may be compatible with the general impression of symmetry that the two hands give us when printed from.

Faulds went on to explain how he took copies of these intrigu-ing lines:

> A common slate or smooth board of any kind, or a sheet of tin, spread over very thinly and evenly with printer's ink, is

all that is required. The parts of which impressions are desired are pressed down steadily and softly, and then are transferred to slightly damp paper. I have succeeded in making very delicate impressions on glass. They are somewhat faint indeed, but would be useful for demonstrations, as details are very well shown, even down to the minute pores. By using different colors of ink useful comparisons could be made of two patterns by superposition. These might be shown by magic lantern. . . . A little *hot* water and soap remove the ink. . . .

I am sanguine that the careful study of these patterns may be useful in several ways.

Faulds then discussed other possible uses of prints—for instance, in historical or anthropological research. And then he made this great leap into forensic history, writing:

When bloody finger-marks or impressions on clay, glass, &c. exist, they may lead to the scientific identification of criminals. Already I have had experience in two such cases, and found useful evidence from these marks. In one case greasy finger-marks revealed who had been drinking some rectified spirit. The pattern was unique and fortunately I had previously obtained a copy of it. They agreed with microscopic fidelity. . . . Other cases might occur in medico-legal investigations, as when the hands only of some mutilated victim were found. If previously known they would be much more precise in value than the standard *mole* of the penny novelists. If unknown previously, heredity might enable an expert to determine the relatives with considerable probability in many cases, and with absolute precision in some.

And then, making it clear that he knew the Tichborne case well, Faulds wrote, "Such a case as that of the Claimant even might not be beyond the range of this principle. There might be a recognizable Tichborne type." Faulds was basing this statement on his observation that there are similarities in print patterns in some families, although hardly enough to provide definite identification. (However, if Lady Tichborne had preserved an unwashed object she was certain her son had handled from which clear prints could have been obtained, it could have served as an exemplar. If no prints on the object matched the Claimant's, perhaps it might have influenced her opinion.) Faulds continued:

> I have heard, since coming to these general conclusions by original and patient experiment, that the Chinese criminals from early times have been made to give the impressions of their fingers, just as we make ours yield their photographs. I have not yet, however, succeeded in getting any precise or authenticated facts on that point. . . . There can be no doubt as to the advantage of having, besides their photographs, a nature-copy of the for-ever-unchangeable finger-furrows of important criminals.

Henry Faulds was not the first person to have noticed ridge patterns on human fingers. As he mentioned, finger marks had been used in Asia. And in the West, as early as 1686, Marcello Malpighi, an anatomist at the University of Bologna, had mentioned the marks. In 1823, Professor John Evangelist Purkinje, a pathologist and physiologist at the University at Breslau, had presented a paper on finger impressions, listing nine types and suggesting a method of classifying them, but Faulds was the first to express the idea that finger marks could aid criminal investigation.

Only a month after Faulds's letter was published in *Nature*, Sir William Herschel, a British civil servant stationed in India, wrote to *Nature* that he had been using fingerprints for identification since 1860. There is no evidence that he foresaw the forensic use of prints, however.

Sir Francis Galton, a cousin of Charles Darwin and a well-known anthropologist, had never been convinced that bertillonage was the perfect solution to the problem of identification. Reading the reports in *Nature*, he quickly saw the advantage of fingerprints and devoted himself to studying the subject. He corresponded frequently and at length on the subject with Herschel (although he ignored Faulds's contribution, infuriating that gentleman). Galton satisfied himself that just as no leaf is exactly duplicated and no two snowflakes are precisely alike, each fingerprint is unique. Further, he determined that an individual's prints never change. He wrote:

> There appear to be no bodily characteristics other than deep scars and tattoo marks comparable in their persistence to these markings; at the same time they are out of all proportion more numerous than any other measurable features. The dimensions of the limbs and body alter in the course of growth and decay; the color, quantity and quality of the hair, the tint and quality of the skin, the number and set of the teeth, the expression of the features, the gestures, the handwriting, even the eye color change after many years. There seems no persistence in the visible parts of the body except in these minute and hitherto disregarded ridges.

This, of course, was a direct contradiction of Bertillon's concept, which held that most bodily measurements did not change.

Galton was championing fingerprinting as the identification process that should be used in Britain. The one great remaining problem, as he saw it, was exactly how it was established for a presentation at court that two prints matched. Merely announcing that they looked alike wouldn't do—hanging a man on the basis of such a vague statement would be feckless even for the enthusiastically punitive judiciary of the time.

In his book *Finger Prints*, published in 1892, Galton presented the results of his research as well as a system he had devised for classifying the patterns of whorls, loops, and triangles found on fingertips. This method was to eventually form the basis for the identification process adopted by Scotland Yard.

The same year, in Argentina, Juan Vucetich, the head of the Statistical Bureau of the La Plata police, was hard at work establishing his own method of print classification. It was put to the test quickly. Two children were found on their blood-soaked bed battered to death by a heavy object. Their distraught twenty-six-year-old mother, Francisca Rojas, accused a neighbor of the crime. He had threatened to kill what she most loved if she would not succumb to his romantic overtures, she told the police. But the neighbor had an unshakable alibi.

The investigators heard rumors that Francisca had a lover who had often been heard to say he would gladly marry her if only she weren't saddled by her two children. The detective in charge, Alvarez, remembering Vucetich's system, carefully combed every inch of the crime scene and finally came upon a small brownish spot on the door. It appeared to be dried blood, which held the print of a thumb. The piece of the door was taken to the station, as was Francisca. Her thumbprint was taken with the aid of a stamp pad. It was compared to the bloody print through a magnifying glass. It was clear they matched.

Confronted with the evidence, the loving mother confessed that in the interest of romance she felt compelled to crush her children's heads with a rock. She had then disposed of the weapon in a well. It was the first murder known to be solved by the use of fingerprints.

(A hauntingly similar clue would appear years later in Conan Doyle's story "The Adventure of the Norwood Builder" when Watson says, "With dramatic suddenness he struck a match, and by its light exposed a stain of blood upon the whitewashed wall. As he held the match nearer, I saw that it was more than a stain. It was the well-marked print of a thumb.")

In France, Bertillon cast a baleful eye on the new identification procedure. He saw it as a threat to his method and his prestige.

He was resentful of Vucetich and Galton. He would tolerate the science of fingerprints, or dactyloscopy, as it was commonly called, only as an adjunct to bertillonage. Within this limit, he grudgingly allowed the Identification Bureau to record and file the fingerprints along with the anthropometric measurements of criminals. Perhaps it was Bertillon's resistance to fingerprinting that kept him from establishing an efficient method of classifying fingerprints, and that led to an excruciating embarrassment in August 1911: the French nation awoke to the hideously momentous news that the *Mona Lisa* had been abducted from the Louvre.

It had happened on a Monday, when the museum was closed to the public. The glass case that contained the wooden panel on which the picture was painted stood open. Examination by the police located a fingerprint on the glass. If it appeared in the great Bertillon's files, the culprit would be identified. France and the world held their collective breaths, but there was no match to be found. It was assumed that the daring thief had no record.

Two years passed, and then an approach was made to an art dealer in Italy from someone who claimed to have the *Mona Lisa*. He turned out to be a house painter named Vincenzo Perugia, who had been keeping the most famous missing painting in the world under his bed since he had casually hidden it under his smock and taken it out of the Louvre. Perugia had an arrest record in France. His prints had to have been among Bertillon's files. Why had they not been found?

Bertillon was forced to explain that he had classified prints of the right thumb only, and Perugia, who seemed to have had a particularly poor sense of occasion, had left behind only a clear print of his left. The case left the stubborn Bertillon with even more resentment toward the fingerprinting process, but in spite of him, outside of France the new science had been growing in strength.

Since 1893, Edward Richard Henry, the chief of police in Bengal, India, having read Galton's book, had been using fingerprints in addition to Bertillon's method of anthropometry. He grew to favor the use of prints and eventually, collaborating with Galton, developed the Galton-Henry system of fingerprint classification still used today in much of the English-speaking world.

By 1900, the British government, which had adopted a combination of anthropometry and fingerprinting, appointed Lord Belper to head a committee to study the "Identification of Criminals by Measurement and Fingerprints." Edward Henry was called as an expert witness and gave testimony supporting fingerprinting as a method superior to bertillonage, a position with which the committee ultimately agreed. The following year, Henry was placed in charge of the new fingerprint branch at Scotland Yard.

It might have appeared that England was the new leader in identification techniques, but France still had extraordinary contributions to make. Edmond Locard, a student of Bertillon, was an assistant to Alexandre Lacassagne. Dr. Locard was qualified in both medicine and law, and in spite of his great respect for Bertillon, he became an early enthusiast of fingerprinting. He was a passionate researcher, and in the interest of acquiring accurate data, he had been known to burn his fingertips merely to satisfy himself that prints were truly indelible. He was a reader and an admirer of both Hans Gross and Conan Doyle, and he suggested that students of forensic science read the Sherlock Holmes tales as examples of proper scientific approach and to obtain a perspective on the new directions forensic science might take.

Appointed in 1910 as head of what was then a tiny police laboratory in Lyon, France, Locard proceeded to build it into a highly efficient and creative facility. He established the first rules for the minimum number of ridges that must concur before a fingerprint match might be declared. Basing his opinion on Galton and Henry's work, he stated that if twelve concurring points are present in a sharp, clear print, the identity is certain. (Often referred to as "Galton's Details," the number of points that must match vary from country to country. On the federal level in the United States, no minimum number of points is required.)

Addressing the difficulties raised when prints recovered from a crime scene are blurred or only partial, Locard stressed that the accuracy of identification depended on multiple factors including the clarity of the prints, the rarity of their pattern, and the visibility of pores and of the core, or center, of the figure.

In 1913, his research led him to discover that it was possible to plant fraudulent fingerprints by the use of a finger modeled of gutta-percha (a rubberlike gum made from the sap of a tree in Malaysia), with ridges molded realistically upon it. A story most likely more amusing than true made the rounds among the police that a skilled Parisian burglar always left the fingerprint of the police chief at the scene of his crimes. To make sure that this did not become a reality, Locard developed a new method of identification to supplement fingerprinting. He called it poroscopy, and it depended on the observation of the patterns formed by thousands of pores between the ridges of fingerprints. There being many more pores than ridges, pore patterns would be infinitely more difficult to counterfeit.

Latent prints (those not visible to the naked eye) were made visible by iodine fumes and then photographed, because the revealed prints would soon fade. Fine-grained powders in colors that contrasted with the background of the prints were also used; the powders were delicately brushed on the latents and then photographed. Since the prints would be shown in court only in a copy, it was important that each step of the process be recorded, to avoid charges of planting prints.

Locard's highly astute mind, imaginative flair, and reputation for integrity made the Lyon laboratory a highly respected facility. It also trained a number of world-class forensic scientists, among them the Swedish criminalist Harry Söderman.

Söderman, both in his memoir and in his conversations, recalled a strange case that took place in Lyon during the 1920s. (He did not specify the exact dates.) A series of burglaries were committed, always during the daytime, through windows that were about a foot open. Although the thief often took the risk of climbing to the second or even the third floor, only one or two objects were stolen, usually of shiny real or imitation gold or silver. In one case, a set of false teeth disappeared while the apartment owner was out of the room for just a few minutes. Police considered the possibility of youngsters daring each other in some sort of initiation rite, or of an individual with a bizarre sexual compulsion to enter forbidden space and abscond with a souvenir.

Eventually, the detective assigned to the case discovered a fingerprint on a windowpane. It was photographed and taken to the laboratory, but not only did it prove impossible to find a match with any print on file, the print was also most peculiar, as the ridges all appeared to run vertically.

Locard pondered the problem and came up with a startling idea. Perhaps he remembered Faulds's original paper, "On the Skin-furrows of the Hand," in which he had discussed studying the prints of primates. Perhaps, as an admirer of Sherlock Holmes, Locard thought of the description in "The Adventure of the Creeping Man":

> As we watched him he suddenly began with incredible agility to ascend it. From branch to branch he sprang, sure of foot and firm of grasp, climbing apparently in mere joy at his own powers, with no definite object in view. . . . It was the monkey, not the professor, whom Roy attacked, just as it was the monkey who teased Roy. Climbing was a joy to the creature.

Edmond Locard ordered all the local organ grinders and their simian employees brought to his laboratory. A number of the monkeys, perhaps concerned about an infringement of their civil rights, resisted fingerprinting and had to be restrained. The organ grinders were more cooperative. When the burglarizing beast had been identified, his companion's rooms were searched and there the missing items were found.

The organ grinder, who had trained his pet to enter empty

rooms on command and return with small glittering objects, spent several months in prison. The monkey served his sentence at the local zoo.

By the time of Bertillon's death in 1913, fingerprinting had been clearly established as the dominant method of identification in police work, even in France. From that day on, those who made crime their living would bear in mind the declaration made by the local inspector of Harrow Weald, speaking of a piece of evidence he did not understand but had preserved, in "The Adventure of the Three Gables": "There is always the chance of finger-marks or something."

WHATEVER REMAINS

- In the United States, the first official use of fingerprinting was in New York State in 1903.

- Even though fingerprinting became the gold standard for identification, it is well to remember that earlier forms of identifying marks continued to remain important. In 1935, in Melbourne, Australia, a recently caught fourteen-foot shark was on display at the aquarium when it suffered a violent attack of dyspepsia. It finally relieved itself by vomiting a mass that contained, among other items, a human arm that had been severed at the shoulder. The arm sported a tattoo of two boxers. The wife of a missing man named James Smith identified the arm as his, and prints at his home matched those of the arm. Although an arrest was made, the accused was acquitted, the jury evidently not being satisfied that the severed arm was definite proof that Smith was dead.

- Recent research indicates that natural residues on prepubescent children's fingers differ from those of adults. Children's latent prints are extremely fragile and can be destroyed by sunlight in just a few hours.

- Although identical twins have identical DNA, their fingerprints differ. Within the womb, as the fetuses float and move their limbs, the still malleable ridges of their fingers are affected by what they touch, and they acquire different shapes.

- There are those who argue that the uniqueness of fingerprints has not been conclusively proven, since each and every fingerprint has not been compared with every other fingerprint, past or present. Clearly this is an impossible standard to achieve. As millions of fingerprint comparisons have been made without any duplication being found, it is reasonable to assume that fingerprints are unique. The usefulness of fingerprints as identifiers in crime investigation is often limited as a practical matter because it is common for fingerprints gathered at crime scenes to be blurred, and often only partial fingerprints are obtained. It is often difficult, as a result, to positively determine a match. The careful training of fingerprint experts is of great importance, as is their strict adherence to scientific ethics.

For centuries, the bodies of executed criminals had been left in the hands of the executioners. Occasionally, anatomists were favored with a subject, whole or in part.

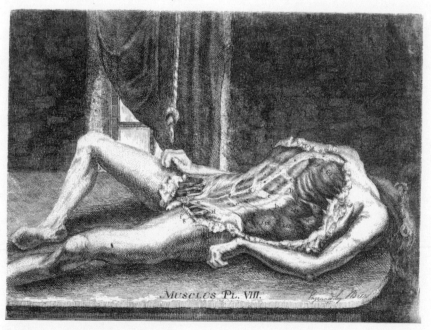

In the nineteenth century, dissection tables were still the flat wooden ones in use during the eighteenth century.

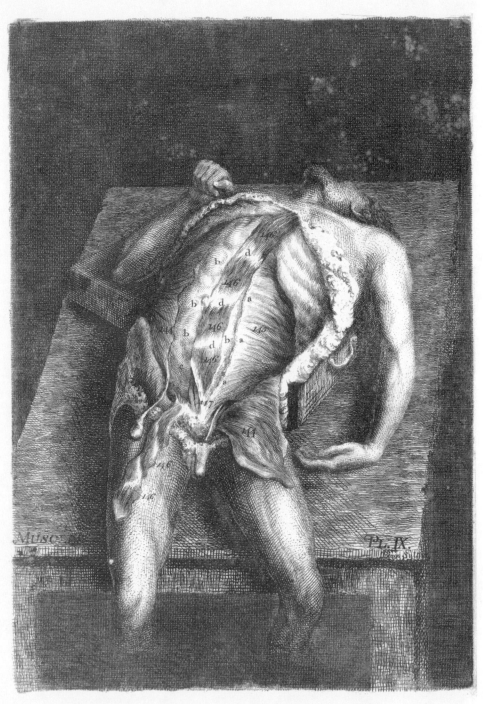

The dissection tables were often too short, and there was no drainage available.

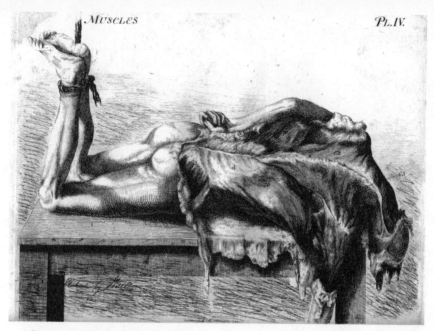

Sometimes the bodies were propped up by ropes to keep the subject intact.

Ropes were also used to demonstrate the way the limbs extended in life and to allow medical artists to draw different views.

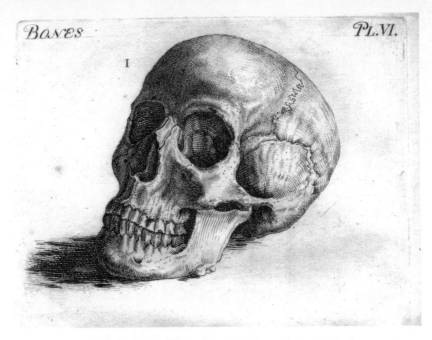

Skulls and bones were boiled to free them of flesh.

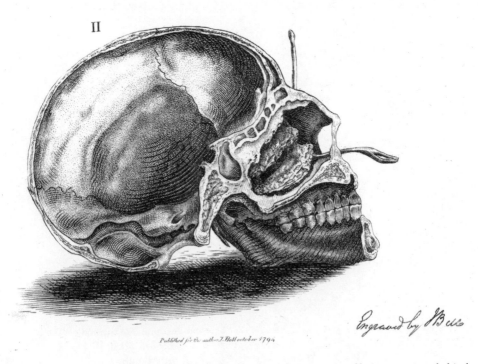

Without the rotating saws available today, skulls were opened by means of knives, saws, and chisels.

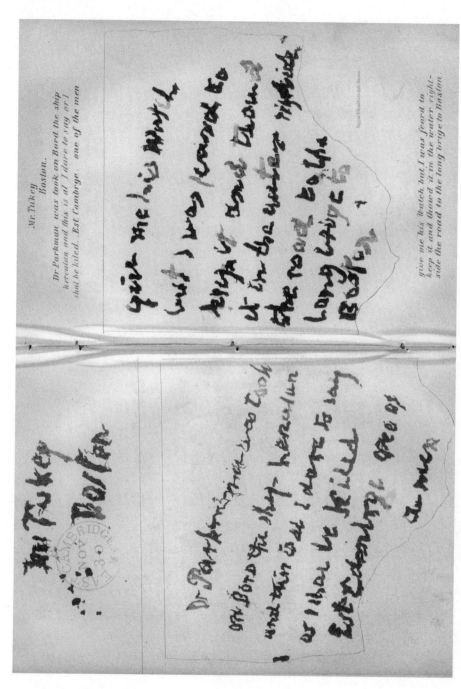

One of the barely legible scrawls the prosecution suspected was the disguised hand of the defendant in the Parkman/Webster case.

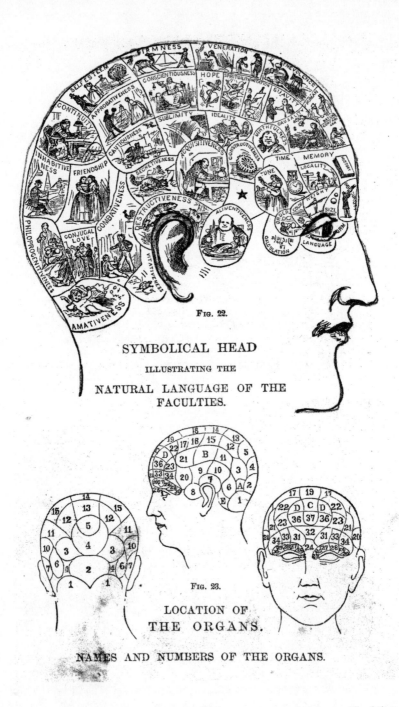

Fig. 22.

SYMBOLICAL HEAD

ILLUSTRATING THE

NATURAL LANGUAGE OF THE
FACULTIES.

Fig. 23.

LOCATION OF
THE ORGANS.

NAMES AND NUMBERS OF THE ORGANS.

Phrenology held that specific parts of the skull were associated with specific abilities.
Heads like these were used for guidance.

An example of a Bertillon card used in the United States in 1910. Curiously, the identity of the subject is not given, except for the listed occupation of "theatrical promoter."

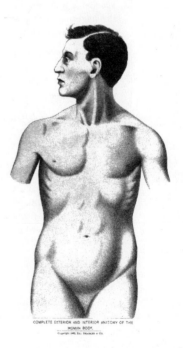

The nineteenth-century fear of sexual behavior sometimes resulted in drawings like this—of a human without genitalia. It appeared in a book of medical advice.

COMPLETE EXTERIOR AND INTERIOR ANATOMY OF THE HUMAN BODY.

Imaginatively awful treatments abounded during the Victorian era.

118

CHAPTER 8

Shots in the Dark

"The bullets alone are enough to put his head in a noose."
—Sherlock Holmes in "The Adventure of the Empty House"

SHERLOCK HOLMES's eye for detail never closes. As he reminds Watson in "The Boscombe Valley Mystery," "You know my method. It is founded upon the observance of trifles." And the trifles he observes and weaves through his reasoning include not only traces of tobacco ash and varieties of earth but also the effects of bullets. Holmes, hot on the trail, remarks in "The Adventure of the Dancing Men," "It is now necessary that we should try to throw some light upon this third bullet, which has clearly, from the splintering of the wood, been fired from inside the room."

Observations of the direction of a bullet's path and its individual characteristics are the basis for the science of ballistics. Coupled with Holmes's vast knowledge of scientific esoterica, these observations often lead to the unraveling of intricate crimes. In using ballistic evidence as a detection tool, the fictional Holmes is following a path already blazed by real-life detectives, such as the dashing Vidocq of the Sûreté and the indomitable Henry Goddard of the Bow Street Runners.

Vidocq is credited by a number of biographers with ordering, in 1822, the removal of a bullet from an aristocratic murder victim's body in order to compare it with her husband's dueling pistols. Observing that the bullet was much too large to fit the suspected firearms, Vidocq turned his attention to a weapon owned by the deceased's lover, which proved to be the appropriate size. The lover confessed and was promptly escorted to the guillotine, to the great relief of the bereaved husband.

Across the channel thirteen years later, Henry Goddard was exploring a gunshot case with even greater rigor on behalf of the London-based Bow Street Runners. The Runners constituted the first government-authorized organization of detectives in Britain and was founded by the novelist Henry Fielding in 1749. Before that time, citizens were expected to enforce the law on their own, and people in the countryside privately hired constables or watchmen to protect them and their property. The very idea of a police force controlled by the government was repellent to most English citizens—they viewed it as a limitation of their freedom and a craven creep toward the embrace of tyranny.

But life in London was more complex than in the country, where everyone knew their neighbors. As the city's population grew, crime kept pace, and it soon became evident that private citizens required some professional help in maintaining order. Fielding had begun by organizing, on his own authority, a small group of constables. He managed the men's activities from his Bow Street residence. Eventually, he was granted some funds by the prime minister to give a stipend to members of his group, now popularly referred to as the Bow Street Runners. They were well established by 1835, the year in which Henry Goddard was called to consult on a mysterious case of attempted murder in the seaside town of Southampton.

In his *Memoirs*, Goddard describes his adventure with a detective's flair for the salient detail. The chief magistrate had been informed that the Southampton home of Mrs. Maxwell, a lady of independent means, had been invaded by burglars in the still hours of the night. Guns had been fired, evidently in an attempt to slaughter the butler as he lay asleep in his bed. Intensely irritated by a bullet piercing both his repose and his pillow, the butler had leapt from his bed and valiantly fought off the intruders. In their haste to escape the righteously enraged servant, the thieves had left behind the large amount of household jewelry and silver plate that they had already securely wrapped.

Saying that this was "a grave matter," the magistrate ordered Goddard to travel to the scene by that night's mail coach and investigate. By nine the following morning, Goddard was at the Maxwell home interviewing the lady of the house and the intrepid butler, Joseph Randall. He found Mrs. Maxwell prostrate with fear.

Goddard examined the brave butler's room and his bed, which stood opposite stoutly shuttered windows. The shutters each had a hole near the top about the size of a saucer to admit air and light.

The butler explained to Goddard that on the night of the attack, he had secured the doors and windows as usual before going to bed. He had been awakened at about one in the morning by an unfamiliar sound outside the pantry windows, which he likened to that made by a chain being dragged over gravel. He thought he heard footsteps inside the house and then heard the door to his bedroom being slowly opened. He could see, reflected on a small picture that hung opposite his bedroom door, a lantern held at arm's length "and the shadow of a man before it and a man behind the one that carried the lantern."

Randall said he pretended to sleep and heard the men back away. Thoroughly alarmed, the butler reached under his pillow for his pistol, when a gun was fired into his room from the outdoors through one of the holes in the shutters. The bullet passed through the butler's pillow and pierced the headboard of the bed. If Randall had not turned to reach for his pistol when he did, he excitedly told the detective, he would "have been left a corpse." The butler then jumped from his bed and chased the masked burglars into the hallway, where he struggled with them, frightening them into escaping and leaving behind the household goods.

The local watch, who had been promptly summoned by Mrs. Maxwell, discovered that the back door had been forced and that the house was in a state of disarray. Goddard, who had listened with great care, was uneasy with the butler's description of the lantern that cast "the shadow of a man *before it*." He examined the back door as minutely as Holmes ever examined a door and found it had been forced by a Jemmy (a short crowbar favored by well-schooled burglars for gaining entry), but he thought the impression on the outside of the door "did not correspond with the inside."

He discovered still another inconsistency. In 1835, bullets were not mass produced but were formed in individual molds by the gun owner. Goddard asked Randall for his pistols, his molds, and the bullet that had been fired through the headboard of the bed and recovered.

Upon examination, each of the bullets, including the slightly flattened one that had been fired, possessed a very tiny, round pimple that corresponded with an equally tiny hole in the mold. It appeared clear to Goddard that all the bullets had been made by the same hand, but he asked for a second opinion from a local gunsmith, who agreed with Goddard's conclusion.

The Runner wrote that this was clearly a matter of "a breaking out, not a breaking in." It appeared that just as in the Sherlock Holmes tale "The Reigate Squires," written more than four decades later, the burglary was a fake.

Strongly pressed for an explanation, Randall finally confessed he had staged the entire incident in hopes of obtaining a handsome reward from Mrs. Maxwell and of ensuring his continued employment. He managed to achieve neither goal. As Mrs. Maxwell preferred to avoid "a scene" (the bête noire of nineteenth-century British life), no charges were brought against him. The shifty servant was allowed to sidle off into obscurity.

Fifty years before Sherlock Holmes first appeared, the Bow Street Runner had used the Sherlockian method of careful observation of trifles. The Randall matter was the first case of ballistic identification to be documented, and Henry Goddard remains forever inscribed in forensic history as the man who proved that the butler did it.

The years that followed were not particularly fruitful for the study of guns and bullets as a part of criminal investigation, and it was largely by happy accident that there was an occasional success. In 1860, a policeman found a paper wad torn from the March 24, 1854, issue of the *Times* of London near the body of a gunshot victim. It smelled of powder and had evidently been used to stuff powder and a bullet down the barrel of a muzzle-loaded firearm. A man named Richardson was under suspicion, and a search of his residence disclosed a double-barreled pistol, one barrel of which had been recently fired. The other was still loaded and furthermore contained a paper wad similar to the one found at the scene. The clever policeman checked with the editor of the *Times* and determined that the second wad came from the same six-year-old issue of the paper. The evidence was damning, and Richardson confessed.

Here and there, there were a few similar cases, but while they were morally satisfying, they were unfortunately no harbingers of great strides in ballistics. The nineteenth century witnessed many changes in the design and manufacture of firearms, including the use of spiraling grooves within the barrel, which gave the weapons greater accuracy and range. Spiraling grooves also produced distinctive markings on the spent bullets. Since each gun maker had a different number and type of rifling grooves, the key existed for determining which bullet was fired from which gun. But the key was not systematically used.

Ballistics research was spotty and uncoordinated. As there was no consensus as to which branch of science the subject belonged to, different specialties dabbled in it from time to time. Pathology made an early attempt when, in 1889, Professor

Alexandre Lacassagne noticed the distinctive striations on a bullet he removed from a murder victim. Examining the revolvers of a number of suspects, he matched the bullet's seven grooves to one of the guns. But Lacassagne studied only the weapons shown to him by the police. If the bullet had come from a different gun, his conclusion would be incorrect. Lacassagne was evidently able to live with the ambiguity, but the unfortunate owner of the revolver, who was convicted of murder, was not.

Jürgen Thorwald, in his *Century of the Detective*, provides an account of a contribution made by the famous German chemist Paul Jeserich in 1898. Dr. Jeserich was asked to determine whether the bullet removed from a murder victim had come from the gun owned by the defendant. He proceeded by firing a test bullet from the suspect's gun and then taking microphotographs of both the test bullet and the murder bullet. Comparing the pictures, he observed small defects in the markings of the lands and grooves on both bullets that he believed were unusual and that matched each other.

Although Jeserich had little experience with firearms, and, like Lacassagne, had examined only the gun given to him by the police, he gave solid testimony for the prosecution. The chemist had only a moderate interest in ballistics and did not actively pursue the subject further. But the defendant, convicted on Jeserich's testimony of a capital crime, no doubt found the subject worthy of thought as he faced his death sentence.

In 1913, Victor Balthazard, a noted French expert in medical jurisprudence, published a paper in the *Archives of Criminal Anthropology and Legal Medicine*. His research established that every fired bullet shows a variety of distinguishing marks influenced by many parts of the firearm. Therefore, Professor Balthazard argued, each bullet has its own fingerprint and is unique.

This conclusion was theoretically fascinating, but in 1913 the world was trembling on the starting edge of the Great War. Research into single murders seemed unimportant and had to take a back seat to the manufacture of engines of mass death.

Sir Sydney Smith, the eminent British forensic pathologist and a great admirer of Sherlock Holmes, noted in his 1959 memoir, *Mostly Murder*, that in 1919 little progress had been made in the field of ballistics since the days of Henry Goddard. "As far as I was concerned," Sir Sydney wrote, "it was still a virgin field." Maintaining that bullets were the concern of the pathologist, since the damage they do to the human body is obviously a medical issue, he proceeded to devote himself to the subject. He had been appointed the principal medicolegal expert in Egypt in 1917, and since murder by gunshot was regularly practiced in that time and place, he had ample opportunity to study it.

The invention of the comparison microscope in 1923 made it possible as never before to evaluate the patterns on two bullets simultaneously in greatly enlarged detail, reducing the chance of error. Sir Sydney made prompt use of this microscope. He published a highly successful textbook in 1925, and his research on ballistic evidence was very influential in the English-speaking world.

But even Sydney Smith's expertise would not prevent the judicial debacle that occurred in Edinburgh, Scotland, in 1926, when a fifty-six-year-old lady named Bertha Merrett, quietly writing a letter in her sitting room, suffered a nasty encounter with a pistol. Mrs. Merrett was an Englishwoman of the upper middle class who had spent much of her married life abroad with her engineer husband. She had followed him diligently wherever his professional interests led him, from New Zealand to St. Petersburg, Russia. But their only child, a son named John Donald, was somewhat delicate. The severe climate of Russia eventually stressed the child's health, and his mother took him to Switzerland to recover, thus missing the excitement of both the Great War and the Russian Revolution. Her husband, who had remained behind, disappeared in the maelstrom.

By 1924, when the boy was sixteen, Mrs. Merrett had brought him to the British Isles to complete his education. In 1926 (which was to prove the Merrett annus horribilis), they were living in a modest flat in Edinburgh, and John was enrolled at Edinburgh University, a nonresident school. They had acquired the regular services of a maid who came in each morning.

According to all accounts, Bertha Merrett was a woman of great intelligence with a fine eye for business and total devotion to her son. John Donald Merrett had a quick mind, charming manners, and good looks, but he balanced these fine qualities with an impressive degree of self-absorption. Careful not to strain his academic ability by excessive study, he avoided actually attending class whenever possible. He kept this from his credulous mother, just as he kept from her the fact that he spent his pocket money on gambling, drinking, and ladies of the evening.

On March 17, 1926, the maid arrived at 9 A.M. as usual and greeted mother and son, who seemed in ordinary cheerful spirits. Mrs. Merrett was writing letters, and her son was reading on the opposite side of the room. The maid was in the kitchen when she heard the sound of a pistol shot, a scream, and a thud. Young Merrett entered the kitchen and said, "Rita, my mother has shot herself!"

In the sitting room, the appalled maid saw Mrs. Merrett lying supine on the floor, still alive, but bleeding profusely from a head wound. A pistol lay on the bureau a few feet away.

Two constables, the memorably named Middlemiss and Izatt, responded to the scene, but instead of being content to merely conduct a methodical investigation, they vigorously set about creating a disturbance. They moved furniture, papers, and books with abandon while diagramming nothing. They did manage to note John Donald's statement that his mother had suddenly shot herself as she was writing letters because "she was worried about money matters" and that he had purchased the gun to "shoot rabbits." They ignored the letter the lady had been in the process of writing and the fact that it was a simple, amiable letter to a friend that contained no suicidal overtones. The police assault on the scene reached its apogee when one officer picked up the weapon and stuffed it in his pocket without recording where he had found it.

Mrs. Merrett, still breathing but unconscious, was removed to the infirmary, where she was placed in the locked ward with barred windows where those who had attempted the criminal offense of suicide were confined. She regained consciousness and complained of a terrible pain in her right ear. This was quite understandable, as an x-ray had disclosed a bullet in the base of her skull. The location of the wound made it inoperable. The patient was told only that she had had a "little accident," as it was considered unwise to alarm her.

Unprompted, she told hospital personnel and friends repeatedly that she had been calmly writing letters, that her son had stood too close to her, that she had told him, "Go away, Donald, and don't annoy me," and that she had heard a sudden bang in her head, "like a pistol." She had no memory of a pistol being in the house. So unaware was Mrs. Merrett of the true nature of her injury that she asked a friend to arrange a consultation with an ear specialist. At one point, she said with admirable maternal forbearance, "Did Donald do this? He's such a naughty boy." None of this information was recorded by police investigators.

Young Merrett, evidently too exhausted by filial concern to visit the hospital regularly, inquired of the doctor, "Is it in the cards that she might recover?" The answer soon came. On April 2, Bertha Merrett's obituary appeared in the *Scotsman*. John Donald Merrett was now officially due the sympathy given to an orphan.

A postmortem was performed by Professor Harvey Littlejohn, who was both chair of forensic medicine at Edinburgh and a former teacher of Sydney Smith. The immediate cause of death was determined to have been basal meningitis, the result of the infection of a bullet wound. Littlejohn's report included the words:

> There was nothing to indicate the distance at which the discharge of the weapon took place, whether from a few inches or a greater distance. So far as the position of the wound is concerned, the case is consistent with suicide.

But Bertha Merrett's family and friends were insistent that suicide would have been abhorrent to her. There had been nothing in her demeanor prior to the shooting that indicated depression. Her statements in the hospital supported their view. Further, self-inflicted gunshots are unusual in females (although not unheard of), and the angle of the wound at the back of the head seemed awkward. The discovery by the bank that the young orphan had been embellishing his pocketbook by forging his mother's name appeared suggestive.

Littlejohn, reconsidering, and aware of his former student's expertise with gunshot wounds, asked for the opinion of Sydney Smith. Sir Sydney, going over the evidence, noted that the doctors at the infirmary had observed the lack of tattooing, or powder marks, around the bullet wound. The question was, he felt, would the weapon that made the wound leave such marks if discharged close enough to the head as to indicate suicide.

He suggested that Littlejohn experiment with the weapon that shot Bertha Merrett. Littlejohn procured the gun, which was a six-cartridge .25 Spanish automatic, loading it with the same type of ammunition used in the Merrett shooting. He fired it at a number of targets, including one made of the skin of a recently amputated leg. He measured the distance each time and discovered that at three inches or less, very obvious powder and burn marks appeared on the target. Marks appeared at six inches. These marks were not only evident to the naked eye, they were exceedingly difficult to remove. It took a distance of nine inches before no marks appeared, and certainly no one could shoot themselves behind the ear at such a long range. (The importance of powder marks was well known to Sherlock Holmes, who says in "The Reigate Squires": "The wound upon the dead man was, as I was able to determine with absolute confidence, fired from a revolver at the distance of something over four yards. There was no powder-blackening on the clothes. Evidently, therefore, Alec Cunningham had lied when he said that the two men were struggling when the shot was fired.")

Littlejohn, to his great credit, wrote a new report, stating that accident was "inconceivable, suicide in the highest degree improbable," and that the circumstances "pointed to homicide."

John Donald Merrett now received the rapt attention of the Scottish judicial system and was indicted on charges of both murder and forgery. Littlejohn, of course, would testify for the Crown. A guilty verdict seemed inevitable. And then Merrett's attorney made an amazing announcement. The expert witness for the defense would be Sir Bernard Spilsbury.

Sir Bernard, the English Home Office pathologist, had a sterling reputation as a brilliant expert on homicide in general and shooting cases in particular. His fame, since his early foray into the public's awareness during the Crippen case, had grown enormous, and his ability to impress a jury was formidable. His official position meant that in England he usually appeared for the Crown, so his appearance in Scotland on the side of the defense was startling. Further, Sir Bernard shared the burden of the defense evidence with Robert Churchill, a well-known gunsmith who frequently collaborated with Spilsbury on shooting cases.

They firmly stated their belief that Bertha Merrett had committed suicide and that the absence of powder burns or tattooing was unimportant. They testified that they had carried out repeated experiments that showed that powder marks need not have been left around the wound even if the shot was at close range.

The problem was that the weapon and ammunition they had experimented with were entirely different from the gun and bullets that had killed Bertha Merrett. Spilsbury and Churchill stubbornly refused to reconsider their position in spite of intense cross-examination. Regardless of the superiority of Littlejohn's experiments, the fact that he had changed his opinion suggested a weakness of his position to the jury. The impact of Spilsbury's determined testimony and the sloppiness of the police investigation all aided the aggressive defense.

After deliberations that lasted for one hour and five minutes, the jury returned. On the charge of murder, they announced the equivocal Scottish verdict: "Not proven." On the charge of forgery, Merrett was found guilty. Sentence of imprisonment for one year was pronounced by the lord justice-clerk.

Sir Sydney Smith, hearing of the verdict, famously remarked, "That's not the last we'll hear of young Merrett." Unfortunately, he was right.

John Donald Merrett served his sentence in a low-security institution. Officially guilty of no capital crime, he was able to inherit from both his mother's estate and his grandfather's. He married young, and to please his wife, he settled a large sum of his inheritance on her. Tiring of her after a while, he casually abandoned the lady. He spent the ensuing ten years in smuggling, gunrunning, drug dealing, and other creative enterprises. He served in the British Navy during World War II, under the name Ronald Chesney. He served well, as far as is known.

By 1954, Merrett/Chesney was living in Germany with his mistress when he noticed he was short of funds. He recalled having given the woman to whom he was still legally wed a sum of money. She strongly preferred not to return it.

Merrett/Chesney concluded that strong measures were needed. He took a boat to England, stole a passport from a man in a pub, and returned to Germany, making certain that his departure from the British port was noticed. He then returned to England with the stolen passport and entered the house where his cast-off spouse lived. He drowned her in the bath, where he left her corpse, intending for her death to appear an accident. His plan was spoiled when, as he left, he met his mother-in-law on the stairs. He promptly and violently dispatched the inconvenient lady, thereby destroying any hope that he might appear to have been widowed by accident.

He raced back to Germany, but the police, sharper than they had been in 1926, were on his trail. Knowing that arrest was inevitable, Merrett (perhaps thinking of Mother) shot himself in the head.

There are few figures as dangerous as that of an expert witness who is brilliant, persuasive, famous, obstinate, and absolutely mistaken. Sir Bernard Spilsbury and Robert Churchill had between them made possible the murder of two harmless women.

In "The Yellow Face," Sherlock Holmes, acknowledging a rare error, says:

> "Watson, if it should ever strike you that I am getting a little over-confident in my powers, or giving less pains to a case than it deserves, kindly whisper 'Norbury' in my ear, and I shall be infinitely obliged to you."

Someone needed to say the equivalent of "Norbury" to Sir Bernard.

WHATEVER REMAINS

- There are many accounts, in a number of languages, of the Henry Goddard case, that claim that the crime solved by the bullet mold was a murder. Goddard's book, *Memoirs of a Bow Street Runner*, make it very clear that this is not accurate.

- The Merrett case was mishandled, but the publicity it generated provided the catalyst for the further study of ballistics. The field developed rapidly in the period after the last Holmes stories were published in 1927. At the present time, the analysis of ballistic evidence is for the most part divided into three specialized areas:

  Interior ballistics: how the bullet moves within the firearm after it is fired.

  Exterior ballistics: how the bullet moves after it leaves the barrel.

  Terminal ballistics: the effect of the bullet on the object it strikes.

- In the story "The Problem of Thor Bridge," Sherlock Holmes proves that a gunshot death is a suicide staged as a murder. As Leslie S. Klinger, the noted Holmes scholar, recounts in his *The New Annotated Sherlock Holmes*, there are striking similarities between the plot of "The Problem of Thor Bridge" and a case described by Hans Gross in his *Handbook for Criminal Investigation*. Suicide deliberately dressed as murder is seen by crime investigators from time to time. The usual motives are to ensure that the next of kin receive insurance payments, as in the Gross case, or to frame and so punish an enemy, as in "The Problem of Thor Bridge."

CHAPTER 9

Bad Impressions

"There has been murder done, and the murderer was a man. He was more than six feet high, was in the prime of life, had small feet for his height, wore coarse, square-toed boots and smoked a Trichinopoly cigar."
—Sherlock Holmes in *A Study in Scarlet*

SHERLOCK HOLMES is a walking repository of eclectic information. All sorts of arcane tidbits interest him, but he holds nothing of greater importance than the study of footprints. In the novel *A Study in Scarlet* he observes, "There is no branch of detective science which is so important and so much neglected as the art of tracing footsteps. Happily, I have always laid great stress upon it, and much practice has made it second nature to me."

The study of footprints was one of the first tools of forensic science. (In his *Memoirs*, Vidocq mentions recording footprints, although he doesn't discuss their use in detail.) The identification and tracing of track marks were part of humankind's repertoire since we first learned to hunt both four-footed animals and each other. It was only natural that this skill be adopted by the new field of criminal science, and it was vigorously if primitively exercised by the Glasgow police during their investigation of the famously bizarre murder of Jessie M'pherson in 1862.

On Monday, July 7 of that year, John Fleming, a respectable accountant of middle age, returned with his son from a weekend in the country to his home at number 17 Sandyford Place in Glasgow. He found his father, James Fleming, who shared the residence, alone and unable to explain the apparent absence of Jessie M'pherson, the servant girl who looked after him. Old Fleming said he hadn't seen her all weekend.

Growing alarmed, the younger Fleming searched the house. One of the doors to the maid's basement bedroom was locked from the inside, but access was gained through a second door that connected the bedroom to the pantry.

Jessie lay prone on the floor near her bed. She was nearly naked, and a piece of carpet covered the upper part of her body. She had been hacked and battered by numerous blows. One of them was deep enough to have exposed her brain. There was a great deal of blood in the room, and what appeared to be three bloody prints of a naked human foot were impressed on the floor.

Old Fleming held his hands up in horror and exclaimed, "She's been lying there all this time—and me in the house!"

A doctor was sent for, and, as in those well-ordered days house calls were expected, a doctor promptly arrived. His name was Watson. He pronounced life extinct, and then, contemplating the extensive sanguinary signs of slaughter, he perspicaciously observed, "This is evidently not a suicide—you had better call the police."

The police surgeon, Dr. Joseph Fleming (no relation to the now unhappy residents of 17 Sandyford Place), together with Dr. Watson, noticed the presence of bloodstains all through the kitchen and the basement hall, and a trail of blood leading to the bedroom, suggesting that the corpse had been dragged. There were bloody fingerprints on the wall, but as fingerprints were not utilized in Scottish police work in 1862, they were ignored. The doctors were struck by the discovery that the kitchen and bedroom floors, and the neck, chest, and face of the dead woman had all been recently washed. The floors were still damp. The bloody footprints lay just beyond the washed area. A drawer in the kitchen proved to contain a butcher's cleaver, which bore traces of blood.

The police were initially highly suspicious of the elderly Mr. Fleming. The medical judgment was that the blows could have been performed by a weak man, and his behavior was most peculiar. He stated that he had heard "squeals" coming from the maid's room on Friday night but had made no effort to investigate. In spite of claiming that he had no idea where Jessie had been for three days, he had not mentioned this interesting fact to the many people with whom he had contact during the weekend, including Jessie's "young man," who had come to the house during that period.

The milk boy had called at the house on Saturday, and the door had been opened by the old man, although this had always been Jessie's function. Asked why he had done so, old Fleming replied, "On Saturday morning, ye ken, Jessie was deid, she couldna' open the door when she was deid!" This was clearly at variance with his claim that he was ignorant of her fate until Monday afternoon. Old Fleming was placed under arrest and confined to jail. But the elderly gentleman pled a shaky memory to account for any discrepancies, and the discovery that some silver and a few dresses of Jessie's were missing suggested robbery as a motive for the killing.

The police suspected that the three footprints etched in blood were a vital clue—if they could determine who had left them, they might solve the case. Unlike the Great Detective—who was perfectly competent in "The Boscombe Valley Mystery" to identify footprints by sight alone and who announced to Watson, "That left foot of yours with its inward twist is all over the place. A mole could trace it"—the Glasgow detectives needed to proceed with caution.

The problem for them was that there was no established protocol for the examination and comparison of footprints in a criminal case. The detectives, however, were flexible and inventive, although sadly ill-equipped.

Alexander M'Call, an assistant superintendent of police in Glasgow, compared the size of the bloody footprints to those of both the deceased and old Mr. Fleming. Lacking a foot rule, he used a stick, keeping his finger and thumb at the appropriate place. It was his conclusion that the footprints had been made by someone outside the Fleming ménage. But who and where was that "someone"?

Advertisements inquiring about the missing items were answered by a pawnbroker who provided a description of a young woman who had brought the silver to him. A railroad clerk located the missing dresses in a trunk that had been mailed to a nonexistent address by a woman of similar description. Old Mr. Fleming thoughtfully told the police that the description sounded like that of Jessie M'lachlan, who had worked as a domestic servant for the Flemings before her marriage and who was a close friend of the murdered woman. Mrs. M'lachlan denied being in the Fleming house on the weekend of the murder and claimed that the missing items had been given to her by old Fleming, along with a tip and instructions for her to dispose of them as she had.

Finding this explanation unlikely and wanting to construct a solid case for the prosecution, the detectives asked the police doctors to examine the new suspect's feet scientifically and compare them with the bloody prints. Dr. George Husband Baird MacLeod, a professor of surgery at Glasgow University, who had already advised the police to cut out and preserve as evidence the floorboards that bore the prints, now accepted the challenge of identifying them. In an article that appeared in the *Glasgow Medical Journal* in 1864, he explained exactly how he did it:

> When Mrs. M'lachlan was taken into custody it was thought most important that a very carefully made comparison should be instituted by a professional man between the impressions and her foot. . . . [T]he author . . . tried

several experiments on his own foot to test the accuracy of several agents to produce impressions on wood which could be comparable with that under consideration. . . . Nothing was found which was not open to objection except blood; and so, having obtained a small phial of bullock's blood, a thin coating of it was placed on wax cloth and the prisoner asked to place her left foot on it and then step on a plank of wood. The accused repeated this several times without the slightest objection. . . . The early impressions were not suitable as the . . . wood had been oiled for some other purpose; but when the writer had as closely as possible imitated the conditions in which the original impressions had been made, i.e., had placed the blood on one side of the room, a piece of carpet between, and then an old dry plank of wood ([as at the crime scene] at 17 Sandyford Place . . .) on which to stand, two impressions were got which corresponded with a degree of accuracy which was quite marvelous with the marks taken from the house. In the minutest detail of measurement and outline did they tally with the original, and in fact each of them was, if possible, closer to the Sandyford footmark than they were to one another.

Further, several witnesses stated that Jessie M'lachlan had told them that she was planning to visit the deceased at Sandyford Place on the significant Friday, and that, having been gone from her own domicile all that night, she was seen returning home at nine o'clock on Saturday morning. Jessie M'lachlan was charged with murder, and old Fleming was set free to offer testimony against her. (According to Scottish law at the time, this made him immune from future prosecution.)

The accused pled not guilty, and the prosecution pressed its case vigorously, leaning heavily on the footprint evidence. "We can do nothing . . . that does not leave its impress behind, for good or for evil, for a blessing or a curse," declaimed Adam Gifford, the prosecutor. "Our footprints are left," he thundered, "in whatever we do. . . . The traces of our actions, good or bad, have life, and they will testify for or against us. And crimes have always left their footprints. In Jessie M'pherson's bedroom, gentlemen, there are bloody footprints! *Whose are those footprints?*"

But although the case against Mrs. M'lachlan seemed damning, it contained huge inconsistencies. There appeared to be no rational motive. The victim's sister testified that the two women had been close friends. There was no history of a quarrel between them. The missing silver was of little worth, and much more valuable and portable items in the house had been left untouched.

If the crime had been committed on Friday night and the old man had been unknowingly alone with the corpse until Monday afternoon, who had washed the floor and the dead woman's face? And why? If Mrs. M'lachlan had done so after the crime to try to hide the blood, why was the floor still wet on Monday? And then there were those diligently preserved footprints. If the floor was washed to eliminate evidence, why was no attempt made to erase those clearly damning prints? What about the testimony of a friend of the deceased to the effect that old Fleming had made his maid's life a misery with his obsessive interest?

On the last point, Lord Deas, the judge, who had clearly decided from the start of the trial not to allow the proceedings to be tinged by impartiality, did his best to prevent the jury from hearing the sordid details of old Fleming's debauched habits, although half of Glasgow had gossiped about them. A number of his old acquaintances insisted that he was not eighty-seven years old as he claimed but merely a sprightly seventy-eight, which might serve to explain his energy.

What is certain is that old Fleming often drank to excess, and when he did (evidently in the grip of incurable optimism), he pressed his amorous attentions on a number of young women. Ten years before, old Fleming, the eldest member of the Anderston United Presbyterian Church, had been chastised by the Kirk

Session for the "sin of fornication" with Janet Dunsmore, a domestic servant whom he had impregnated.

These embarrassing issues were avoided at the trial. As the prosecutor tartly observed, "The guilt of James Fleming is not the subject of this inquiry." The judge delivered a four-hour charge to the jury that contained not one word favorable to the accused but did discuss at length the "bloody marks of naked feet."

The trial had lasted three days. The jury, deliberating with dispatch, returned a guilty verdict in just fifteen minutes. The judge, who had arrived at court handily equipped with the black cap worn when pronouncing a death sentence, was irritated by the defense counsel, who slowed the proceedings by the announcement that the accused wished to have a statement read. The judge had to agree. This was her right, although defendants were not allowed to testify during the trial.

Jessie M'lachlan was only partially literate, and her statement, which she had dictated, was read aloud by her counsel, Rutherford Clark. She admitted she had visited the deceased on the fatal Friday night and had spent a good part of the evening in the kitchen drinking whiskey with her and old Mr. Fleming. They ran out of the libation by eleven, and Fleming sent her to the pub to purchase more. The pub was closed. On her return to Sandyford Place, she found Jessie M'pherson on the floor of her bedroom, half undressed, stunned, and bleeding from cuts on her brow and nose. Mrs. M'lachlan asked her host to bring water so that she could aid the injured woman. While Fleming was attending to this, the victim regained her senses and confided that he had made a sexual advance toward her that she had repulsed, as she had previous such attempts, and that in a rage he had struck her with something sharp.

Fleming returned with a basin of water, some of which spilled, drenching Mrs. M'lachlan's dress, shoes, and stockings, so she removed them and was barefoot as she washed her friend's bloody wounds. Fleming refused her request to send for a doctor, saying he would send for one in the morning and that he would make amends to the injured woman by making her comfortable the rest of her life. Helped into the warmth of the kitchen, Jessie M'pherson lay down in front of the fire but seemed to grow weaker.

Mrs. M'lachlan, now determined to have a doctor, dressed herself to go out and find one, only to discover that the front door had been locked. She heard a noise in the kitchen and rushed back to it, where, she said, "I saw the old man striking her with something which I saw afterwards was the meat chopper . . . he was striking her on the side of her head . . . he took the body by the oxters [armpits] and dragged it . . . [to the bedroom] . . . and took the sheet and wiped the blood with it. . . . I saw the chopper all covered with blood. I beseeched and begged of him to let me go away and I would swear I would never reveal what I had seen."

The statement goes on to say that the old man claimed he was sure that his maid would die anyway, and if a doctor came and heard her story, he would be arrested, so he had to kill her; that if Mrs. M'lachlan were to report the matter to anyone, she would be blamed, too; and that she was to take the silver and sell it so that he could claim a burglary.

In his incisive 1938 account of the case, the great legal historian William Roughead commented, "On each and every point in which Mrs. M'lachlan's statement was capable of confirmation, its truth was clearly established; in no single instance was it in any respect contradicted. It fitted the proven facts so perfectly as to render its fabrication incredible."

But Lord Deas, having brought the black cap with him, was determined to wear it. Denouncing Jessie M'lachlan's statement as "a tissue of wicked falsehoods," he condemned her to die at the end of a rope in three weeks' time. He expressed the wish, in traditional fashion, that "the Lord will have mercy upon your soul." Mrs. M'lachlan cried in response, "Aye, He'll hae mercy, for I am innocent!"

The statement became public knowledge, and sentiment rapidly grew in favor of the convicted woman. The newspapers were inundated with letters on her behalf, several of them making the point that the wet floor must have been the result of the old man washing it just before the body was discovered and that he had deliberately spared the footprints with the purpose of incriminating Mrs. M'lachlan. "When once your point of view is changed, the very thing which was so damning becomes a clue to the truth," Sherlock Holmes says in "The Problem of Thor Bridge," and so it was in the Sandyford case.

Within a month, a formal inquiry found that legal ethics required that Mrs. M'lachlan's life be spared, but that as she was an accessory after the fact, the judicial view of simple decency required a sentence of life at penal servitude. She served fifteen years before she was released. She had been a model prisoner who never ceased to insist on her innocence. Her son had been three years of age when she was sentenced. At her release he was eighteen. Mrs. M'lachlan eventually emigrated to America and died in Michigan in 1899.

No legal charges could be brought against old Mr. Fleming, but the stigma that attached itself to the priapic paterfamilias made life in Glasgow socially unpleasant. As a result, he and his family felt it wise to move away and so vacated the atmospheric premises of number 17 Sandyford Place.

Although the footprints in the M'lachlan affair had pointed in the wrong direction, the publicity elicited by the case aroused interest in footprints as evidence. In 1882, when the British forensic pathologist Charles Meymott Tidy published his text, *Legal Medicine*, he included a lengthy section titled "Marks of the Hands and Feet." He reported that having made numerous experiments, he had established that footprints may be larger or smaller than the boot or foot that produced them. In the case of a footprint made in soft sand or soil, he noted, the particles at the edge of the print collapse into the impression as the foot is withdrawn. In wet clay, the impression is larger, as the foot is lifted in the opposite direction from the one in which it was first placed. Therefore, not only is the print important, but the material in which it is left is also highly relevant.

Tidy suggested methods for taking plaster casts of footprints—a technique Sherlock Holmes perfected, as the Great Detective modestly implies in *The Sign of Four*: "Here is my monograph upon the tracing of footsteps, with some remarks upon the uses of plaster of Paris as a preserver of impresses"—as well as for examining them for bloodstains or other biological markers, and advised removing floorboards that show bloody footprints to serve as evidence, just as had been done in the Sandyford case.

Tidy evidently would have disagreed with the footprint evidence offered in the Sandyford case, as he was dubious about the worth of naked footprints. He wrote, "In the case of a naked foot, supposing the blood to have been washed off, and there be no peculiarities in the conformation of the foot and toes corresponding to the stain, the evidence of a blood impress on a floor can of itself be of very little value re identity." (This, of course, was before the study of skin ridges was developed.)

There was also a great deal of disagreement among specialists in medical jurisprudence as to the relationship between footprints and the feet that produced them. Tidy remarked, "[Dr.] Mascar of Belgium contended that the footprint is generally smaller than the foot, while [Dr.] Caussé claimed it was generally larger."

Although in the nineteenth century most footwear was individually made, and the marks left by boots and shoes were therefore distinctive, evidence drawn from these marks was not effectively used in court. Through the end of the nineteenth century, there was still no generally accepted protocol for the collection and study of footprints. Sherlock Holmes might have been able to draw definite conclusions about the physical size of individuals from their foot marks, but physicians disagreed with each other on the subject. Paul Topinard, the French anthropologist, included in his text, *Anthropology* (which appeared in English in 1890), a section titled "The Proportions of the Hand and Foot." It contained a table that concerned the ratio between foot size and height, but the variations were so wide that they had little practical use in forensic work.

The legal effectiveness of footprint evidence was further limited by creative criminals who made use of footprints to foil investigators. Allan Pinkerton, the American private eye, wrote in his 1884 memoir, *Thirty Years a Detective*, that clever burglars, when attempting to enter homes that were "surrounded by soft and yielding ground, in which the shoes they wear would make an impression which might lead to detection, wear [as a form of disguise] extraordinarily large shoes." They would discard the misleading shoes in a nearby well after the job was completed.

Infrequently, a less than astute burglar would leave behind his own compromising footwear, to the delight of law enforcement. An instructive example of this occurred in Falkirk, Scotland, in the autumn of 1937. A particularly agile thief was found inside a shop that he had illegally entered. He was in his stocking feet. His shoes had been left outside near the drainpipe that he had climbed to gain access. There had been two similar burglaries in the area in which the police had collected discarded shoes, but the climbing burglar denied any knowledge of them. The pathologist Sir Sydney Smith was asked if he could determine whether the footwear left at the other scenes had been worn by the same man.

Sir Sydney observed that in each case, right and left shoes showed wear very differently, and he suspected that the owner had a deformity of his left leg. He had gelatin casts made of the inside of the shoes. Evaluating these carefully, Sir Sydney found that the casts were identical to each other and had been worn by the same individual. Also, "from an examination of his footwear, I was able to build up quite a distinctive picture of the man . . . he walked with a limp," the doctor wrote. Although Sir Sydney had never seen the accused burglar until he testified in his case, the elaborate description of spinal curvature and a shortened leg he had constructed proved to be accurate.

The burglar confessed. His severe deformity had been the result of childhood polio, and his dexterity with drainpipes could only have been the result of grim determination. After his conviction, he agreed to be photographed and x-rayed, and so he made a helpful contribution to the forensic use of footwear.

But this was an unusual case. Through the early years of the twentieth century, the study of footprints continued to be merely the ill-treated stepchild of medical jurisprudence, and many of the doctors asked to give evidence in the matter did not share Sydney Smith's interest or creativity.

Writing at the end of the nineteenth century about the importance of footprint evidence, Hans Gross made the sensible suggestion that footprints should not be primarily the province of physicians, although he agreed that the opinion of "interested" medical men would be useful. He pointed out that an "intelligent shoemaker" could be of great help in matching boot to owner as well, and he insisted that the final responsibility for putting all the evidence together must remain with the investigator of a criminal case. In spite of Dr. Gross's belief in the usefulness of footprint evidence, the development of footprint comparisons continued to lag behind research in other branches of forensic science. In this discipline, Sherlock Holmes was clearly ahead of his time.

In the 1940 edition of *Modern Criminal Investigation* by Söderman and O'Connell, the chapter on footprints states, "Footprints are generally not used sufficiently by investigators of crime. Experience is needed. . . . [O]nce the eye has become accustomed to observe minute details a composite picture of interesting facts will stand out very clearly."

Sherlock Holmes no doubt would have agreed.

WHATEVER REMAINS

- When man landed on the moon for the first time in July 1969, astronaut Neil Armstrong photographed the mark made by a booted human foot on the lunar surface.

- Footprints are still an important part of criminal investigation, but properly identifying them at a crime scene may be complicated by the footmarks made by first responders. Solutions to this difficulty include plastic bands with identifying marks slipped over shoes, distinctive treads on police shoes, and plastic booties slipped over footwear.

- A number of law enforcement agencies including the FBI now maintain computerized programs that are designed to match unknown footwear impressions with the brand and manufacturer of the footwear.

- A Florida medical examiner was able to determine that a drowning death in a submerged vehicle was a suicide because of the firm imprint of the deceased's foot on the accelerator.

- Thomas Noguchi, while chief medical examiner for Los Angeles, was puzzled by a bullet wound in the forehead of a corpse. There was no exit wound, and no bullet in the head. He concluded that the wound had been made by a spike-heeled shoe, and a shoe with dried blood on the heel that matched the wound was found nearby.

CHAPTER 10

The Real Dirt

Knowledge of Geology.—Practical, but limited. Tells at a glance different soils from each other. After walks has shown me splashes upon his trouseres, and told me by their colour and consistence in what part of London he had received them.

—from Dr. Watson's description of Holmes's
abilities in *A Study in Scarlet*

SHERLOCK HOLMES is as obsessive about interpreting the subtle marks left on victims or suspects by their habits as he is about the observation of dust and fiber left at crime scenes. "Here, too, is a curious little work upon the influence of a trade upon the form of the hand," he tells Watson in *The Sign of Four*, "with lithotypes of the hands of slaters, sailors, cork-cutters, compositors, weavers, and diamond-polishers. That is a matter of great practical interest to the scientific detective—especially in cases of unclaimed bodies, or in discovering the antecedents of criminals."

Holmes was absolutely correct. During the very period in which Conan Doyle was constructing the Sherlock Holmes Canon, trace evidence was becoming a vital part of criminalistics.

Hans Gross, writing in 1893, six years after *A Study in Scarlet*, stressed the importance of "occupational dust." "There are," he wrote, "a surprising number of callings which leave their traces on the clothing and under the fingernails of those who practice them. The clothing of the chimney sweep will contain soot, finely powdered cinders and coal, and possibly traces of mortar." He discussed the varieties of dust that might be found on the clothes of miners, bricklayers, hairdressers, brewery workers, and pigeon breeders, as well as the importance of fibers, hair, plant life, and even excreta that might be found at a crime scene. The preferred method of gathering such material was first to examine the clothing carefully in a good light with a magnifying glass and to carefully remove visible material and label it. Then the clothing was inserted in a bag, which was shaken or struck vigorously to release any clinging fragments that needed microscopic examination. (In later years, this step was simplified by the use of a vacuum cleaner.)

In 1904, by which time Dr. Gross's innovative book had gone through several printings, the importance of its contribution to the field of trace evidence was made overwhelmingly clear. In October of that year, near the town of Wildthal in Germany, the strangled body of a woman was found lying in a bean field. Her hands bore the tiny pinprick marks typical of a person who sews for a livelihood. Her scarf, made of bright red and blue silk, had been tied in a killing twist about her neck. She was quickly identified as Eva Disch, a local seamstress. She had evidently been killed where she lay. Searching the area, the police found only a heavily soiled handkerchief as probable evidence. A few years before, this would have yielded little, but the ideas of Hans Gross had influence in the Freiburg im Breisgau district attorney's office, which had charge of the case. The office contacted Georg Popp, a chemist who owned a commercial consulting laboratory in Frankfurt. Dr. Popp's specialty originally had been the analysis of tobacco, ashes, and the residues left in cases of suspected arson. Having been consulted in a few forensic cases that touched on these matters, he had developed an intense interest in police science.

Now, presented by the police with the stained handkerchief from the bean field crime scene, Dr. Popp peered at it through his microscope. Red and blue silk threads, consistent with the scarf used to strangle Eva Disch, clung to the handkerchief, glued to it by shiny strings of nasal secretion. The mucus also held bits of sand, coal, snuff, and crystals of the mineral known as hornblende.

The police were suspicious of a Karl Laubach, a former Foreign Legionnaire. He had two different jobs, one at a gasworks and one at a gravel pit, which would have exposed him to the varied substances found on the handkerchief. Laubach was also known as a habitual user of snuff.

As Sherlock Holmes would advise in "The Adventure of the Creeping Man," "Always look at the hands first, Watson. Then cuffs, trouser-knees, and boots." Popp scraped under Laubach's fingernails, examined the gleanings under the microscope, and was richly rewarded. He found coal dust, sand, and crystals of hornblende. He found bits of red and blue fiber that corresponded with fiber from the murder scarf. The trousers of the suspect provided additional encouragement. Loam, bits of crushed mica coal particles, and traces of vegetation clung to the garment, and were consistent with the soil at the scene of the crime. Similar traces were found on a path leading from the crime scene to Laubach's home. Laubach resisted at first but eventually succumbed to science and confessed.

Georg Popp continued to wield his microscope in the interest of the law and helped to establish Germany's place as a primary developer of forensic analysis. He influenced many scientists of the next generation, including the Swedish Harry Söderman. Söderman tells us in his memoir, *Policeman's Lot*, that in spite of Popp's contributions to Germany's prestige, he and his wife spent their last years secluded in a Black Forest hunting lodge, loathing the Nazi government, and bitter at the struggle they were forced to endure in order to save the life of their Jewish daughter-in-law. Georg Popp died just before the start of the Second World War.

While Popp was establishing the forensic usefulness of chemistry and the natural sciences in Germany, Edmond Locard, head of the forensic laboratory in Lyon, France, was pursuing similar ideas. Dr. Locard, like Sherlock Holmes, was a man of wide-ranging interests, and, like Holmes, he had a passion for music. Even while he was developing the forensic laboratory, Locard served as music and theater critic for the Lyon newspaper. (It was said that his office was visited more frequently by apprehensive actors than it was by criminal suspects.) His eclectic interests led him to consider the forensic application of a variety of materials and techniques. He maintained a collection of soil, mineral, fiber, and animal hair samples in the hopes of simplifying the identification of trace evidence recovered at crime scenes.

Every crevice and fissure in the human body was considered a possible hiding place for trace evidence. Ear wax was of special interest, as small particles of dust will adhere to it even in the face of stringent hygiene. The ears of suspects were often swabbed and the results placed on a slide for examination under a microscope. If pertinent debris was observed, microchemical analysis could be performed. In Locard's view, "The microscopic debris that covers our clothing and bodies are the mute witnesses, sure and faithful, of all our movements and all our encounters."

In 1912, the practicality of this approach became evident when Marie Latelle, a young citizen of Lyon, was found dead of unknown causes in her parents' home. From the state of rigor, it was clear she had died before the previous midnight.

Her suitor, Emile Gourbin, a clerk at a local bank, was questioned, but he had a firm alibi: he had been miles away with several friends playing cards until after one in the morning. The friends, who gave every appearance of telling the truth, confirmed his account.

Dr. Locard was asked to consult. Examining the corpse, he found clear marks of strangulation on the neck. He then examined Gourbin, carefully scraping under the young man's fingernails and taking the results to his laboratory, where he subjected them to the sort of microscopic examination Holmes performed in "The Adventure of Shoscombe Old Place":

Sherlock Holmes had been bending for a long time over a low-power microscope. Now he straightened himself up and looked round at me in triumph.

"It is glue, Watson," said he. "Unquestionably it is glue. Have a look at these scattered objects in the field!"

I stooped to the eyepiece and focused for my vision.

"Those hairs are threads from a tweed coat. The irregular gray masses are dust. There are epithelial scales on the left. Those brown blobs in the centre are undoubtedly glue."

Locard had similar good fortune. Peering through his microscope, he discovered tiny flakes of epithelial cells, which might have come from the victim's neck. This was not certain, as they might instead have come from Gourbin. There was, however, an unusual pink dust that clung to the skin cells. Locard found the pink dust to contain magnesium stearate, zinc oxide, and iron oxide pigment, also known as Venetian red. Traces of rice powder were also present in the sample. The sophisticated, theater-loving Locard believed that the pink dust was a cosmetic.

Facial makeup had been variously acceptable and unacceptable in Europe for centuries. In the eighteenth century, even men had worn it. During the early Victorian period, makeup had been used discreetly by ladies, but after 1890, it was considered both racy and passé among "nice" women, although tiny dustings of white starch were allowed to produce an "interesting" fashionable pallor.

Ladies made do by using burned matches to darken lashes, flower petals to stain lips, and occasionally arsenic-laden flypaper to improve their complexions. At the turn of the twentieth century, the purchase of makeup was a surreptitious undertaking.

By 1910, things had begun to change. Sergei Diaghilev's Ballets Russes had created a sensation in Europe, and the dramatic makeup used by the dancers influenced fashion. Middle-class women began to experiment with creams, powders, and even mascara. But as these fripperies were not yet mass produced, the source of a cosmetic was important evidence.

A diligent search in Lyon located the chemist who had custom-made Marie Latelle's powder. Confronted with this information, Gourbin confessed. He had constructed his alibi by setting the clock ahead an hour and a half so that it appeared he was with his friends at the time of the killing. His friends, glowing with wine and gambling with cards, had not noticed. Gourbin's trick of playing with time provided the prosecution with convenient evidence of premeditated murder.

Edmond Locard's reputation and that of his laboratory were burnished by the Latelle case and attracted both students and research funds to Lyon. Locard wrote a classic seven-volume study of forensic science, *Traité de criminalistique*, which would influence generations of scientists. He stated, "*Il est impossible au malfaiteur d'agir avec l'intensité que suppose l'action criminelle sans laisser des traces de son passage*" (It is impossible for a criminal to act, considering the intensity of a crime, without leaving a trace), and so he became known among forensic scientists as the originator of Locard's Exchange Principle, which states that every contact leaves a trace. Although Locard evidently never phrased his idea in just that way, it is implicit in the underlying philosophy of his work, just as it is in Sherlock Holmes's remark in "The Adventure of Black Peter," "As long as the criminal remains upon two legs so long must there be some indentation, some abrasion, some trifling displacement which can be detected by the scientific searcher."

In 1949, a case that began in the genteel environs of the Onslow Court Hotel in South Kensington, London, provided an interesting example of the exchange principle as well as the value of basic geology in forensic detection. The hotel was home to a number of very respectable retired people, among them Mrs. Henrietta Helen Olivia Roberts Durand-Deacon, a sixty-nine-year-old widow. Although Mrs. Durand-Deacon was financially comfortable, she entertained both enterprising ambition and an idea for the manufacture of artificial fingernails. Being a friendly sort, she shared her thoughts with a fellow resident, the forty-year-old, dapper John George Haigh. Mr. Haigh listened attentively and then suggested that Mrs. Durand-Deacon visit a factory he owned in Crawley, West Sussex, to see if those premises might be appropriate for the production of cosmetic nails. She accepted, and the date for this venture was set for February 18.

Two days later, during breakfast at the Onslow Court Hotel, Haigh expressed his concern about Mrs. Durand-Deacon's whereabouts to other guests. He explained that he had arranged to meet the lady at the Army Navy store where she had an errand and planned to drive her to his factory from there, but she had not kept the appointment. The other guests were alarmed, and a decision was made to contact the police.

A female officer, Police Sergeant Lambourne, interviewed Haigh. His unctuous manner made her uneasy at once, and she industriously checked police records to see if his name appeared. It did. He had served time for fraud and theft repeatedly in Nottingham, Surrey, as well as in London. Perhaps Mrs. Durand-Deacon's friendly trust in Haigh had been unwise.

The now highly suspicious police visited Haigh's factory on Leopold Road in Sussex and discovered that it was little more than a storeroom. The storeroom did contain a few objects of interest: a .38 Enfield revolver, eight rounds of the appropriate ammunition, some rubber protective clothing, a dry-cleaning receipt dated February 19 for a Persian lamb coat much like one owned by Mrs. Durand-Deacon, and three carboys (special containers for corrosive liquids) of sulfuric acid.

A few days after the examination of the "factory," the jewels that the missing lady had been wearing turned up in a shop, which had purchased them for one hundred pounds. Mr. Haigh was invited to "help the police with their inquiries."

At an interview with Detective Inspector Webb on February 28, Haigh suddenly leaned forward and said, "Tell me frankly.

What are the chances of anyone being released from Broadmoor [an institution for the criminally insane]?"

Webb didn't respond. Haigh then told him that the truth was too fantastic for belief. Webb delivered the formal caution, and Haigh responded, "Mrs. Durand-Deacon no longer exists. She has disappeared completely, and no trace of her can ever be found again. I have destroyed her with acid. You will find the sludge which remains on Leopold Road. But," he said, smiling confidently, "you can't prove murder without a body."

Mr. Haigh was mistaken on this point, as many others have been. The law does not require a corpse to prove murder; it requires a corpus delicti—the body of evidence that establishes that the crime has taken place. Haigh, not understanding this, his ego racing at full gallop, proceeded to dictate a complex confession. He had killed Mrs. Durand-Deacon and at least five other people over the years, but he had a very good reason for his bad behavior.

He was, he explained, a vampire, and was in dire need of their blood. He had shot Mrs. Durand-Deacon in the back of the head at the storeroom at Crawley, then made an incision in the side of her neck, collected a glass of blood, and drank it. Removing her fur coat and jewels, he then put her clothed body into a vat, poured acid over it, and went to tea, at which meal he ate a poached egg. Returning to his labors, he refilled the vat with acid a number of times over the next few days and then, judging his project complete, emptied the vat into the street. He had used the same methods on his other victims, all of whom, he happily reported, were also beyond recovery.

The police were not impressed. Some of his reported victims were indeed missing, but others appeared to be completely imaginary. Haigh had fraudulently collected funds from the genuine victims, and the police believed that his motive was purely monetary and that the vampire tale was merely setting the stage for an insanity defense. Sherlock Holmes had remarked in "The Adventure of the Sussex Vampire," "The idea of a vampire was to me absurd. Such things do not happen in criminal practice in England." That was very much the feeling among the police investigating Haigh.

A great deal of circumstantial evidence was already at hand, and the police improved on it. Keith Simpson, the eminent forensic pathologist, was asked to inspect the sludge that was spread outside the Crawley "factory." He went carefully over the ground in very much the same way Holmes examined the ground in Boscombe Valley:

> For a long time he [Holmes] remained there, turning over the leaves and dried sticks, gathering up what seemed to me to be dust into an envelope and examining with his lens not only the ground but even the bark of the tree as far as he could reach. A jagged stone was lying among the moss, and this also he carefully examined and retained.

Dr. Simpson observed small pebbles covering the area just outside the six-by-four-foot greasy mass of sludge. He examined the pebbles with a magnifying glass. He wrote later, "I picked one up and examined it through the lens. It was about the size of a cherry, and looked very much like the other stones, except it had polished facets." Stones with polished facets were not indigenous to the area, and Dr. Simpson concluded that the unusual specimen was a gallstone, originally belonging to the late Mrs. Durand-Deacon. And so it proved. Gallstones, it seems, are very resistant to acid.

The sludge, which was carted off to the laboratory, weighed 475 pounds, and within it were found dentures, part of a plastic handbag, a few bone fragments, and more gallstones. The dentures were firmly identified by Mrs. Durand-Deacon's dentist as belonging to the victim.

The defense, which pled insanity, presented psychiatric evidence that Haigh had been reared in a grim atmosphere of religious fanaticism and cruelty and had been plagued since childhood by dreams of blood and an urge to drink his own urine.

The unimpressed jury wasted no time in arriving at a guilty verdict. Haigh, sentenced to death, willed his clothing to Madame Tussaud's wax museum, with the stipulation that his effigy be shown properly attired, trousers neatly creased, shirt cuffs showing, hair properly parted. The "vampire" had a concern for detail.

The value of subtle trace evidence, demonstrated by Keith Simpson, Edmond Locard, and their fictional counterpart Sherlock Holmes, has only increased with time. In 1974, in the second edition of *Crime Investigation*, the criminalist Paul Kirk wrote of the criminal:

> Wherever he steps, whatever he touches, whatever he leaves even unconsciously, will serve as silent witness against him. Not only his fingerprints or his footprints, but his hair, the fibers from his clothes, the glass he breaks, the tool marks he leaves, the paint he scratches, the blood or semen he deposits or collects—all of these and more bear mute witness against him. This is evidence that does not forget. It is not confused by the excitement of the moment. It is not absent because human witnesses are. It cannot perjure itself. It cannot be wholly absent. Only its interpretation can err. Only human failure to find it, study and understand it, can diminish its value.

And Holmes, of course, makes certain that the "mute witness" is made to speak. As he tells Inspector Lestrade in "The Adventure of the Norwood Builder," "I pay a good deal of attention to matters of detail, as you may have observed."

WHATEVER REMAINS

- "The hero of the Long Island Cave Mystery?" inquires Sherlock Holmes when he is introduced to Mr. Leverton of Pinkerton's American Agency in "The Adventure of the Red Circle." Holmes thus launched endless speculation among Sherlockians, as it is generally accepted that there are no caves on Long Island in the United States. But in geological terms this is debatable. An old, somewhat obscure definition of "cave" is "any hollow." About 15,000 years ago on the northern half of Long Island, chunks of ice broke off from a glacier and were imbedded in the earth. Eventually these frozen masses melted, and great hollows in the ground formed in their place. These are known as "kettles." Perhaps these are the mysterious "Caves of Long Island."

- Another possibility often mentioned by Conan Doyle scholars is that the Long Island referred to is not the one in New York. If that is the case, an excellent candidate in terms of earth evidence is the Long Island in the Bahamas. Eighty miles long and one to three miles wide, it boasts a rough, rocky shore and many limestone caves.

- Alfred Swaine Taylor, the pathologist, wrote as early as 1873 of the importance of collecting diatoms and other microscopic plant life in drowning cases in order to match them to the body of water in which the corpse was found. He mentioned a case in which the discrepancy between the diatoms in the body and those in the water tank in which the body was discovered indicated that the drowning had occurred elsewhere.

CHAPTER 11

Notes from the Devil

"Let us now see the letter."
—Sherlock Holmes in "The Man with the Twisted Lip"

Just as he is fascinated by footprints, Sherlock Holmes is intrigued by the study of ambiguous documents. The Sherlockian eye for detail is most penetrating on this subject, as he demonstrates in "The Man with the Twisted Lip" when he says to the wife of a missing man:

> "The name, you see, is in perfectly black ink, which has dried itself. The rest is of the grayish color, which shows that blotting-paper has been used. If it had been written straight off, and then blotted, none would be of a deep black shade. This man has written the name, and there has then been a pause before he wrote the address, which can only mean that he was not familiar with it. It is, of course, a trifle, but there is nothing so important as trifles."

Holmes's interest in the evidence provided by letters written by hand or by typewriter is well placed. Forgery has an old and dishonorable history, and the evaluation of questioned documents is one of the most complex disciplines in the forensic sciences. The subject was addressed early in English legal proceedings, and the Scottish-born Arthur Conan Doyle no doubt learned as a schoolboy of the notorious Casket Letters, which influenced the fate of a Scottish queen.

The January 1569 court papers of England's Elizabeth I refer to the subject. Mary Stuart, Queen of Scots, fleeing political and military chaos in her country, had traveled to England in the hope of support and succor from her cousin Elizabeth. Mary was accused by English nobles of having had a part in the murder of her dissipated second husband, Lord Darnley. The evidence of her complicity was said to be contained in letters of hers found among the possessions of her third husband, James Hepburn, the Earl of Bothwell.

Mary denied her guilt. She and her advisers were allowed to examine only copies of the letters, and the courtiers who testified as to their authenticity had no particular expertise in the matter. The arrangement of characters and use of language in the copied letters were not typical of Mary. (Holmes takes note of a similar anomaly centuries later in *A Study in Scarlet*: "The A, if you noticed, was printed somewhat after the German fashion. Now, a real German invariably prints in the Latin character, so that we may safely say that this was not written by one, but by a clumsy imitator.")

Elizabeth, who for political reasons wished to avoid a conviction at the time, pronounced an equivocal verdict: "Nothing had been sufficiently proved, whereby the Queen of England should conceive an evil opinion of her good sister." But the issue of the letters tempered sympathy for Mary, making her eventual execution more palatable to the public.

The original letters have long been lost, so a scientifically informed opinion as to whether they were forgeries promoted by the English court is impossible. What is certain, however, is the authenticity of the extraordinary letter of condolence that Elizabeth I sent to Mary's son, James of Scotland, after his mother was beheaded. "My dear Brother," she wrote, pretending that the entire miserable business had been engineered by her nobles against her will, "I would you knew (though not felt) the extreme dolor that overwhelms my mind, for that miserable accident which (far contrary to my meaning) hath befallen." (The "accident" had included the attentions of a particularly inept executioner who needed three blows with an axe to get the job done.) After a few pages of similar warm familial sentiment, it was closed with "Your most assured loving sister and cousin. Elizabeth R."

Royal blood did not protect one from suspicions of forgery, and neither did being a member of the social elite. In the middle of the nineteenth century, within the pristine precincts of Boston, Massachusetts, a murder case that riveted the attention of the public on both sides of the Atlantic hinged partially on suspect documents.

In 1849, Harvard Medical School was housed in a two-story brick building that squatted at the edge of the Charles River. The rear of the building was supported by wooden pilings sunk deep in the riverbed. The dissecting room and its disposal vault lay in the back, on an earthen floor. When the river rose, water entered the vault and flowed over the human debris inside, so the discarded bits and pieces, the shards and scraps, rose and fell with the tide.

Just before Thanksgiving, George Parkman, a well-known physician, businessman, and philanthropist, disappeared. He had last been seen entering the College of Medicine, and it was searched by the police, but to no avail.

As the search widened, a number of letters offering advice and commentary about the case arrived for the authorities. Three in particular aroused the interest of Marshal Francis Tukey, the head of law enforcement in Boston. One was signed "Civis," was clearly written by an educated person, and suggested that the river as well as the outhouses be searched. The other two were barely legible, seemingly illiterate scrawls: one advising that Parkman had been kidnapped and taken aboard a ship, while the other opined that Parkman's dead body was to be found on Brooklyn Heights. None of these suggestions bore fruit.

The police may have been stalemated, but not so Ephraim Littlefield, a dissecting room porter of extraordinary industry. Littlefield's suspicions were aroused, he later claimed, by the unusual gift of a coupon for a Thanksgiving turkey presented to him by John Webster, professor of chemistry. Possibly the porter was motivated by the thought of a reward promised for information regarding the missing man. Whatever his reason, late one night while the students were absent and the laboratories empty, the silence of the medical school was broken by the chink of Littlefield's chisel, chipping away relentlessly at the brick wall that enclosed the privy vault beneath Dr. Webster's laboratory. Littlefield's discovery of a pelvis and other body parts in the privy led to the indictment of Dr. Webster, who, it was discovered, owed Parkman a large sum of money that he couldn't repay.

At the trial, the prosecutor, George Bemis, argued that Dr. Webster had written the letters in order to distract suspicion from himself. The trial record of that case is one of the first documents we have of expert testimony offered on the subject of handwriting. The first expert to testify was Nathaniel D. Gould, who said:

> I am a resident of this city. . . . I know the prisoner and have known him for a long time by sight but have no personal acquaintance with him. . . . I have never seen him write but have seen what I suppose to be his handwriting. I am familiar with his signature. I have seen it appended to diplomas given by the Medical College for twenty years. I have been employed as a penman to fill out these diplomas. . . . I have paid particular attention to the subject of Penmanship, having practiced it in every way and instructed in it for some fifty years. I have also published on the subject.

Mr. Bemis then directed the witness, "Please look at the three letters and state if you can in whose handwriting they are."

Edward Sohier, the defense counsel, argued that a proper foundation had not been laid for the testimony. He pointed out that the witness hadn't seen the prisoner write and that "this class of evidence was exceedingly liable to error."

The court ruled that Mr. Gould was allowed to respond. "I think," Gould said, "it is Dr. Webster's handwriting. . . . [T]here are some circumstances which may appear trifling to a person who has not attended the subject, but yet I consider them important." (Here he seems to be foreshadowing Holmes's remark about printed evidence in *The Hound of the Baskervilles*: "But this is my special hobby, and the differences are equally obvious.")

Gould continued, "Every man who undertakes to disguise his hand must do it either by . . . carelessly letting his hand play entirely loose . . . or by carefully guarding every stroke that he makes." He goes on to say that it is impossible to keep this up very long: "[A] single particle or character, will furnish a key for detection of the real writer . . . [such as] in these letters the small letter 'a' the small 'r' . . . and the character '&' which Dr. Webster almost uniformly makes in one peculiar manner and which he almost always uses in lieu of the written word."

Gould points out a number of other peculiarities he identifies with Webster. "I can detect similarities, which may escape the eyes of another, just as a naturalist can see peculiarities in a shell which would escape my observation. . . . My practice in comparing handwriting is to look first . . . to see how many letters are similar and then how many are dissimilar."

Another expert, George G. Smith, was called by the prosecution. "I am an engraver," he said. "I have been called frequently, to give an opinion of handwriting, as an expert in court. . . . In regard to the Civis letter I am compelled to say . . .that it is in Professor Webster's handwriting. . . . I am very sorry to say that I feel quite confident of this." Smith was not confident of the origin of the other letters.

The testimony concerning the letters, while not the most crucial of the case, was extremely damaging to the defense. In spite of Dr. Webster's contention that Littlefield was a body snatcher who had planted the grim remnants of his trade in the privy, Dr. Webster was convicted of murder. Webster then dictated a confession of sorts to a helpful minister, claiming that the killing was an unplanned act of passion. Since the body had been dismembered and parts of it burned, it could not provide supporting evidence for the lesser crime of manslaughter. Although the evidence as well as the confession was riddled with enough inconsistencies to keep crime historians busy to the present day, the Commonwealth of Massachusetts was not distracted and hanged Dr. Webster on August 30, 1850.

The scientific evaluation of written evidence stood on a somewhat shaky foundation in the nineteenth century, but its importance was beginning to be recognized. And then an explosive case in France dealt a serious blow to the growth of the discipline.

In 1894, a "bordereau," or memorandum, listing French military secrets, was recovered from a wastepaper basket in the German embassy. Casting about for the culprit who had written the document, a cabal of French military officers decided a convenient scapegoat would be Captain Alfred Dreyfus. Dreyfus was favored as a suspect—in spite of compelling evidence that the bordereau had been written by an officer named Esterhazy—because he was fluent in German (he had been born in Alsace), was reserved in his manner, and, most importantly, was Jewish. One could be a staunch French patriot and at the same time indulge a hidden taste for anti-Semitism.

Handwriting experts gave conflicting evidence as to the authorship of the bordereau, and the famous Alphonse Bertillon was called on for his opinion. Questioned documents were far from his area of expertise, but he felt this was no reason to decline. He delivered a complicated, meandering opinion, complete with diagrams. He concluded that the suspect writing was that of Dreyfus and that it differed from Dreyfus's usual hand in some respects because Dreyfus had forged his own handwriting. Just for good measure, Bertillon threw in some mathematical formulae on the subject of probability. Wrapped in the mantle of scientific certainty, he exercised his prejudices.

No one understood what Bertillon said, but his stature was such that conviction was assured. Alfred Dreyfus, stripped of his rank and separated from his family, was sent to Devil's Island to suffer solitary confinement. His guards were forbidden to speak to him.

All of France took sides on the trial, and violent demonstrations resulted. Emile Zola, the novelist and journalist, wrote a passionate dissection of the entire affair in the paper *L'Aurore* in the form of an open letter to the president of the French Republic. Entitled *"J'Accuse"* (I Accuse), it said about the evidence:

> How flimsy it is! The fact that someone could have been convicted on this charge is the ultimate iniquity. I defy decent men to read it without a stir of indignation in their hearts and a cry of revulsion, at the thought of the undeserved punishment being meted out there on Devil's Island. He knew several languages. A crime! He carried no compromising papers. A crime! He would occasionally visit his birthplace. A crime! He was hard-working, and was well informed. A crime! He did not become confused. A crime! He became confused. A crime!

After marshaling arguments against the members of the military who had engineered the trial, Zola focused on the handwriting experts:

> I accuse the three handwriting experts, Messrs. Belhomme, Varinard and Couard, of having submitted reports that were deceitful and fraudulent, unless a medical examination finds them to be suffering from a disease that impairs their eyesight and judgment.

Why Bertillon was not included in this cri de coeur is not clear—perhaps Zola concurred with a popular view that the father of anthropometry had simply lost his mind.

Eventually, public opinion roused on behalf of Dreyfus, and he was retried. Incredibly, he was once again found guilty. Riots ensued. Proof that French Intelligence had manufactured evidence against Dreyfus was found. Officially, Dreyfus was "pardoned." The guilty verdict against him was finally overturned in 1906.

Bertillon's reputation was tarnished, and the public's trust in document examination was severely shaken. It would take the genius of Edmond Locard to change things.

During World War I, in the year 1917, citizens of the French city of Tulle began receiving nasty anonymous letters. The recipients found themselves accused of a variety of repellent acts, usually of an interesting sexual nature. Women were informed that their husbands away at war were unfaithful; men from Tulle who were in the service got mail accusing their wives of general debauchery.

The letters and their envelopes were subjected to the sort of scrutiny that Holmes applied in "The Man with the Twisted Lip" ("The envelope was a very coarse one and was stamped with the Gravesend postmark and with the date of that very day, or rather of the day before, for it was considerably after midnight. 'Coarse writing,' murmured Holmes"), but it didn't solve the case. The first letters had been mailed, but when the post office was placed under surveillance, the letters began to be surreptitiously delivered by hand. Everyone was suspected, but no one was caught.

Söderman, writing of the case, tells us that a priest, walking down the street, found a letter tucked into the door of the apothecary. Thinking it might be important, he retrieved it and brought it inside. Waving aside a thank-you drink, he insisted that the apothecary read it first, as it might be important news. The apothecary did so, then, with a cry of anguish, leaped upon the priest, clearly intent on doing bodily harm. The two were separated by neighbors who heard the sounds of fierce battle amid the breaking of medicine bottles. It seems the letter had accused the innocent priest of sleeping with the apothecary's wife. Less amusing was the plight of a man who grew so depressed after receiving a letter that he had to be placed in an asylum, where he eventually died.

The letters continued throughout the war, into the early twenties, poisoning the atmosphere. Finally, a clue emerged. A young woman of sterling reputation and strong religious principles, Angèle Laval, was heard discussing the contents of a letter before it had been received. Suspicion focused on her, but proof was needed. Dr. Locard was asked to consult. Locard perused over three hundred of the anonymous letters, as well as samples of Angèle Laval's writing and those of her mother, since the two women lived together.

The suspect missives were printed in block characters, so Locard needed to see similar specimens written by the Lavals. To obtain these he dictated to Angèle for most of a day, removing the samples as she finished them. At intervals she had hysterics. It was soon obvious that the writing was hers in most cases. Even though she tried to disguise her penmanship, she couldn't remember from hour to hour what she had improvised, and a distinctive *Y* soon made an appearance. In similar fashion, Locard established that the other letters had been written by Angèle's mother. Knowing that arrest was near, the two women decided on suicide by drowning and jumped into a reservoir. The elder died instantly. Angèle was fished out by passersby and stood trial. She was sentenced to only two months in prison and fined 500 francs.

Commenting on the prisoner's vaunted piety, Locard remarked, "*Il n'y a rien plus sale que le rêve d'un saint*" (There is nothing dirtier than the dream of a saint).

By the end of the nineteenth century, the poison pen was often replaced by a machine. But if malefactors thought this would serve to disguise their handiwork, they were disappointed. In 1891, when "A Case of Identity" was published, Conan Doyle has Holmes note:

> "It is a curious thing . . . that a typewriter has really quite as much individuality as a man's handwriting. Unless they

are quite new, no two of them write exactly alike. Some letters get more worn than others, and some wear only on one side."

This was an exceedingly clever, if not entirely accurate, observation. Typewriters that used both lowercases and uppercases were not in common use until 1878, and their usefulness as evidence was not yet established when "Identity" was written. As it happens, typewriters, even when spanking new, showed enough individual quirks to firmly establish identity. Locard, devoted admirer of the Great Detective that he was, managed to prove the point.

Poisonous letters began to appear in the city of Lyon nailed to the doorways of houses. They drew so much attention that the Sûreté was asked to investigate. Some of the letters were typed, others constructed of letters cut from newspapers. Locard—reasoning as Holmes did in *A Study in Scarlet* that if a man writes on a wall or pins something there, he instinctively does it at eye level—focused his inquiries on a father and son who were of appropriate height and who had access to typewriters. One of the typewriters in the father's office was identified as the one used in constructing the obscene posted letters. Fingerprints discovered on one of the letters provided additional evidence.

The crime, committed by parent and offspring with no clear motive, was very similar to the case in Tulle. The penalty was precisely the same—two months in prison and a fine of 500 francs. (As Holmes observed in *A Study in Scarlet*, "There is nothing new under the sun. It has all been done before.")

The storytelling skills of Conan Doyle sparked the imagination of scientists and provided a great contribution by making the public aware of the function of police laboratories. But when it came to handwriting, or chirography, as it was called in the nineteenth century, Sherlock Holmes was sometimes a bit overly enthusiastic. In spite of popular belief, even a highly trained forensic document examiner cannot reliably tell handedness, gender, or age from handwriting. The additional claim, largely made by graphologists, that psychological traits can be deciphered from handwriting has no basis in empirical evidence. Like astrology, it belongs to the realm of pseudoscience.

Scientifically oriented forensic document examiners test ink, paper, styles of writing, and impressions made on written material. They photograph and enlarge specimens so that they can observe tiny discrepancies. They are wisely cautious in drawing conclusions.

Consider the embarrassment of the graphologists asked to examine the doodles found on British prime minister Tony Blair's desk at the Davos World Economic Forum. As Reuters gleefully reported in January 2005, the "handwriting experts" concluded that Mr. Blair was "struggling to concentrate, . . . stressed and tense," and, most damning, "not a natural leader." It was later discovered that the doodles were not the work of Mr. Blair but of Bill Gates, the founder of Microsoft, who had shared a table with the prime minister at the summit.

As Mr. Holmes once remarked in "The Adventure of the Six Napoleons," "The Press, Watson, is a most valuable institution, if you only know how to use it."

WHATEVER REMAINS

- In 1910, Albert S. Osborn published his reference work on the examination and identification of handwriting. It became the unofficial bible of the subject in the United States.

- In 1935, at the trial of Bruno Richard Hauptmann for the kidnapping and murder of the infant son of Colonel Charles A. Lindbergh, Osborn's testimony on the ransom notes proved devastating for the defense.

- In 1945, the mutilated body of a woman named Frances Brown was found on her bed. Scrawled in lipstick on the wall above the corpse were the words "For God's sake catch me before I kill more, I cannot control myself." A student named William Heirens was arrested for the murder. He confessed to the killing of Brown as well as to other homicides. The writing on the wall was compared to Heirens's usual hand and considered in terms of the height of the suspect, just as Holmes and Locard would have suggested. It was believed to be corroborative evidence. Heirens, still in prison, now insists that his confession was coerced and that the handwriting experts were mistaken.

- In the 1950 trial of accused traitor Alger Hiss for perjury, the American elder statesman was found guilty largely on evidence given by document experts who testified that the stolen papers were typed on an old Woodstock typewriter belonging to Hiss. The *e*'s and *g*'s on the machine were said to be distinctive by FBI laboratory examiner Ramos Feehan.

CHAPTER 12

A Voice in the Blood

"Let us have some fresh blood."
—Sherlock Holmes in *A Study in Scarlet*

Sherlock holmes's passion for science and his innovative intellect are displayed with striking clarity as he announces his development of a chemical test for hemoglobin. Watson describes this amazing event in the 1887 *A Study in Scarlet*:

> Broad, low tables were scattered about, which bristled with retorts, test-tubes, and little Bunsen lamps, with their blue flickering flames. There was only one student in the room, who was bending over a distant table absorbed in his work. At the sound of our steps he glanced round and sprang to his feet with a cry of pleasure. "I've found it! I've found it," he shouted to my companion, running towards us with a test-tube in his hand. "I have found a reagent which is precipitated by hemoglobin, and by nothing

else." Had he discovered a gold mine, greater delight could not have shone upon his features. . . .

"Why, man, [said Holmes,] it is the most practical medico-legal discovery for years. Don't you see that it gives us an infallible test for blood stains?"

Holmes was understandably elated. Determining whether a stain was truly blood was an old and difficult problem in criminal investigation. All sorts of attempts had been made to establish a reliable test. In France in the early nineteenth century, Ambrose Tardieu had even experimented with an olfactory method, but although a number of blindfolded volunteers had sniffed diligently at various sanguinary specimens, the results were too erratic to be of use.

Blood is a marvelously changeable fluid. When fresh it is usually frankly red, but its odor as well as its appearance may be modified by a number of things, including the kind of material on which it has fallen. Blood on a polished metal surface glistens, for instance, while on soft fabric it is usually absorbed quickly and takes on a stiffened aspect. The color can change rapidly, from red to brown to gray-green. If attempts to remove the stain have been made by the use of water or chemicals, the color will be affected and the stain may not be easily visible. Blood is often adulterated by other bodily fluids or contaminated by poison, which may also affect its appearance. Some foods, such as garlic, affect its odor. Even a meticulous Sherlockian examination of suspicious stains with a magnifying glass is not sufficient to definitely identify blood.

Medical jurisprudence addressed the problem in three basic ways. Sherlock Holmes is aware of two of them, as he makes clear when he says, "The old guaiacum test was very clumsy and uncertain. So is the microscopic examination for blood corpuscles. The latter is valueless if the stains are a few hours old."

The guaiacum test, which Holmes disdains, was based on the fact that the resin of the West Indian guaiacum tree turns the deep blue color of sapphires when oxidized. This change in color will result as well if a mixture of blood and hydrogen peroxide is added to the guaiacum. The difficulty with this test lies in the fact that a number of substances besides blood may produce positive results, including bile, saliva, and red wine. As wine would take several hours longer than blood to achieve the blue color, a careful operator could distinguish it from blood. Still, the existence of blood was not directly established by the guaiacum test, but the presence of hemoglobin was inferred by a positive result. There were a number of other chemical tests in use at the time, but they were no more conclusive.

The microscopic test for blood was also, as Holmes said, by itself of limited value. Charles Meymott Tidy described the laborious process in 1882, advising the experimenter to cut out a small portion of the stained fabric and place it on a microscope glass and then moisten it with an appropriate solution before covering it with a coverslip. He warns against using water, which will cause the corpuscles to swell. (Tidy lists chloral hydrate solution along with a few other choices as adequate.)

The slide, he says, should then be examined with a ¼-inch power and the corpuscles measured with a micrometer. "All structures associated with a blood stain should be examined with great care," he continues, explaining that if hair, biliary or fecal matter, spermatozoa, epithelial cells, or brain tissue are found mixed with the sample, they may help in determining the origin of the stain. Charts were available that listed, more or less accurately, the size and shape of corpuscles in a variety of creatures. Researchers were expected to compare the cells under their microscope with the chart to attempt to identify the source. The problem lay in the wide range of possibilities. Tidy writes:

> The blood-corpuscles in man and in all mammalia (excepting the camel tribe) are circular, flattened, transparent, non-nucleated cells presenting (as generally seen) concave sides with a central bright spot. This bright spot, however, by a small change of focus or of light may be made to appear shaded.

The diameter of the blood-corpuscles in a man varies from 1-2800th of an inch to 1-4000th.

These corpuscles vary in size and shape in different animals.

It was a very complex system, and when the cells were dehydrated, they lost their shape, making identification even more difficult. And dried bloodstains were often precisely the issue in criminal cases, as Holmes informs Watson:

"Criminal cases are continually hinging upon that one point. A man is suspected of a crime months perhaps after it has been committed. His linen or clothes are examined and brownish stains discovered upon them. Are they blood stains, or mud stains, or rust stains, or fruit stains, or what are they? That is a question which has puzzled many an expert, and why? Because there was no reliable test. Now we have the Sherlock Holmes's test, and there will no longer be any difficulty."

His eyes fairly glittered as he spoke, and he put his hand over his heart and bowed as if to some applauding crowd conjured up by his imagination.

Alas, the Great Detective overstates the case. In 1887, when Holmes made this claim in *A Study in Scarlet*, there was already one very reliable test in use for the presence of blood, which he left unmentioned—spectrum analysis. Dr. Tidy, in his text, tells us that this method was used by Henry Letheby, professor of chemistry at London Hospital, as early as 1864, in the celebrated murder trial of Franz Müller.

On July 9 of that year at a quarter after ten in the evening, two bank clerks boarded an empty first-class train compartment at the Hackney station of the North London line. One of the pair casually placed his hand on the seat, only to feel it was coated with an upsettingly sticky substance. In the dim light of the oil lamps, he could just make out its red color. The guard was called before the train started and the car was searched. What appeared to be more blood was found on the cushions, the window, one of the door handles, and a walking stick. A small black bag and a black beaver hat stamped with the maker's name, J. H. Walker, completed the scene. If the sticky red fluid was really blood, what and where was its source?

There were no witnesses to what might have occurred in the carriage. In those days, there was no corridor connecting railway cars and there were no windows between them. Robberies, some of them violent, were not infrequent, particularly at night. Suspecting this was a similar event, the police ordered the car locked, detached, and sent first to Chalk Farm and then to Bow Station for further examination. The hat, stick, bag, and cushions were given to the Metropolitan Police so that the stains could be tested and identified as blood if possible.

At roughly the same time that the carriage was being searched, the driver of a train going in the opposite direction saw a figure slumped on a six-foot-wide stretch of ground that ran along the tracks between Hackney Wick and Bow Stations. Stopping the train, the driver got out and discovered an unconscious man who had obviously been severely beaten. Taken to a nearby public house, he was identified by the contents of his pockets as Thomas Briggs, the seventy-year-old head clerk at the banking house of Robarts on Lombard Street. Mr. Briggs had a fractured skull, among other injuries, and died the following morning without regaining consciousness. His distraught son, summoned by the police, identified the bag and walking stick as belonging to his father but said he had never before seen the hat found in the carriage. A top hat, which Mr. Briggs had worn to the train, was missing, and so were his gold watch and chain.

Inspector Dick Tanner reasoned that the crime was an unplanned robbery and that the assailant had, in the stress of the moment, taken the wrong hat away with him. He put out a description of the hat left behind as well as of the watch and chain.

As the attack on Mr. Briggs was the first known homicide in an English railway car, the resultant publicity was enormous. It was quickly rewarded when a jeweler, with the singularly appropriate name of Death (disappointingly, it is pronounced "Deeth"), came forward with the missing jewelry and explained that a customer had exchanged them for a similar set of the same value.

Hearing of this, a cab driver named Matthews told the police that a family friend named Franz Müller had given Matthew's ten-year-old daughter a jewel box to play with that bore the label "Death," and that Müller owned a beaver hat made by J. H. Walker. A photograph of Müller was given to the police by Matthews, and Death identified it as that of his customer.

But Müller was gone. Inspector Tanner questioned Müller's landlady and was told he had left for New York on the sailing ship *Victoria*. Foreshadowing Inspector Dew's efforts forty-five years later in the Crippen case, Tanner boarded the steamship *City of Manchester* and arrived in New York weeks before the arrival of the *Victoria*. Müller was apprehended still in possession of Mr. Briggs's hat, which had been cut down to allow the removal of Briggs's name. The suspect was promptly extradited and returned to England to stand trial at the Old Bailey on October 27.

Dr. Henry Letheby testified concerning the blood evidence. He had not examined the bloodstained scene until July 26, and the walking stick was not subjected to his scrutiny until October 6. By that time, the stains were dried and hard to identify. The issue was important because the position and shape of the blood spots and stains would aid Letheby in reconstructing the crime.

Holmes relies on similar evidence in "The Adventure of the Bruce Partington Plans," saying to Watson, "Either the body fell from the roof, or a very curious coincidence has occurred. But now consider the question of the blood. Of course, there was no bleeding on the line if the body had bled elsewhere. Each fact is suggestive in itself. Together they have a cumulative force."

Dr. Letheby used several techniques to determine which spots were blood. He testified:

I have measured the globules of blood, and I believe it to be human blood. . . . There was blood on the glass. . . . It had the characteristics of human blood, and, from the coagulum in it, had been living when it came on the glass. It contained particles of brain matter. There were two spots like splashes. They were about the size of sixpences. Such an effect would have been produced by a blow if a person had been sitting on that part of the carriage and had been struck on the left side of the head; as he was leaning against the glass that effect might have been produced.

Dr. Letheby stated, "I used a microscope [as we gather from Dr. Letheby's notes, which were inherited by Dr. Tidy, a spectroscope was attached to the microscope] and also chemical tests to determine the character of the stains."

No doubt it was the desiccated quality of the stains that prompted the chemist to include the use of the spectroscope in his arsenal of tests. He relied on a technique that had a venerable past. Some of the early experiments were done by a maker of lenses and physicist named Joseph von Fraunhofer. Leaning on the previous work of Isaac Newton and William Wollaston, among others, Fraunhofer, in the early part of the nineteenth century, constructed a device composed of a lens, a prism, and a small telescope. He placed these in front of a window shade that had a slit through which light passed. The light then traveled through the lens and prism and was examined through the telescope. Fraunhofer observed not only separated bands of color but dark lines running among them. Although the lens maker's interest lay in understanding color rather than criminal science, he inadvertently made a great contribution to the latter. The dark lines he observed, now known as Fraunhofer lines, provided the idea.

In 1859, Robert Wilhelm von Bunsen, professor of chemistry at Heidelberg (the very man credited with the invention of the Bunsen burner often used by Holmes), and his colleague, the physicist Gustav Robert Kirchoff, attached the spectroscope to a microscope and developed a highly accurate method of detecting hemoglobin. Henry Chapman, a nineteenth-century American pathologist, described the concept:

> The spectroscopic method of investigating blood-stains is based on the fact that blood interferes with the transmission of certain rays of light, and that it gives rise to what are known as the dark absorption bands of the blood spectrum. . . . [W]hen light is transmitted through a prism it is decomposed into the seven colors: Violet, indigo, blue, green, yellow, orange, red. If, however, a weak solution of . . . blood be placed between the source of light and the prism, dark bands will appear [their location depending on whether the blood is venous or arterial].

Another advocate of the method was Alfred Swaine Taylor, who explained:

> We simply examine the light as it traverses a solution of the red coloring matter, and with a proper spectral eyepiece attached to a microscope we notice whether the colored spectrum has undergone any change. If the red liquid owes its color to recent or oxidized blood, two dark absorption bands will be seen breaking the continuity of the colored spectrum. These are situated respectively at the junction of the yellow with the green rays, and in the middle of the green rays. If the blood is quite recent and of a bright red color the two absorption bands are distinct and well defined.

Spectral analysis was highly sensitive and could detect blood in stains that were years old. While other substances such as dark red dyes could produce dark lines, they did not appear in the same place in the spectrum. The technique took great skill, but it worked very well.

In his testimony in the Müller case, Dr. Letheby had been definite as to the location of the bloodstains and had provided a vivid word picture of how Mr. Briggs met his death. The jury found Franz Müller guilty, and he was publicly hanged outside of Newgate Prison in November 1864.

The Müller case influenced a number of changes in England. The dangerous isolation of train passengers was mitigated by the installation of small windows in the front and back of railway carriages—these were sometimes referred to as "Muller lights." The Regulation of Railways Act required the installation of communication cords on trains by 1868. The victim's top hat that Müller had cut down sparked a dashing new fashion among stylish young men, affording the executed man a sartorial remembrance.

In the forensic world, the spectroscope grew in importance, but it was not universally put to use. Information as well as technical training spread slowly in those days. Although Alfred Swaine Taylor was arguing in 1873 that if a "well-trained person skilled in micro-spectral observations" used the method, the "minutest traces of blood would be disclosed," we find a number of historically important cases in which only older, less sensitive techniques were relied on.

The case of the infamous Borden murders in Fall River, Massachusetts, provides a glimpse into the approach toward blood evidence in 1892 New England courtrooms. The Borden family lived discordantly in a narrow, inconveniently constructed house on Second Street. The household consisted of seventy-year-old Andrew Borden, a former undertaker who was currently a successful but compulsively frugal businessman; his two daughters from his first marriage—Emma, who was forty-two, and Lizzie, ten years Emma's junior; and Abby Borden, Andrew's second wife, who was sixty-four. A maid named Bridget lived with them; she was referred to by the family as Maggie, since the previous maid had been called Maggie, and it evidently required too much effort of the Bordens to change the name by which they addressed their servant.

The Borden daughters bitterly resented their stepmother, to the point where they declined to dine with her and referred to her as Mrs. Borden. Suspicion simmered among the family members—upset stomachs gave rise to talk of poison; missing items from Mrs. Borden's bedroom resulted in interior doors being locked. On the steaming hot day of August 4, 1892, Emma was out of town visiting friends. The elder Bordens, who with Maggie were recovering from a bout of intestinal problems, breakfasted unpleasantly on reheated mutton soup, bananas, and coffee. Lizzie, rising later, sipped only coffee. Mrs. Borden went upstairs to change the bed linen; Mr. Borden went into town on business; Maggie washed the windows between bouts of nausea.

By ten forty-five, Mr. Borden returned home and stretched out on the parlor sofa to nap. Maggie went up to her stifling attic room to do the same. At about eleven o'clock, Maggie was startled by a cry from Lizzie on the ground floor.

"Maggie—come down here! Father's dead! Somebody's come in and killed him!"

Lizzie was not exaggerating. Mr. Borden lay on the sofa, his head bleeding profusely. One eye dangled from its socket, and his nose was severed. He had been struck in the face at least eleven times, and fresh blood still ran from the wounds. The doctor and a neighbor were sent for. After a quick examination of the corpse, the doctor covered it with a sheet.

Lizzie had told Maggie that Mrs. Borden had, in response to a note, gone out to visit an unnamed sick person in town, but that Lizzie thought she had since heard her stepmother return. The neighbor and Maggie went upstairs to investigate and found Mrs. Borden on the floor of the guest room, her head crushed by repeated blows from an axe or a hatchet. The dead woman lay face down in a large pool of congealing and drying blood.

Lizzie delivered herself of a number of contradictory statements about where she had been during the crucial time. A local pharmacist informed police that the day before the murders he had refused Lizzie's request to sell her prussic acid, which she claimed she wanted to preserve a fur cape. As Lizzie was the only person with both motive (she stood to inherit her father's estate) and opportunity to commit the crime, she became a person of interest to the police.

Had Lizzie, they wondered, expressed her displeasure with her parsimonious father and inconvenient stepmother by dispatching them with a hatchet? Medical opinion was that Mrs. Borden had died at least an hour before her husband. Was it possible that respectable, churchgoing Lizzie Borden had crouched on the stairs of that narrow house (which must have been still redolent of mutton soup and blood) waiting for her father to come home to a violent death? There was a great deal of evidence that she had, and to the shock of Fall River, the wellborn Lizzie Borden stood trial for the double murder.

It is not our purpose here to savor all of the dark delights of the Borden mystery—it is the voice in the blood that is our current concern. So we will only mention the first, hasty autopsy, which was performed on the dining room table, chez Borden. (Home autopsies were still common at the time. It is probable that the table was protected by undertaker's boards during the operation, which makes the exercise much more palatable.)

The second, more thorough postmortem was performed alfresco at the grave site following the service, after the mourners had taken their sorrowful leave. As this occurred a week after the murders, the bodies were somewhat decomposed, but the open air made the odor tolerable, and there was sufficient light for a series of photographs to be taken. The heads were removed, to be stripped of their flesh, the better to disclose the horrendous wounds they bore when they were exhibited in court.

At trial, the blood was a subject of much importance. Which stains at the scene were blood and which were not? Where blood had fallen and where it hadn't, how fast it coagulated, and how slowly it dried were all at issue. Was the lack of visible blood on Lizzie the day of the murder evidence of innocence? Or was it evidence of guilt, as it could easily be argued that a loving daughter innocent of the assault would have approached her injured father and inevitably been stained with his blood? What was the weapon? And where was it now?

William Dolan, the medical examiner for Bristol County, was one of the first at the scene. By an incredible coincidence, Dr. Dolan was walking past the Borden home at eleven forty-five, just after the discovery of the bodies. His testimony at the preliminary hearing and trial gives us an idea of how the physical evidence was evaluated:

I have practiced medicine in Fall River for eleven years; received my education in the medical department of the University of Pennsylvania. I have been in general prac- tice, with probably more surgery than medicine. Have had several cases of fracture of the skull. Have been medical examiner for Bristol County for two years; for one year, when these murders took place. . . .

There was very little blood on his [Andrew Borden's] clothing, except on his bosom, his shirt bosom, and of course the back where the blood ran down, that is, in the back of his cardigan, and his clothes were soaked, where it had run down from his face to the lounge, as it lay on the lounge. . . .

There was not a great deal on the floor. It was drop- ping when I was there, dropping from the lounge in two places on to the carpet. . . .

[Dolan then describes a number of separate blood spot clusters.] Taking first the wall behind the sofa, there were in one cluster of spots, as it were, radiating, describing the arc of a circle, there were seventy eight blood spots. . . .

I believe there were eighty six spots. The highest of those of that particular cluster I think were three feet seven inches from the floor.

Some very minute, some the size of a pin head, others were the size of a pea, and varying from that. . . . I then found on the paper above the head of the lounge, the highest spot except one upon the ceiling; that was six feet one and three quarters inches from the floor.

Those spots, I did not exactly measure them [a great many details were not exactly measured by Dr. Dolan], but they must have been half an inch in their longest axis by quarter of an inch in width. . . .

On that picture and frame were in all forty spots. The highest spot there was fifty eight inches from the floor. . . .

I found the carpet underneath the head of the lounge in two spots two pools there of blood. I found on the par-lor door west of the head of the lounge about seven drops, that is on the door and on the jamb.

I think about five feet . . . I did not measure it accu-rately [again no measurement, no photograph, no diagram—Sherlock Holmes as well as Hans Gross would have been no doubt displeased] . . . one very large one in the center division of the upper two panels of the door. . . . The top one was quite a large one. . . . Taking the one I told you above the lounge as the biggest one, about half an inch in length, this would be about two-thirds the size of that. . . .

We saw two spots upon the ceiling immediately above, not exactly above the head of the lounge. I do not think it was human blood; I think it was some insect that had been killed there. There was another spot . . . that was in all probability human [but he is not sure]. . . .

It was not a spot; it was a string, as it were, of blood. Instead of being a spot of blood, that was long, it would probably measure, if drawn out, two inches or two and a half inches. . . .

The one in the groove was a medium spot. I could not give you the measurement . . . it was probably the size of a huckleberry, a small huckleberry. . . .

All the others were spots, were real spots, you could

tell from the way they struck. They drew down just as a spot of water on a piece of paper would do where it struck. It made a larger spot and pressed downward and made a neck. The other one there was a line, without much width.

It could be made by swinging from an instrument used in murdering Mr. Borden.

It seems evident that Dr. Dolan was primarily concerned with the physical distribution of the blood. Even so, he did not make precise measurements, and the photographs taken at the scene are blurred and indistinct.

Concerning the body of Mrs. Abby Borden, Dr. Dolan testified:

Under her head, and pretty well down on her breast, she was lying in a pool of clotted blood, quite dark, as if it had been there sometime. It was not in the fluid condition that Mr. Borden's was.

The front of the clothing was very much soaked, that is, down to the chest, and also the back, down about half way, of course going right through to her underclothing.

On the pillow sham, immediately above, about a foot or eighteen inches in front were about three spots. On the rail of the bed I should judge there would be from thirty to forty, probably fifty spots of blood.

The medical testimony of a Dr. Edward Wood was presented:

I am a physician and chemist—since 1876 professor of chemistry in the Harvard Medical School. Have given special attention to medical chemistry, to medico-legal cases, involving poisons and bloodstains. Have been called upon in several hundred trials, including a large number of capital cases.

Dr. Wood then testified that he had examined the stomachs and intestines of the victims, had found them to be normal, and could locate no sign of poison. We should recall, however, that a chemist will find only the poison he suspects and specifically tests for. Dr. Wood's testimony does not report tests for any other drugs or sedatives—a dose of which might have accounted for the nausea and sleepiness of the Borden ménage.

Dr. Wood's testimony continued:

On August 10, at Fall River, I received from Dr. Dolan the large hatchet known as the claw-hammer hatchet; the two axes; the blue-dress skirt and waist; the white skirt [Lizzie's clothing]; the sitting-room carpet; the bedroom carpet; . . . three small envelopes, one labeled "hair of Mrs. Borden, 8/7/92, 12.10 P.M.," one labeled "hair from A. J. Borden, 8/7/92, 12.14 P.M.," one labeled "hair taken from the hatchet."

The claw-hammer hatchet had several stains on it which appeared like bloodstains, on handle, side and edge. All the stains on the head of the hatchet were subjected by me to chemical and microscopic tests for blood, and with absolutely negative results. The two axes, which I designated A and B, had stains which appeared like blood, but tests showed them absolutely free from blood. [The hairs, he said, were most likely cow's.] . . .

The blue skirt has, near the pocket, a brownish smooch, which resembled blood, but a test showed it was not. [The test is not specified, and no question concerning this is raised. Lack of detailed questioning of expert witnesses on scientific matters is common in this period.] Another, lower down, proved not to be blood. The waist had not even a suspicion of bloodstain. The white skirt had a small blood spot, six inches from the bottom of the skirt. It was $\frac{1}{16}$ inch in diameter: the size of the head of a small pin. The corpuscles, examined under a high-power microscope, averaged $\frac{1}{3243}$ of an inch, and it is therefore consistent with its being human blood. Some animals show a similar measurement: the seal, the opossum and one variety of guinea pig. The rabbit and the dog come pretty near. [Dr. Wood mentions the measurements of the corpuscles but does not mention spectrum analysis.] . . .

Experiments which I made with the two carpets, from the sitting room and the guest chamber, showed that blood dried on them with equal rapidity. . . .

There is the small hatchet, which I should have mentioned in connection with the claw-hammer hatchet. The latter has a cutting edge of $4\frac{1}{2}$ inches; the small one an edge of $3\frac{1}{8}$ inches. . . .

Q. I will ask you the same question I did with reference to the other hatchet, whether in your opinion that hatchet could have been used and then cleaned in any manner so as to remove any trace of blood beyond the power of your discovery, as you examined it?

A. It couldn't have been done by a quick washing.

Q. Why not?

A. It would cling in those angles there and couldn't be thoroughly removed. The coagula would cling. It would have to be very thoroughly washed in order to remove it. It could be done by cold water, no question about that. But it couldn't be done by a careless washing. . . .

[Dr. Wood is shown a hatchet head found with its handle broken off.] Both sides of this hatchet were rusty. There were several suspicious spots on the side of it, but they were not blood. When I received it, there was a white film, like ashes, on it.

The murder weapon was never definitely identified, although most Borden scholars believe it to have been the handleless hatchet. The very absence of positive tests for blood raises questions about the thoroughness of the forensic procedures. A few

weeks before his death, Mr. Borden, using a hatchet, had decapitated a number of pigeons that Lizzie was keeping in the barn, as
he claimed they attracted vandals. Why was there no sign of
pigeon blood? Hatchets and cleavers were routinely used to divide
cuts of meat, which would explain the cow hairs on one hatchet,
but where was the blood? The handles were wood, and blood
would have clung to the crevices. One might suppose that a test as
sensitive as spectrum analysis would have provided useful information. Certainly the lack of a proven weapon made it easier for
the jury to do what it clearly wanted to do—find Lizzie (who was,
after all, the treasurer of the Young Woman's Christian Temper-
ance Union) not guilty and free to share the Borden estate with
her sister, Emma.

As Sherlock Holmes told Watson, determining the presence
of blood was only part of the problem. Even spectral analysis
would not tell the examiner whether the blood was that of a
human. The first attempts at solving the difficulty relied on photography. Dr. Paul Jeserich made important contributions in this
area. His technique was discussed in the 1893 *Albany Law Journal*:

> A murder had been committed, and D. was the man sus-
> pected; suspicion being strengthened by the circumstance
> that an axe belonging to him was found smeared with
> blood, which had been partly wiped off. The man denied
> his guilt, and accounted for the bloodstained weapon,
> which he declared he had not taken the trouble to wipe, by
> saying that he had that day killed a goat with it. The blood
> was examined microscopically, and the size of the corpus-
> cles proved his statement to be false. A photo-micrograph
> of it, as well as of goat's blood, was prepared for compari-
> son by the judge and jury. Another photo-micrograph was
> also made from part of the blade of the axe, which showed
> very clearly by unmistakable streaks, that the murderer
> had done his best to remove the traces of his crime. It is
> certain that these photographs must be far more useful for

purposes of detection than the original microscopic prepa-
rations from which they are taken; for it requires a certain
education of the eye to see through a microscope properly,
and still more to estimate the value of the evidence it
offers. It is certain too that counsel on either side would
see through the microscope with very different eyes.

This was an important advance, but it still did not address two
problems: if the blood was old and dry, the corpuscles lost shape;
and some animals had corpuscles similar to those of humans. The
evidence produced by photomicrographs was useful but not infallible.

By 1900, solutions were beginning to be found in Europe.
Karl Landsteiner, assistant professor at the Institute of Pathology
and Anatomy in Vienna, discovered that the reason early attempts
at transfusions often failed was that different types of blood
existed. If a patient was infused with the wrong type of blood, it
caused a clumping or agglutinating of the recipient's blood, with
fatal results. At first it was thought that only two blood types
existed. Landsteiner found a third. Eventually, four separate blood
types were distinguished.

The usefulness of blood typing in legal matters was not realized until 1915, when Leone Lattes of the University of Turin
established that the blood on the shirt of one Renzo Girardi was
Girardi's type and not that of the woman with whom Signora
Girardi accused the unfortunate man of making violent love. In
1916, Dr. Lattes reported on the case in the *Archivo di Anthropolo-
gia Criminale, Psichiatria, e Medicina Legale*.

In 1901, the forensic world was galvanized by the announcement of a new accomplishment. Paul Uhlenhuth, assistant
professor at the Institute of Hygiene in Greifswald, Germany, had
developed a method for distinguishing human blood from animal
blood. It rested on the fact that if an animal, such as a rabbit, was
injected with blood from another species, a defensive reaction to
that other species' blood would be produced in the rabbit's blood.

This defensive serum was known as precipitin. The serum from a rabbit previously injected with human blood would react to another such exposure and would react just as strongly to human bloodstains. But the injected rabbit's serum would react only to the blood of a species to which it had been previously exposed. This made it possible to determine precisely which species was the source of a bloodstain.

By the end of 1901, the new discovery would be put to the ultimate test when a ghastly crime on the island of Rugen terrified the inhabitants. Rugen lies in the Baltic Sea, off the northwest coast of the German province of Pomerania. The island's irregular shape affords it many coves and beaches, and its landscape is rich as well with woods and white chalk cliffs. Prehistoric graves are common on the island. Rugen had in its past been conquered and ruled by various peoples, among them the Danes and the Slavs, and its complex folklore reflected that history. Trolls and dwarfs, giants and pagan gods were the stuff of the island's superstitions.

Even at the dawn of the twentieth century, a stubborn belief in werewolves still gripped some of the population. The local version of the lycanthropy legend was that one could become a werewolf by girding oneself with a strap cut from the back of a hanged man. Werewolves were believed to attack and kill horses, sheep, and children, mutilating their bodies in a lupine frenzy.

The ancient legend seemed to stir to terrifying life in July 1901. Herman and Peter Stubbe, eight and six years old, did not return home for supper. A search party set out to find them that night, pressing deep into the forest by the light of torches but without success. The following morning, with the daylight to guide the searchers, a large rock stained with blood was discovered. A stench hovered in the air, leading them to a thicket not far away. There they found what remained of the children. The boys' limbs had been severed and their bodies slit open. The internal organs had been removed and scattered throughout the woods. The children had been decapitated. The anguished search party plodded through the forest, gathering the bloody pieces.

It was remembered that on June 11, only a month before, a number of sheep had been killed in a field on Rugen. The animals had been cut open and their parts scattered. The farmer who owned the sheep had seen the perpetrator running away but had been unable to catch him.

The vicious bloodiness of the crimes and the utter lack of understandable motive inevitably evoked memories of the old werewolf stories. Rugen was in a turmoil, and suspicion was everywhere.

A fruit seller told police that she had seen a carpenter named Ludwig Tessnow talking to the dead children on the afternoon before they disappeared. Tessnow, who traveled about doing odd bits of carpentry, had been seen by another witness shortly after the crime. The witness stated that Tessnow's clothes had been covered with brown stains. Tessnow was arrested. The clothes he was wearing did indeed bear a mixture of stains of various shades of brown. He explained that they were wood stains, acquired as he worked, except for some stains on his hat, which were cattle blood.

The mention of wood stains reminded the examining magistrate of another murder that had occurred in September 1898 in the small village of Lechtingen. Two little girls, aged seven and eight, named Hannelore Heidemann and Else Langmeir, had not returned from school. Their worried parents discovered that the children had never arrived at the schoolhouse that morning. By dusk, a search party had found the little girls' bodies in a nearby wood. As in the Rugen case, the corpses had been dismembered and some of the organs scattered. A man whose behavior was suspicious and whose clothing was covered with dark spots had been arrested. There were no forensic facilities in the little town, and once the suspect explained the spots were only wood stains, he had been freed for lack of evidence. The suspect's name had been Ludwig Tessnow.

The Rugen authorities now holding Tessnow displayed him to

the owner of the mutilated sheep. The farmer promptly and firmly identified Tessnow as the sheep killer. Convinced that Tessnow was a compulsive, sadistic murderer, the Rugen prosecutor pondered how to prove his theory.

A magistrate in Greifswald read of the case. He was aware of the new test for human bloodstains and arranged to have the suspect clothing sent to Uhlenhuth. There were over a hundred spots and stains that needed examination. After four days of effort, it was determined that although a large number of spots were wood stains, nine of them were sheep's blood, and seventeen of them were the blood of human beings. Ludwig Tessnow was convicted and sentenced to death. There were no more sadistic killings of children on the island—science had shown that there was no werewolf on Rugen. There had been instead an even more frightening predator—a twisted human being.

By 1904, the precipitin test was a basic instrument of forensic laboratories. Science was learning to understand the voice in the blood.

Sherlock Holmes may have overlooked some details, but his belief in the usefulness of a reliable test for blood was vindicated. It's a great pity it took so long to develop it. What Holmes said to Watson about the fictional "Holmes" test was exactly true of Uhlenhuth's test: "Now, this appears to act as well whether the blood is old or new. Had this test been invented, there are hundreds of men now walking the earth who would long ago have paid the penalty of their crimes."

WHATEVER REMAINS

- The domestic postmortems carried out in the Borden case were not unique to American medical practice. They were performed frequently enough in Britain at the end of the nineteenth century to justify a chapter on the subject in *Practical Pathology*, a text published by Professor Sims Woodhouse in 1883. He was of the opinion that a firm kitchen table covered with a "stout macintosh" was useful, and that the physician's hands should be washed with water and turpentine, followed by a dash of carbolic acid.

- Rubber gloves did not come into common medical use until well after 1890.

- Home autopsies required different instruments from those ordinarily carried in a doctor's black bag. Desirable portable equipment included a saw, a spine wrench, scissors, assorted scalpels and knives, and needle and suture for tidying up afterward. Most instruments used for postmortems were discards from the operating theaters.

- Franz Müller may have been the first to commit murder on an English train, but he was not the last. Percy Mapleton, a writer of short stories, shot and stabbed Frederick Gold in 1881 on a train going from London to Brighton. The motive appears to have been robbery. In 1887, on the train from Feltham to Waterloo Station in London, a dead woman occupied one of the second-class compartments. Although the police identified her as a Miss Camp, and located a blood-stained pestle on the train tracks, the murder was never solved. In 1910 a porter noticed blood running from under the seat of a train when it arrived at Alnmouth and traced its source to the huddled corpse of John Nesbit, who had been shot five times. Nesbit had been carrying a large sum of money, which was missing. John Alexander Dickman was convicted and executed for the murder.

CHAPTER 13

Myth, Medicine, and Murder

"Is it something in the blood?"
—Ferguson to Holmes in "The Adventure of the Sussex Vampire"

T HE QUESTION OF WHY some individuals seem driven to crime is one of the great unresolved issues in criminal investigation. Sherlock Holmes was certainly aware of one creative nineteenth-century attempt to solve the problem, the "science" of phrenology, or craniology, as it was originally called. Invented by the Viennese anatomist Franz Joseph Gall in the late eighteenth century, the system was based on the belief that both intellectual ability and moral character are innate and can be observed in the shape of the skull. (Holmes refers to the concept in "The Adventure of the Blue Carbuncle" when he says, "It is a question of cubic capacity; a man with so large a brain must have something in it.")

Gall published his ideas in 1796, and in 1804, accompanied by his dissectionist and disciple, J. G. Spruzheim, he began touring Europe to lecture on the subject. By 1814, Spruzheim and phrenology had arrived in Britain, where they aroused much controversy. Interest in the system waxed and waned, but by the time Sherlock Holmes and his magnifying glass sprang from the pen of Arthur Conan Doyle, it was once again in favor.

In "The Final Problem," Holmes describes his first meeting with his nemesis, the archcriminal Professor Moriarty:

> "His appearance was quite familiar to me. He is extremely tall and thin, his forehead domes out in a white curve, and his two eyes are deeply sunken in his head. He is clean-shaven, pale, and ascetic-looking, retaining something of the professor in his features. His shoulders are rounded from much study, and his face protrudes forward and is forever slowly oscillating from side to side in a curiously reptilian fashion. He peered at me with great curiosity in his puckered eyes.
>
> "'You have less frontal development than I should have expected,' said he at last."

In phrenological terms, this remark is less than complimentary. Specific parts of the skull were associated with specific abilities, and "frontal development" referred to the area that was associated with comparison, or analytic ability. Samuel Wells, in his 1873 work, *How to Read Character: A New Illustrated Hand-Book of Physiology, Phrenology, and Physiognomy*, explains why, in this matter at least, size counts: "[If] Comparison [frontal development, is] Very Large, [it indicates] you possess remarkable powers of analysis; ability to reason from analogy and to discover new truths by induction; can clearly trace relations between the known and the unknown which escape common investigators"—the very qualities upon which Holmes prides himself. Clearly Moriarty was not only the "Napoleon of Crime" but also an adherent of phrenology, as were an amazing number of educated people at the time.

The British Phrenological Society was established in 1881. The distinctive model heads designed by the American exponent, Lorenzo Fowler, illustrating the various "organs of the faculties," were a common sight in physicians' consulting rooms. Young couples often had "readings" before marriage to determine their compatibility, and "gentleman scientists" collected interesting skulls with "bumps" that delineated the arcane traits of their original owners.

James Mortimer, the surgeon who brings the problem of the Baskerville hound to Holmes's attention, is such a collector, as he forthrightly says to Holmes when he first consults him:

> "You interest me very much, Mr. Holmes. I had hardly expected so dolichocephalic a skull or such well-marked supraorbital development. Would you have any objection to my running my finger along your parietal fissure? A cast of your skull, sir, until the original is available, would be an ornament to any anthropological museum. It is not my intention to be fulsome, but I confess that I covet your skull."

Phrenology might have acquired a new acceptance in the late nineteenth century, but it rested on an extraordinarily shaky foundation. It is quite true, as Gall first postulated, that there are individual parts of the brain that control particular functions, but the corollary he suggested—that the brain influences the shape of the skull and that the talents and moral qualities of a human being can be determined by measuring the contours of the head—is without merit.

How was it possible for so many intelligent researchers and physicians to accept a pseudoscience as a realistic approach to explaining character? The troubling fact is that medicine has had a long history of dancing with myth and magic. In ancient times, terrified by death and disease, and having little understanding of the causes of either, human beings tried desperately to find explanations that might quell their fear. They were highly motivated to understand that which threatened, but they had not developed a logical method for doing so. Quacks, alchemists, and primitive physicians armed with anecdotes and herbals were dangerous guides. They convinced a credulous public, among other things, that the wounds of a murder victim bled in the presence of the murderer, that the heart turned black if poison was the cause of death, and that a souvenir bottle of urine from a faraway loved one would provide a clue to his emotional and physical well-being.

During the Middle Ages, when repeated waves of the Black Death destroyed millions of Europeans, no one observed that the teeming hordes of flea-bearing rats that arrived with the sailing ships carried the dread plague. Instead, popular opinion offered a number of inventive explanations as to the cause of the disease. One was that witchcraft, promulgated, of course, by elderly women, was to blame. (The elderly who survived the plague were suspect simply because they did not succumb, but it is very likely that they had acquired resistance during previous cycles of disease.) The second explanation rested on the common understanding that dragons spread plague. Winged dragons, some dark folktales explained, copulated only while airborne. Their preferred trysting places were over still bodies of water: lakes, ponds, or wells. As the mating dragons hovered, quivering in reptilian ecstasy, dragon semen, which was well known to be highly poisonous, sometimes escaped into the water below, making the water a source of death. Less sophisticated citizens insisted that the water poisoning was carried out by the Jews. Mass murder by burning of the Jewish population resulted.

The study of disease was largely a matter of reasoning from one or two incidents to a large and erroneous conclusion. In the middle of the seventeenth century, an English knight, Sir Kenelme Digby, provided posterity with a perfect example of this manner of problem solving when he experimented with a new approach to the treatment of wounds acquired on the battlefield. He knew that such injuries had once been treated by the application of complicated unguents that included ingredients such as eunuchs' fat and crocodile dung, sometimes delicately moistened with urine. In spite of what was strongly believed to be cutting-edge medicine, some of the wounded stubbornly did not respond to the treatment.

Military physicians then switched to the use of weapon ointment, which involved leaving the patient in peace and baptizing the instrument that had made the wound with the ominous elixir instead. This was an apparent success, as fewer of the wounded died, but there was great difficulty in locating the correct weapon in the postbattle chaos. As a result, the technique faded from use, army physicians went back to spreading the unsavory salve directly on the wound, and the death rate rose.

At this juncture, Sir Kenelme had his groundbreaking idea. He would treat the clothing of the wounded, thus avoiding the tiresome search for the weapon, and would apply a powder made mostly of copper sulfate, avoiding the similarly tiresome search for crocodiles and eunuchs. The experiment worked—the death rate among the troops plummeted, and in 1658, the proud Digby published *A Late Discourse, Made in Solemne Assembly of Nobles and Learned Men at Montpellier in France, Touching the Cure of Wounds by the Powder of Sympathy, with Instructions how to make the said powders whereby many other Secrets of Nature are unfolded.* Originally written in French, it was translated into English by "R. White, Gent."

The "Digby effect" is the sort of erroneous reasoning that Holmes warns about when he says in "The Reigate Squires": "It is of the highest importance in the art of detection to be able to recognize, out of a number of facts, which are incidental and which vital."

Holmes, however, is not completely immune from accepting superstition as science. We can see this clearly when in "The Final Problem" he describes Moriarty's moral deficiencies as being the result of biological inheritance: "[T]he man had hereditary tendencies of the most diabolical kind. A criminal strain ran in his blood, which, instead of being modified, was increased and rendered infinitely more dangerous by his extraordinary mental powers." Holmes's evaluation of Moriarty was wholly in keeping with nineteenth-century theories of criminology, which in turn were influenced by the faulty research techniques of previous times.

The Italian physician Cesare Lombroso published a small book titled *L'uomo delinguente* in 1876 and later expanded it to explain his views of some criminals as atavistic creatures who bore distinctive physical signs of their shortcomings. His opinions acquired international notoriety, and although he later modified them somewhat, his original writings won many adherents. In 1906, he presented a paper at the Sixth Congress of Criminal Anthropology at Turin, Italy, which affords us a striking picture of his methods:

> In 1870 I was carrying out research in the prisons and asylums of Pavia upon the cadavers and living persons in order to determine the substantial differences between the insane and criminals without succeeding very well. At last I found in the skull of a brigand a very long series of atavistic anomalies, above all an enormous middle occipital fossa [depression] and a hypertrophy of the vermis [the median part of the cerebellum] analogous to those found in inferior vertebrates.
>
> At the sight of these strange anomalies the problem of the nature and of the origin of the criminal seemed to me resolved; the characteristics of primitive men and of inferior animals must be reproduced in our times. Many facts seemed to confirm this hypothesis.
>
> Above all the psychology of the criminal; the frequency of tattooing and of professional slang, the passions as fleeting as they are violent, the lack of foresight which resembles courage and courage which alternates with cowardice, and idleness which alternates with the passion for play and activity.

It is evident that Lombroso's research did not encompass what we today consider the proper scientific method of stating a problem, forming a hypothesis, predicting the results of future observations, and having independent researchers duplicate the results. Lombroso was basing his views on a very small sample, and he most likely confused cause and effect by tossing cultural artifacts such as tattooing and the use of slang into the anthropological hopper.

Lombroso also argued that crime is incited by the press, saying:

> Morbid stimulation is increased a hundred-fold by the prodigious increase of really criminal newspapers, which spread abroad the virus of the most loathsome social plagues simply for sordid gain . . . and excite the morbid appetite and still more morbid curiosity of the lower social classes. . . . In New York in 1851 a woman murdered her husband, a few days afterward three other women did the same thing.

While it may be true that a venal and salacious media is an unpleasant addition to society, it is quite a leap to assume that the report of a single murder in New York was the direct cause of those that followed. After all, spouses had managed to murder each other with efficient energy for centuries before the advent of newspapers.

Lombroso was quick to accept new ideas and was the first to make use of an early form of lie detector. He was also an enthusiastic admirer of the work of Richard L. Dugdale, the "gentleman sociologist" from Ulster County, New York, who in 1877 published *The Jukes: A Study in Crime, Pauperism, Disease and Heredity*, which described several generations of what was purported to be a family group of criminals and mental defectives. Lombroso wrote in *Crime: Its Causes and Remedies*, "The most striking proof of the heredity of crime and its relation to prostitution and mental diseases is furnished by the fine study which Dugdale has made of the Juke family." To be fair to Dugdale, he included the concept that a poor environment was a major cause of the Jukes's criminality, but proponents of eugenics who wished to "improve" the human race by controlled breeding grasped Dugdale's work and Lombroso's admiration for it as weapons for their cause. In the United States, this led to the forced sterilization of a number of people who were adjudged imbeciles or idiots.

In recent years, historical research has led to the discovery of old records that have made it clear that the Jukes were not all related to each other but were a composite of several families, and that they were not universally either criminals or mentally defective. What they seem to have been was poor. In the late nineteenth century, however, the belief that heredity was a major cause of criminality was dominant. We see it reflected in "The Boscombe Valley Mystery" when Turner explains his violent rejection of a suitor for his daughter's hand by saying that the suitor's father was amoral, and he says to Holmes, "I would not have his cursed stock mixed with mine; not that I had any dislike to the lad, but his [the suitor's father's] blood was in him, and that was enough."

The skewed logic that pretended to be science at the end of the nineteenth century was not limited to criminology. Just as in the days of Kenelme Digby, understanding of the root causes of disease, diagnosis, and treatment was often mired in myth. "Brain fever" was a catchall convenient diagnosis for physicians and a useful narrative device for writers of fiction. It is mentioned repeatedly in the tales of Sherlock Holmes, including "The Adventure of the Copper Beeches," "The Musgrave Ritual," "The Crooked Man," "The Naval Treaty," and "The Adventure of the Cardboard Box." The phrase with which Holmes refers to the condition in "The Crooked Man" is typical: "No information could be got from the lady herself, who was temporarily insane from an acute attack of brain fever."

The disease most likely to cause "temporary insanity" is encephalitis, or inflammation of the brain or the meninges (the membranes that envelop the spinal cord and brain). Symptoms include headache, fever, vomiting, weakness, and irritability. Common treatments included leeches, hot footbaths, and the ever-popular strong laxatives. Since encephalitis does not occur in fact as often as it does in fiction (where it appears to be as frequent as the common cold) or as often as it is discussed in old medical books, it is fair to suspect that any illness that produced feverish delirium was diagnosed and treated as brain fever.

The great difficulty in arriving at an accurate diagnosis and avoiding a disease that had no known cause led to a kind of medical terrorism in which any practitioner could make wild statements as to the cause of an illness, imply that the patient's habits triggered it, and prescribe unpleasant treatments to alleviate it.

The nineteenth-century obsessive concern with masturbation is a prime example. The 1891 edition of *Warren's Household Physician* included the following on what he called "Self Pollution, or Onanism":

> There is probably no vice to which so many boys and young men, and even girls and young women, are addicted, and from which so many constitutions break down, as self-pollution. . . .
>
> Symptoms . . . are very numerous. . . . The principal ones are headache, wakefulness, restless nights, indolence, indisposition to study, melancholy, despondency, forgetfulness, weakness in the back and private organs, a lack of confidence in one's own abilities, cowardice, inability to look another full in the face.

Treatments proffered included tonics and frequent washing of the genitals with icy water. *Warren's Household Physician* also advised avoiding solitude and soberly suggested that one "Sleep with some friend" instead.

The great fear was that, along with the myriad symptoms Dr. Warren described, masturbation might be a forerunner of something even more threatening: nocturnal emissions, or "spermatorrhea." This dire condition, delineated in the 1889 edition of *The People's Common Sense Medical Advisor* by R. V. Pierce, M.D., results, we are told, in impotence, premature decay, consumption, St. Vitus's Dance, epilepsy, paralysis, softening of the brain, complete dementia, and insanity. "This form of insanity," Dr. Pierce continues, "is rarely curable, and often results in suicide." To prevent this dread occurrence, it was important to wear only loose clothing and helpful to receive "daily injections of cold water into the bowels." (Dr. Pierce, it is interesting to note, was a U.S. congressman; he resigned that office in 1880 to "serve the sick." Obviously possessed of an eclectic mind, he was also the inventor and purveyor of "Dr. Pierce's Pleasant Purgative Pellets.")

Imaginatively awful treatments abounded during the Victorian era. In the interests of sedating a patient and relaxing a spasm of the lower intestine, nicotine in the form of tobacco smoke introduced into the rectum was considered useful. Dr. George B. Wood, in *A Treatise on Therapeutics and Pharmacology or Materia Medica* published in 1860, explained how to deliver the appropriate dose. The practitioner was advised to light a pipe or cigar, and, by means of a funnel, to direct the smoke into one of the many clever instruments created for the purpose of introducing the smoke into the patient—one of the simplest being a pair of bellows, its muzzle covered with leather to avoid injury to the bowel.

Other parts of the body benefited from tobacco smoke as well. Dr. Wood goes on to describe the case of a woman who was suffering the intense pain of a dislocated jaw. Her doctor felt it was imperative to relax her tense facial muscles, but the lady's general state of health made her a poor candidate for bleeding, which was the usual method of inducing a relaxed state. She was therefore provided with a pint of gin, which she imbibed. The doctor waited hopefully, but she remained tense. Growing desperate, the physician handed her a cigar. She took several puffs, promptly growing sufficiently relaxed to fall off her chair. The alert doctor seized the happy moment to spring upon her and realign the problem mandible.

As useful as the nicotine-laden smoke may have been in desperate situations, it was still very dangerous. Nicotine is a potent poison, as Sherlock Holmes was well aware ("I think, Watson, that I shall resume that course of tobacco-poisoning which you have so often and so justly condemned," he says in "The Adventure of the Devil's Foot"). It was difficult to measure out a proper therapeutic dose, and once the smoke was inserted, there was no way to retrieve it should the subject react badly. Patients were known to have died from an excess of it.

Jürgen Thorwald, in *The Century of the Surgeon*, informs us that some clever practitioners avoided the problem by eschewing the smoke and simply inserted a strong cigar into the sufferer's rectum, the advantage being that the cigar could be quickly withdrawn if need be. Just how efficacious this treatment was, Thorwald doesn't say, but no doubt the patient found it diverting.

Sherlock Holmes may have toyed with phrenology, but when it came to most other myths, he asserted his scientific bias. In "The Adventure of the Sussex Vampire," Holmes is depicted as the epitome of logical skepticism. When he receives the famous letter that begins:

Re Vampires.

SIR,—

    Our client, Mr. Robert Ferguson, of Ferguson and Muirhead, tea brokers, of Mincing Lane, has made some inquiry from us . . . concerning vampires. As our firm specializes entirely upon the assessment of machinery the matter hardly comes within our purview, and we have therefore recommended Mr. Ferguson to call upon you and lay the matter before you.

Holmes reacts with irritation, famously demanding:

"But what do we know about vampires? . . .

    Rubbish, Watson, rubbish! What have we to do with walking corpses who can only be held in their grave by stakes driven through their hearts? It's pure lunacy."

"But surely, [Watson says,] the vampire was not necessarily a dead man? A living person might have the habit. I
have read, for example, of the old sucking the blood of the
young in order to retain their youth."

Watson and Holmes are referring not only to folklore but also to
nineteenth-century literary concepts of vampirism, such as that
fabricated by Bram Stoker in his 1897 novel *Dracula*.

In real life, exhumations of reputed vampires provided helpful
information to medical science. In the eighteenth century, during
a vampire panic in central Europe, a number of graves were
opened by physicians of the occupying Austrian army. Their
reports give a detailed picture of the unexpected effects that burial can have on cadavers—effects that in less educated minds gave
credence to the vampire legends. Bodies of males, for instance,
were sometimes discovered showing "wild signs," or penile erec-
tions, no doubt caused by bloating from gases. The same gases
caused corpses to split open, often with sufficient noise to be
heard aboveground. Some burials were in earth so rich in tannin
that the bodies were extraordinarily preserved, even after centuries underground. All of this served to immortalize the belief in
the "undead."

Dr. R. V. Pierce might have believed that "consumption" or
tuberculosis was caused by solitary sex, but in many nineteenth-
century country villages the disease was instead associated with
vampirism. The latency period before the signs of illness grew
obvious meant that the infected descendants of deceased victims
often showed the first signs of illness after their progenitors were
buried. It was not recognized that the disease was the result of
contagion within the household. The symptoms of weakness and
anemia caused by poor lung function and bloody coughs suggested to the credulous that the dead had returned to feed on
their young.

Opening the graves of the suspected vampires sometimes disclosed that the corpses had changed position, a result of effects of

decomposition and ensuing gas formation. Insect activity affected the visage of the dead, contraction of the skin made it appear that the hair and nails continued to grow, and what was thought to be fresh liquid blood could be found in the mouth or chest cavities. It was not generally realized that blood, which coagulates after death, can subsequently return to a liquid state, so when a stake was driven into the chest of an exhumed corpse and a plume of blood erupted, it satisfied the observers that a vampire had been quelled.

(Some believed that it was more efficacious to remove the head of the corpse. In eighteenth- and nineteenth-century New England, this was the method of choice during outbreaks of tuberculosis. Recently exhumed graves in Rhode Island, Vermont, and Connecticut disclosed skulls buried at the feet of the dead.)

Sherlock Holmes had no patience with these superstitions: "But are we to give serious attention to such things? This agency stands flat-footed upon the ground, and there it must remain," he declares in "The Adventure of the Sussex Vampire," and he proceeds to get to the heart of the matter, determining that the culprit who inflicts injury on a small child is no vampire but his morbidly jealous half-brother.

Holmes, Watson often reminds us, is a passionate collector of books and articles relating to old crimes, and perhaps he solves the vampire problem so handily because he recalls another infamous crime that had taken place in England sixty-four years before the publication of "The Adventure of the Sussex Vampire." In June 1860, Francis Savile Kent, the four-year-old son of Samuel Savile Kent, was found missing from the nursery of the three-story lavish family home in Wiltshire when the household awakened. There was no sign of an intruder. The household included Samuel Kent's second wife, who was pregnant, her three small children, Kent's three children over age fifteen by his first deceased wife, and several servants. A frantic search by the family, local police, and villagers went unrewarded until someone thought to look in a long disused servant's outhouse that was half hidden by overgrown garden shrubbery.

Blood covered the outhouse floor. Wedged in the outhouse vault (receptacle) was the corpse of the missing child, dressed in his nightgown and wrapped in a blanket. There was a wound in his chest, and his throat had been cut so deeply that he was almost decapitated.

The local police responded by arresting the nursemaid, who had no conceivable motive. There was also no evidence against her, and she was eventually released. A bloody handprint was found on a windowpane and wiped off so as "not to upset the family." The closets were not searched so as not to "invade the family's privacy." Mr. Kent was highly unpopular, having an overbearing manner, and a local rumor had it that he had murdered his little son for unspecified reasons. An agitated press demanded results.

The local police were clearly floundering. Scotland Yard responded by sending Detective Inspector Jonathan Whicher, one of their most talented investigators, to assume control of the case. Aware that the present Mrs. Kent, the mother of the dead boy, had first entered the household as the older children's governess during the final illness of their mother, he paid close attention to sixteen-year-old Constance, the child of the first Mrs. Kent. The girl had been known to use the old outhouse as a hiding place. Her mother had a history of mental derangement. Was it possible that this was an inherited tendency? And, as Francis had been the obvious favorite of his mother, might jealousy and revenge be a motive? Could it be "something in the blood?" as the distraught father, Ferguson, wonders in "The Adventure of the Sussex Vampire."

One of Constance's three nightgowns was missing. A bloody "shift" that had been found by the local police near a boiler room had been left there but had disappeared by the time Whicher tried to collect it. Whicher believed the shift to have been the missing nightgown. A search of the young girl's bedroom was rewarded by the discovery of a pile of old newspaper clippings under her mattress—clippings that told the tale of Madeleine Smith, the Scottish lady who had stood trial in 1857 for poisoning her lover. The calm and collected manner in which Miss Smith faced her accusers was detailed in the press, as was the "Not proven" verdict accorded her.

Possibly influenced by Constance's choice of reading matter as well as by the missing nightgown, Inspector Whicher arrested Constance on July 16, to the great shock of the townspeople. In the tradition of Madeleine Smith, Constance remained calm and slightly sorrowful. She immediately became a figure of intense sympathy. Judicial inquiries were held but were largely disorganized. The barrister Mr. Kent hired to defend Constance characterized Detective Inspector Whicher as "a man eager in pursuit of the murderer, and anxious for the reward which has been offered."

Constance was released without trial, as the evidence was considered insufficient, and the nursemaid was rearrested—and also released for lack of evidence. The body of the murdered child was exhumed in the hope that the missing nightgown might have been mistakenly interred with the corpse, but this was not the case. Tormented by rumors, the Kent family moved away, having sent Constance to a convent in France. Whicher, excoriated for having placed under arrest a shining example of English maidenhood, resigned from Scotland Yard. After a while, people forgot about the incident.

And then, five years after the murder, Constance Kent reappeared at a religious retreat in Brighton, England. The retreat housed a home for unwed mothers, and there is some evidence that Constance assisted the midwives. It is certain she spent much time conferring with a minister at the retreat. Perhaps because of that influence, twenty-year-old Constance Kent, in the company of the minister, went to the police and at last confessed to the murder of her little half-brother Francis.

She described stabbing him. "I thought the blood would never come," she said. In response, the court sentenced her to death. Because of her youth at the time of the offense and in view of the fact that she had freely admitted her guilt, her sentence was promptly commuted to life in prison. She served twenty years and was released in 1885 into a world that was utterly strange to her. At her release, the whole tragic tale was told again in the press. (Certainly a young doctor named Arthur Conan Doyle must have read the details. Perhaps they provided the seed for "The Adventure of the Sussex Vampire.")

Constance was forty-one years old, her hair streaked with gray, when she was freed. She possessed a few useful skills, having acquired training as a midwife. We know she was sporadically attracted to religion. (We also know she once had a way with a knife.) There are no available facts as to where she went or how she lived or which of her abilities she put to use. As it was just three years before the Ripper murders terrorized London and the Ripper was believed to be a knife wielder with some medical knowledge, it is tempting to speculate about a connection, but there is no evidence as to how Constance spent the remainder of her life.

By then, Whicher was working as a private detective, having investigated, among other matters, the past of the Tichborne Claimant. After Constance Kent's confession, he had been offered the reward, which he declined. In the Kent matter, he had uncovered a dreadful family flaw, very similar to the one Sherlock Holmes found in the case of the Sussex vampire. But whereas when Holmes confronted the tormented father, saying, "You have to face it, Mr. Ferguson. It is the more painful because it is a distorted love, a maniacal exaggerated love for you, and possibly for his dead mother, which has prompted his action. His very soul is consumed with hatred for this splendid child," and Ferguson sadly but bravely accepted Holmes's verdict, Detective Inspector Whicher was not as fortunate. As the honest messenger bearing very bad news, he was in the right, and for that, he was wronged.

Jonathan Whicher was a talented investigator who reasoned carefully from observable facts and had no more patience with vampire tales than Sherlock Holmes. But this adherence to facts was not a universal approach in the nineteenth and early twentieth centuries. Well-trained medical professionals could embrace myth with amazing alacrity and present it in the language of science, complicating police investigations.

For instance, while the belief that hair and nails could grow after death was taken as evidence of vampirism in some primitive rural communities, some pathologists who rejected vampirism as a cause continued to accept this postmortem growth as a proven phenomenon. Charles Meymott Tidy, usually a careful observer, continued to be taken in by this view to the end of the nineteenth century in spite of well-thought-out papers to the contrary by the pathologists Haller and Chapman. Tidy included in his text, *Legal Medicine*, the note: "May the hair grow after death? That both the hair and the nails may grow for a time after death has been proved by careful observations."

In support of that interesting but untrue statement, he quotes from *The French Dictionary of Medical Sciences*, which includes the concurring opinions of Drs. Good, Pariset, Villarme, and Bichat. Tidy explains that "there may be molecular life and fecundity of the epidermis and therefore of the hair follicles for a time after somatic death, [which] is what theory would lead us to expect, and observations are ample in proof." In further support he describes a case presented in the *New York Medical Record* of August 18, 1877, in which a Dr. Caldwell of Iowa states that he was present in 1862 "at the exhumation of a body which had been buried for four years. The coffin had given at its joints, and that the hair of the deceased protruded. [Caldwell] had evidence to show the deceased was shaved before burial, but the hair of the head [at exhumation] measured 18 inches, the whiskers 8 inches the chest hair 4–6."

Because it has since been well established that the hair and nails do not grow after death, although they may appear to have done so due to the shrinkage of the skin, we may suspect either that Dr. Caldwell's exhumed subject had been the victim of a grossly incompetent barber or that the wrong coffin had been opened.

Another fanciful belief much accepted by lawyers as well as medicos of the period was that the retina of a murdered person would retain the image of the last thing he or she focused on—with any luck, the murderer. Andre Moenssens, in his 1962 paper "The Origin of Legal Photography," quoted from the 1877 case of *Eborn v. Zimpelman*, a civil matter concerning the admissibility of photographic evidence. During this litigation, an attorney happily promoted that extraordinary idea of the dying image, saying:

> Every object seen with the natural eye is only seen because [it is] photographed on the retina. In life the impression is transitory; it is only when death is at hand that it remains permanently fixed on the retina. . . . Science has discovered that a perfect photograph of an object, reflected in the eye of one dying, remains fixed on the retina after death. (See recent experiments stated by Dr. Vogel in the May number, 1877 of the *Philadelphia Photographic Journal*.) Take the case of a murder committed on the highway: on the eye of the victim is fixed the perfect likeness of a human face. . . . We submit that the eye of a dead man would furnish the best evidence that the accused was there when the deed was committed, for it would bear a fact, needing no effort of memory to preserve it . . . the handwriting of nature, preserved by nature's camera.

In spite of the dramatic hyperbole, "science" had discovered nothing of the sort. But facts aren't always allowed to stand in the way of passionate legal advocacy. The idea of the dying retinal image was firmly fixed in the minds of many and perhaps was the reason that it was not uncommon for murderers of the period to destroy the eyes of their victims before leaving the crime scene.

So persistent was this belief that it found its way into a famously mysterious case of murder in New York City as recently as 1920. Shortly after eight on a warm June morning of that year, Mrs. Marie Larsen headed for her Manhattan job as housekeeper to Joseph Bowne Elwell, the very well-known bridge expert and putative author of *Elwell on Bridge* and *Elwell's Advanced Bridge*.

Separated from his wife, Helen (who, it is believed, had actually written much of the highly successful books), Elwell lived alone. He was an avid investor, racehorse owner, and man about town. His charm, his dazzling smile, his glossy chestnut hair, combined with his enormous skill at cards, made him a much sought-after dinner companion. Mrs. Larsen was pleased to be employed by such a famous figure.

Knowing that he had been planning to be out late with friends the previous evening, the housekeeper turned her key in the lock quietly. As she entered the town house, she heard the unexpected sound of desperately labored breathing coming from the small room to the right. The source of the sound proved to be an elderly bald man sitting on a high-backed armchair. He was barefoot and was attired in red silk pajamas. His gaping mouth disclosed three widely separated teeth. A bullet hole was situated in the exact center of his forehead, and blood from the wound dripped onto an open letter on his lap. A cartridge from the offending bullet lay on the floor. The wall behind the stricken man was covered with blood, bone fragments, and brain tissue from the exit wound. As the bullet had passed through the dying man's skull, it had struck the wall and recoiled, and now it rested on a table next to the high-backed armchair.

Racing from the house, Mrs. Larsen found the milkman making deliveries and asked him to send for the police. An ambulance rushed the stertorously breathing man to the hospital, where he died two hours later without regaining consciousness.

A search of the town house made the victim's identity apparent. Hidden in the back of Joseph Bowne Elwell's closet was a collection of forty expensively made wigs. They were of graduated lengths so that their owner could wear them in sequence and create the appearance of growing hair. A gleaming set of false teeth, carefully constructed to accommodate three genuine ones, rested in a glass of water.

The dashing bridge expert had never been seen by his friends without his cosmetic aids. So carefully had he kept them a secret that the police at once wondered whom he might have trusted enough to allow them to see him as he was.

Suicide was considered a possibility, but the .45 caliber gun that had made the wound was missing, and there was no apparent motive. The open letter on the dying man's lap had been delivered at seven thirty that morning (in those happy days, there was such a thing as an early mail delivery), so the shooting had to have occurred after that.

It was up to the chief medical examiner of New York City, Charles Norris, to determine the manner of death—accident, suicide, or homicide. As all of New York was fascinated by the case and everyone seemed to have an opinion (after all, it was one of the many cases described in the news media as "The Crime of the Century"), the pressure was enormous.

The majority of the detectives on the case insisted it was suicide and that the gun had been stolen afterward by an unknown party. This information was leaked to the newspapers, which announced it as fact. Dr. Norris was certain it was murder. In his autopsy report, he had carefully noted the appearance of the entrance wound, examining it in Holmesian fashion with a magnifying glass. There were three inches of powder grains around the wound but no powder burns, which Norris interpreted to mean that the gunshot came from at least four or five inches away. As the wound was centered in the forehead, it was an impossibly awkward angle for a suicidal injury.

In an effort to convince the police and the district attorney, Dr. Norris called on Captain Cornelius W. Willemse, commander of the First Detective Division of New York, to help him demonstrate the impossibility of a self-inflicted wound. In front of an audience that included Assistant District Attorney Dooling, Dr. Norris, and a gunshot expert from the U.S. Army, Captain Willemse repeatedly fired a .45 caliber revolver, similar to the one that killed Elwell, at a piece of human flesh donated from the mortuary. At a distance of four to five inches, the resulting wound exactly resembled that on the victim. A closer range caused powder burns. The police now accepted that the case was a homicide and that there was work to be done.

Time, however, had been lost. And matters grew worse. The newspaper coverage had been intense and now included the dramatic statements of one Roland Cook, an elderly physician, who took to appearing in front of the murder house and delivering himself of opinions to the seething horde of reporters. As crime historian Jonathan Goodman recounts the matter in his book on the Elwell case, Dr. Cook was of the firm view that Dr. Norris had been gravely remiss for not having photographed the dead man's eyeballs at autopsy, as it was a fact that the retinas of the dead retained images of what they last saw. Greatly excited by this news, Mr. Goodman tells us, the *New York Times* printed an article entitled "How Paris Would Treat the Elwell Case," which suggested that Dr. Norris had indeed ignored this important medical procedure.

Reporters then questioned Assistant District Attorney Dooling about the matter. Knowing nothing about the subject, Dooling promised he would look into this "very interesting" theory and said he would "speak to expert photographers and medical men on the subject." This issue provided yet another time-consuming distraction for the hard-pressed medical examiner, who pointed out tartly that the retina retention concept was without merit, but even if it were true, the victim had not died immediately, so any image on his retina would have been of the medical personnel on the ambulance sent to aid him. What we can be sure of is that well into the twentieth century this medical myth was considered worth discussing.

The murder of Joseph Bowne Elwell has never been solved.

It would be heartening to believe that the misalliance between myth and medicine is at an end and that today murders are examined only through the prism of the scientific method, but this is a comfort we may not have. In Britain during the last decade, a much-respected pediatrician formulated what became known as his "law" concerning sudden unexplained deaths of infants for which no cause could be found. This law stated, "One such death in a family was a tragedy, two were suspicious, and three constituted murder." Like many aphorisms, this is pithy, easy to remember, and incorrect. It assumes that there is no underlying hereditary condition as yet undiscovered that might be responsible.

The physician went on to state that the chance of a repeated crib death in a single family was as rare as one in seventy-three million. On the basis of this opinion, in spite of a complete lack of any corroborating evidence of a crime, a number of British women who had lost babies to crib death had their subsequent children taken from them and placed in adoptive homes. Three women, including the solicitor Sally Clark, were convicted of murder and sent to prison. These cases were overturned on appeal, as statisticians came forward and testified that the figure of one in seventy-three million was grossly mistaken. Indeed, having lost a child to crib death makes a family much more likely to suffer an additional loss, and the usually accepted figure for recurrence of this dread event is one in seventy-seven.

The eminent pediatrician, like Bertillon in the Dreyfus case, had reached outside of his specialty to dabble in a field in which he had no expertise. And as in the Dreyfus case, the innocent suffered as a result. As Holmes said in *A Study in Scarlet*, "It is a capital mistake to theorize before you have all the evidence."

But a single physician, perhaps well intentioned but disastrously mistaken, could not cause such a debacle without the aid of a credulous justice system. The easy acceptance of an opinion just because it is offered by a man who claims science as his shield is dangerous, just as myths stated as scientific fact are dangerous. It needs to be remembered, as Sherlock Holmes warned Watson in "The Adventure of the Empty House," that sometimes "we come into those realms of conjecture where the most logical mind may be at fault."

WHATEVER REMAINS

- Madeleine Smith, the determined young lady tried for murdering her lover Emile L'Angelier by lacing his cocoa with arsenic, sat for a phrenological examination, although it is not clear at what period in her interesting career this took place. The findings appear in the published account of her trial. She is credited by the phrenologist with talents in mathematics, engineering, and architecture. He concludes: "Owing to her strong affections and healthy temperament, she will make a treasure of a wife to a worthy husband."

- In an attempt to streamline examinations, nineteenth-century phrenologists developed a dismayingly complex instrument called the psychograph. It contained 1,954 parts cocooned within a walnut case. The device contained calipers used to measure a subject's head. The psychograph would then emit a stream of tape listing twenty-eight personality traits including benevolence, caution, and conjugal love. There are three psychographs in working order in the United States.

- In 1873, the writer and humorist Mark Twain, while visiting London, noticed an advertisement for the phrenological techniques of a fellow American, Mr. Lorenzo N. Fowler. Twain visited Fowler using an assumed name and left the examination room of that worthy with a chart Fowler had made of Twain's head. Three months later, Twain, using still another name, returned to Fowler's lair, and had the exam repeated. He left with a second chart, which bore no recognizable resemblance to the earlier one.

- In nineteenth-century America, bereaved relatives sometimes physically disinterred their own loved ones in the hope of preventing vampire-caused disease. Such cases have been reported not only in New England but as far west as Chicago, and as recently as 1875.

Glossary

algor mortis. The cooling of the body after death.

Aqua Tofana. Literally, Tofana's water; a poisonous mixture containing arsenic reportedly concocted and sold in Rome and Naples by the murderous seventeenth-century entrepreneur Teofania di Adamo.

autopsy. Medical examination of a dead human body; from the Greek meaning "to see for one's self."

bascule. The wooden seesaw plank of the guillotine on which the convicted was strapped for execution.

bezoar stone. Stones formed in the intestinal organs of animals such as goats; believed in former times to be an antidote to poison.

body snatchers. Grave robbers; an illicit source of human anatomical specimens.

bordereau. A form, docket, list, or covering memorandum; commonly used to refer to the list of French military documents found in the German embassy in Paris that Dreyfus was accused of writing.

cadaveric spasm. Instant rigor at the moment of death. It is rarely encountered.

carboy. A large bottle of green glass enclosed in basketwork or boxed for protection, used especially for carrying corrosive liquids.

chirography. Penmanship, or the art of handwriting.

coroner. From "crowner," originally a representative of the Crown who was responsible for conducting inquests. In some jurisdictions, the term is used interchangebly with medical examiner; in others, a coroner is simply a layman with no medical training who is responsible for engaging a forensic expert to consult when needed.

corpus delicti. The body of evidence that establishes that the crime has taken place.

craniology. Old term for phrenology.

dactyloscopy. The science of fingerprints.

declic. The blade release lever on the guillotine.

exudates. Substances such as liquids or odors released from a gland, pore, membrane, or cut.

forensic. Of the court, relating to legal proceedings; sometimes used as an abbreviation for "forensic science" or to refer to the application of science to decide questions arising from legal proceedings.

forensic science. Any academic science applied to legal proceedings.

graphology. The study of handwriting for the purpose of judging psychological attributes of an individual.

guaiacum. A West Indian tree whose resin was used in the old guaiacum test for the presence of blood.

hemoglobin. A component of animal blood cells that carries oxygen and gives red blood cells their characteristic color.

homicide. The killing of one human being by another human being.

hyoscine. An alkaloid sedative.

infarct. Alternatively, infarction. Recently dead tissue due to sudden loss of blood supply, as from a heart attack.

Jemmy. A short crowbar used by burglars to gain entry, today called a jimmy in the United States.

lividity. Gray-blue discoloration caused by the settling of blood after death.

livor mortis. The discoloration of death, which occurs as the circulation ceases.

lunette. Wooden collar on the guillotine in which the neck of the convicted was held for execution.

luz bone. The part of the body believed in ancient times to be that from which the entire body of a dead individual would be resurrected at the day of judgment.

medical jurisprudence. The original term for "forensic medicine." It is still used on occasion.

not proven. A verdict available to juries in Scotland in addition to guilty or innocent, resulting in acquittal.

perimortem. At or around the time of death.

phrenology. A pseudoscience that attempted to determine intellectual traits and character by observation of the shape of the skull.

portrait parlé. Literally, "speaking picture." The system devised by Alphonse Bertillon in 1882 to identify individuals with police records.

postmortem. Medical examination of a dead person; from the Latin meaning "after death."

precipitin. Serum produced in blood in a defensive reaction to the injection of blood from another species.

prussic acid. Hydrocyanic acid, a solution of hydrogen cyanide and water.

psychopomp. A spiritual presence whose purpose is to warn of approaching disaster or to accompany a human to the afterworld.

tannin. Tannic acid, often produced by the decomposition of plant matter, especially peat moss. Tannin tans skin and leather and acts as a preservative.

vomitus. Contents of the stomach ejected through the mouth.

Bibliography

PUBLISHED MATERIALS

Adams, Norman. *Dead and Buried? The Horrible History of Bodysnatching*. New York: Bell Publishing Company, 1972.

Ashton-Wolfe, H. *The Forgotten Clue: Stories of the Parisian Sûreté with an Account of Its Methods*. Boston: Houghton Mifflin Company, 1930.

Atholl, Justin. *Shadow of the Gallows*. London: John Long, 1954.

Bailey, James A. "Iodine Fuming Fingerprints from Antiquity." *Minutiæ* (Lightning Powder Company, Jacksonville, FL), issue number 76 (Summer 2003).

Barber, Paul. *Vampires, Burial, and Death: Folklore and Reality*. New Haven: Yale University Press, 1990.

Baring-Gould, William S. *Sherlock Holmes of Baker Street: A Life of the World's First Consulting Detective*. New York: Bramhall House, 1962.

Barker, Richard, ed. *The Fatal Caress: And Other Accounts of English Murders from 1551 to 1888*. New York: Duell, Sloan and Pearce, 1947.

Belin, Jean. *Secrets of the Sûreté: The Memoirs of Commissioner Jean Belin*. New York: G. P. Putnam's Sons, 1950.

Bell, John. *Engravings Explaining the Anatomy of the Bones, Muscles, and Joints*. London: Bell and Bradfute, and T. Duncan; and J. Johnson, and G.G.G. & J. Robinsons, 1794.

Bemis, George. *Report of the Case of John W. Webster: Indicted for the Murder of George Parkman*. Boston: Charles C. Little and James Brown, 1850.

Beneke, Mark. "A Brief History of Forensic Entomology." *Forensic Science International* 120 (2001): 2–14.

Birkenhead [Frederick Winston Smith], Earl of. *More Famous Trials*. Garden City, NY: Sun Dial Press, 1937.

Bishop, George. *Executions: The Legal Ways of Death*. Los Angeles: Sherbourne Press, 1965.

218

Blundell, R. H., and G. Haswell Wilson, eds. *Trial of Buck Ruxton.* London: William Hodge & Company, 1950.

Bolitho, William. *Murder for Profit.* New York: Harper & Brothers, 1926.

Bond, Raymond T., ed. *Handbook for Poisoners: A Collection of Famous Poison Stories; Selected, with an Introduction on Poisons.* New York: Rinehart & Co., 1951.

Boos, William F. *The Poison Trail.* Boston: Hale, Cushman & Flint, 1939.

Booth, Martin. *The Doctor and the Detective: A Biography of Sir Arthur Conan Doyle.* New York: Thomas Dunn Books/St. Martin's Minotaur, 2000.

Bradley, Howard A., and James A. Winans. *Daniel Webster and the Salem Murder.* Columbia, MO: Artcraft Press, 1956.

Bridges, Yseult. *Poison and Adelaide Bartlett: The Pimlico Poisoning Case.* London: Hutchinson of London, 1962.

Brophy, John. *The Meaning of Murder.* London: Ronald Whiting & Wheaton, 1966.

Browne, Douglas G. *The Rise of Scotland Yard: A History.* New York: G. P. Putnam's Sons, n.d., ca. 1955.

Browne, Douglas G., and E. V. Tullet. *Bernard Spilsbury: His Life and Cases.* London: George G. Harrap & Co., 1951.

Brussel, James A. *Casebook of a Crime Psychiatrist.* New York: Bernard Geis Associates, 1968.

Buchan, William. *Domestic Medicine; Advice to Mothers: Treatise on the Prevention and Cure of Diseases by Regimen and Simple Medicines.* Boston: Joseph Bumstead, 1811.

[Bulfinch, Thomas]. *Bulfinch's Mythology: The Age of Fable, The Age of Chivalry, The Legends of Charlemagne.* London: Hamlyn Publishing Group, 1969.

Burroughs Wellcome & Co. *Wellcome's Excerpta Therapeutica*, U.S.A. edition. London: Burroughs Wellcome & Co., 1916.

Burton, John Hill. *Narratives from Criminal Trials in Scotland,* vol. 2. London: Chapman and Hall, 1852.

Byrnes, Thomas. *1886 Professional Criminals of America.* New York: Chelsea House Publishers, 1969.

Caesar, Gene. *Incredible Detective: The Biography of William J. Burns.* Englewood Cliffs, NJ: Prentice-Hall, 1968.

Camps, Francis E. *The Investigation of Murder.* With Richard Barber. London: Michael Joseph, 1966.

Carey, Arthur A. *Memoirs of a Murder Man.* With Howard McLellan. Garden City, NY: Doubleday, Doran, and Company, 1930.

Carr, John Dickson. *The Life of Sir Arthur Conan Doyle.* Harper & Brothers, New York, 1949. Reprint, New York: Vintage Books, 1975.

Cassity, John Holland. *The Quality of Murder: A Psychiatric and Legal Evaluation of Motives and Responsibilities Involved in the Plea of Insanity as Revealed in Outstanding Murder Cases of This Century.* New York: Julian Press, 1958.

Chapman, Henry C. *A Manual of Medical Jurisprudence and Toxicology.* Philadelphia: W. B. Saunders, 1893.

Ciba Foundation. *The Poisoned Patient: The Role of the Laboratory.* Amsterdam: Associated Scientific Publishers/Elsevier, 1974.

Costello, A. E. *Our Police Protectors: History of the New York Police from the Earliest Period to the Present Time,* 2nd ed. New York: A. E. Costello, 1885.

Cullen, Tom A. *When London Walked in Terror.* Boston: Houghton Mifflin Company, 1965.

Dale-Green, Patricia. *Lore of the Dog.* Boston: Houghton Mifflin Company, 1967.

De La Torre, Lillian, ed. *Villainy Detected: Britain in 1660 to 1800.* New York: D. Appleton-Century Company, 1947.

De Quincey, Thomas. *Miscellaneous Essays.* Boston: Ticknor, Reed, and Fields, 1851.

Devlin, Patrick. *The Criminal Prosecution in England.* London: Oxford University Press, 1960.

de Vries, Leonard. *'Orrible Murder: An Anthology of Victorian Crime and Passion Compiled from the Illustrated Police News.* With Ilonka Van Amstel. New York: Taplinger Publishing Company, 1971.

Dewberry, Elliot B. *Food Poisoning: Its Nature, History and Causation: Measures for Its Prevention and Control.* London: Leonard Hill, 1943.

Dilnot, George, ed. *The Trial of Professor John White Webster.* New York: Charles Scribner's Sons, 1928.

Doyle, Arthur Conan. *The Annotated Sherlock Holmes: The Four Novels and Fifty-six Short Stories Complete.* Edited by William S. Baring-Gould. New York: Wings Books, 1992.

———. *The Complete Sherlock Holmes: The A. Conan Doyle Memorial Edition,* 2 vols. Garden City, NY: Doubleday, Doran, and Company, 1930.

———. *The New Annotated Sherlock Holmes.* Edited, with a foreword and notes, by Leslie S. Klinger. Additional research by Patricia J. Chui; introduction by John le Carré. New York: W. W. Norton & Company, 2005.

Dreyfus, Alfred. *Five Years of My Life: The Diary of Captain Alfred Dreyfus.* New York: Peebles Press, 1977.

Duff, Charles. *A New Handbook on Hanging: Being a Short Introduction to the Fine Art of Execution.* Chicago: Henry Regnery Company, 1953.

Duke, Thomas S. *Celebrated Criminal Cases of America.* San Francisco:

James H. Barry Company, 1910. Reprinted with corrections and index added. Montclair, NJ: Patterson Smith Publishing Company, 1991.

Dumas, Alexandre. *Celebrated Crimes*, 8 vols. Translated from the French by I. G. Burnham. Philadelphia: George Barry, 1895.

Edwards, Samuel. *The Vidocq Dossier: The Story of the World's First Detective*. Boston: Houghton Mifflin Company, 1977.

Esterow, Milton. *The Art Stealers*. New York: Macmillan Publishing Company, 1973.

Evans-Pritchard, E. E. *Witchcraft, Oracles, and Magic among the Azande*. Abridged with an introduction by Eva Gillies. Oxford: Clarendon Press, 1983.

Fabian, Robert. *Fabian of the Yard: An Intimate Record by Ex-Superintendent Robert Fabian*, 5th ed. London: Naldrett Press, 1954.

———. *London After Dark: An Intimate Record of Night Life in London and a Selection of Crime Stories from the Case Book of Ex-Superintendent Robert Fabian*. New York: British Book Centre, 1954.

Fatteh, Abdullah. *Handbook of Forensic Pathology*. Philadelphia: J. B. Lippincott Company, 1973.

Faulds, Henry. "On the Skin-furrows of the Hand." *Nature* 22 (October 28, 1880): 605. Available at http://www.galton.org/fingerprints/faulds-1880-nature-furrows.pdf and http://www.eneate.freeserve.co.uk/page3.html.

Felstead, S. Theodore. *Shades of Scotland Yard: Stories Grave and Gay of the World's Greatest Detective Force*. New York: Roy Publishers, n.d., ca. 1951.

Finger, Charles J. *Historic Crimes and Criminals*. Girard, KS: Haldeman-Julius Company, 1922.

Franklin, Charles. *They Walked a Crooked Mile: An Account of the Greatest Scandals, Swindlers, and Outrages of All Time*. New York: Hart Publishing Company, 1969.

Frazer, James George. *The Golden Bough: A Study in Magic and Religion*. Abridged. New York: Macmillan Company, 1941.

Furman, Guido, ed. *Medical Register of the City of New York for 1865: For the Year Commencing June 1, 1865*. New York: New York Medico-Historical Society, 1866.

Gaute, J. H. H., and Robin Odell. *The Murderers' Who's Who: Outstanding International Cases from the Literature of Murder in the Last 150 Years*. Montreal: Optimum Publishing Company, 1979.

Glaister, John. *Medical Jurisprudence and Toxicology*, 9th ed. Edinburgh: E. and S. Livingstone, 1950.

———. *The Power of Poison*. London: Christopher Johnson Publishers, 1954.

Glaister, John, and James Couper Brash. *Medico-Legal Aspects of the Ruxton Case*. Baltimore, MD: William Wood & Company, 1937.

Goddard, Henry. *Memoirs of a Bow Street Runner*. London: Museum Press Limited, 1956.

Gonzales, Thomas A., Morgan Vance, and Milton Helpern. *Legal Medicine and Toxicology*. New York: D. Appleton-Century Company, 1937.

Gonzalez-Crussi, F. *Notes of an Anatomist*. New York: Harcourt Brace Jovanovich, 1985.

Good, John Mason. *The Study of Medicine*, 6th American ed., vol. 1. New York: Harper and Brothers, 1836.

Goodman, Jonathan. *The Slaying of Joseph Bowne Elwell*. New York: St. Martin's Press, 1988.

Gordon, Richard. *The Alarming History of Medicine*. New York: St. Martin's Press, 1994.

———. *Great Medical Disasters*. New York: Dorset Press, 1986.

Gribble, Leonard. *Great Manhunters of the Yard*. New York: Roy Publishers, 1966.

Gross, Hans. *Criminal Investigation: A Practical Textbook for Magistrates, Police Officers and Lawyers; Adapted from System Der Kriminalistik of Dr. Hans Gross*, 4th ed. Translated from the German and edited by John Adam and J. Collyer Adam. Edited by Ronald Martin Howe. London: Sweet & Maxwell, 1949.

Guiley, Rosemary Ellen. *Vampires Among Us*. New York: Pocket Books, 1991.

Guttmacher, Manfred S. *The Mind of the Murderer*. New York: Grove Press, 1962.

Haggard, Howard W. *Devils, Drugs, and Doctors: The Story of the Science of Healing from Medicine-Man to Doctor*. New York: Harper and Row, 1929.

Haining, Peter, ed. *The Gentlewomen of Evil: An Anthology of Rare Supernatural Stories from the Pens of Victorian Ladies*. New York: Taplinger Publishing Company, 1967.

Halasz, Nicholas. *Captain Dreyfus: The Story of a Mass Hysteria*. New York: Simon and Schuster, 1955.

Hall, Angus, ed. *The Crime Busters: The FBI, Scotland Yard, Interpol—The Story of Criminal Detection*. London: Treasure Press, 1984.

Hall, John, ed. *Trial of Adelaide Bartlett*. New York: The John Day Company, 1927.

Hamm, Ernest D. "Track Identification: An Historical Overview." *International Symposium on the Forensic Aspects of Footwear and Tire Impression Evidence*. June 27, 1994. Quantico, VA: FBI Academy, 1994.

Hardwick, Michael, and Mollie Hardwick. *The Man Who Was Sherlock Holmes*. Garden City, NY: Doubleday & Company, 1964.

Harrison, Shirley, and Michael Barrett. *Diary of Jack the Ripper*. New York: Hyperion, 1993.

Hartman, Mary S. *Victorian Murderesses: A True History of 13 Respectable French and English Women Accused of Unspeakable Crimes*. New York: Schocken Books, 1976.

Helman, Cecil. *The Body of Frankenstein's Monster: Essays in Myth and Medicine*. New York: W. W. Norton Company, 1992.

Helpern, Milton. *Autopsy: The Memoirs of Milton Helpern, the World's Greatest Medical Detective*. With Bernard Knight. New York: St. Martin's Press, 1977.

Henry, E. R. *Classification and Uses of Fingerprints*. London: His Majesty's Stationery Office, 1913.

Heppenstall, Rayner. *French Crime in the Romantic Age*. London: Hamish Hamilton, 1970.

———. *Reflections on the Newgate Calendar*. London: W. H. Allen, 1975.

Hertzler, Arthur E. *The Horse and Buggy Doctor*. New York: Harper & Brothers, 1938.

Higham, Charles. *The Adventures of Conan Doyle: The Life of the Creator of Sherlock Holmes*. New York: W. W. Norton, 1976.

Hodge, Harry, and James H. Hodge, eds. *Famous Trials: From Murder to Treason—The Sensational Courtroom Dramas Which Make Up Legal History*. Selected and introduced by John Mortimer. Abridged. Harmondsworth, Middlesex, England: Penguin Books, 1984.

Hoeling, Mary. *The Real Sherlock Holmes: Arthur Conan Doyle*. New York: Julian Messner, 1965.

Holmes, Oliver Wendell. *Medical Essays, 1842–1882*, Riverside ed., vol. 9. New York: Houghton Mifflin Company, 1911.

Holmes, Paul. *The Trials of Dr. Coppolino*. New York: The New American Library, 1968.

Holton, Gerald. *Introduction to Concepts and Theories in Physical Sciences*. Cambridge, MA: Addison-Wesley Publishing Company, 1955.

Honeycombe, Gordon. *The Murders of the Black Museum, 1870–1970*. London: Hutchinson & Company, 1982.

Hoover, John Edgar. *The Identification Facilities of the FBI*. Washington, DC: Federal Bureau of Investigation, U.S. Department of Justice, 1941.

Houde, John. *Crime Lab: A Guide for Nonscientists*. Ventura, CA: Calico Press, 1999.

Houts, Marshall. *Where Death Delights: The Story of Dr. Milton Helpern and Forensic Medicine*. New York: Coward-McCann, 1967.

Hunt, Peter. *The Madeline Smith Affair.* London: Carroll & Nicholson, 1950.

Hussey, Robert F. *Murderer Scot-Free: A Solution to the Wallace Puzzle*, 1st American ed. South Brunswick, NJ: Great Albion Books, 1972.

Hynd, Alan. *Murder Mayhem and Mystery: An Album of American Crime.* New York: A. S. Barnes and Company, 1958.

Infamous Murders. London: Verdict Press, 1975. Reprint, London: Treasure Press, 1985.

Irving, H. B. *A Book of Remarkable Criminals.* London: Cassel and Company, 1918.

Irving, H. B., ed. *Trial of Franz Müller.* Edinburgh and London: William Hodge & Company, 1911.

———. *Trial of Mrs. Maybrick.* Philadelphia: Cromarty Law Book Company, 1912.

Jaffe, Jacqueline A. *Arthur Conan Doyle.* Boston: Twayne Publishers, 1987.

Jardine, David, ed. *The Lives and Criminal Trials of Celebrated Men.* Philadelphia: 1835.

Jarvis, D. C. *Folk Medicine: A Vermont Doctor's Guide to Good Health.* New York: Henry Holt and Company, 1960.

Jefferis, B. G., J. L. Nichols, and Mrs. J. L. Nichols. *The Household Guide or Domestic Cyclopedia: A Practical Family Physician, Home Remedies and Home Treatment on All Diseases; An Instructor on Nursing, Housekeeping and Home Adornments; Also a Complete Cook Book.* Naperville, IL: J. L. Nichols & Company, 1905.

Jesse, F. Tennyson. *Murder and Its Motives.* London: George G. Harrap & Co., 1952.

Jesse, F. Tennyson, ed. *Trial of Madeleine Smith.* London: William Hodge & Company, 1927.

Jones, Ann. *Women Who Kill.* New York: Holt, Rinehart and Winston, 1980.

Jones, Richard Glyn, ed. *Poison! The World's Greatest True Murder Stories.* New York: Berkley Books, 1989.

Joyce, Christopher, and Eric Stover. *Witnesses from the Grave: The Stories Bones Tell.* New York: Ballantyne Books, 1992.

Kahn, David. *The Codebreakers: The Story of Secret Writing.* New York: The Macmillan Company, 1968.

Karlen, Delmar. *Anglo-American Criminal Justice.* In collaboration with Geoffrey Sawer and Edward M. Wise. New York: Oxford University Press, 1967.

Keller, Allan. *Scandalous Lady: The Life and Times of Madame Restell, New York's Most Notorious Abortionist.* New York: Atheneum, 1981.

Keylin, Arleen, and Arto DeMirjian Jr., eds. *Crime: As Reported by the New York Times.* New York: Arno Press, 1976.

Kirk, Paul L. *Crime Investigation*. New York: John Wiley & Sons, 1974.

Knapp, Andrew. *The Newgate Calendar or Malefactors' Bloody Register: Containing Genuine and Circumstantial Narrative of the Lives and Transactions, Various Exploits and Dying Speeches of the Most Notorious Criminals of Both Sexes Who Suffered Death Punishment in Gt. Britain and Ireland*. Edited by B. Laurie. New York: G. P. Putnam's Sons, 1932.

———. *The Newgate Calendar: Comprising Interesting Memoirs of the Most Notorious Characters Who Have Been Convicted of Outrages on the Laws of England; With Speeches, Confessions, and Last Exclamations of Sufferers*. Edited by Edwin Valentine Mitchell. Garden City, NY: Garden City Publishing Company, 1926.

Knowles, Leonard. *Court of Drama*. London: John Long, 1966.

Lambert, Samuel W., Willy Wiegand, and William M. Ivins, Jr. *Three Vesalian Essays: To Accompany the Icones Anatomicae of 1934*. New York: The Macmillan Company, 1952.

Laurie, Peter. *Scotland Yard: A Study of the Metropolitan Police*. New York: Holt, Rinehart and Winston, 1970.

Lefebure, Molly. *Murder with a Difference: Studies of Haigh and Christie*. London: William Heinemann, 1958.

Lenotre, G. *The Guillotine and Its Servants*. Translated from the French by Mrs. Rodolph Stawell. London: Hutchinson & Co., 1930.

Lewis, Alfred Allen. *The Evidence Never Lies: The Casebook of a Modern Sherlock Holmes*. With Herbert Leon MacDonell. New York: Holt, Rinehart and Winston, 1984.

Lincoln, Victoria. *A Private Disgrace: Lizzie Borden by Daylight*. New York: G. P. Putnam's Sons, 1967.

Lindsay, Philip. *The Mainspring of Murder*. London: John Long, 1958.

Loftus, Elizabeth, and Katherine Ketcham. *Witness for the Defense: The Accused, the Eyewitness, and the Expert Who Puts Memory on Trial*. New York: St. Martin's Press, 1991.

Lombroso, Cesare. *Crime: Its Causes and Remedies*. Translated from the Italian by Henry P. Horton. Boston: Little, Brown and Company, 1912.

———. "The Savage Origin of Tattooing." *Popular Science Monthly*. April, 1896.

Lopez, Barry Holstun. *Of Wolves and Men*. New York: Charles Scribner's Sons, 1978.

Lowenthal, Max. *The Federal Bureau of Investigation*. New York: William Sloane Associates, 1950.

Lustgarten, Edgar. *Defender's Triumph: Courtroom Drama and Brilliant Legal Strategy in Four Classic Murder Trials*. New York: Charles Scribner's Sons, 1951.

————. *The Murder and the Trial.* Edited by Anthony Boucher. New York: Charles Scribner's Sons, 1958.

————. *Verdict in Dispute.* New York: Charles Scribner's Sons, 1950.

————. *The Woman in the Case.* New York: Charles Scribner's Sons, 1955.

MacCallum, W. G. *A Text-Book of Pathology.* Drawings chiefly from Alfred Feinberg. Philadelphia: W. B. Saunders Company, 1918.

Makris, John N. (ed.), et al. *Boston Murders.* New York: Duell, Sloan and Pearce, 1948.

Maple, Eric. *Magic, Medicine and Quackery.* New York: A. S. Barnes and Company, 1968.

Maples, William R., and Michael Browning. *Dead Men Do Tell Tales: The Strange and Fascinating Cases of a Forensic Anthropologist.* New York: Doubleday, 1994.

Marten, M. Edward. *The Doctor Looks at Murder.* With Norman Cross [pseud.]. Garden City, NY: Doubleday, Doran & Company, 1937.

Masters, Anthony. *Natural History of the Vampire,* 1st American ed. New York: G. P. Putnam's Sons, 1972.

Matossian, Mary Allerton Kilbourne. *Poisons of the Past: Molds, Epidemics, and History.* New Haven: Yale University Press, 1989.

Maybrick, Florence Elizabeth. *Mrs. Maybrick's Own Story: My Fifteen Lost Years.* New York: Funk & Wagnalls Company, 1904.

Mayhew, Henry. *London's Underworld.* Edited by Peter Quennell. Selections from Those That Will Not Work, the fourth volume of London Labour and the London Poor first published in 1862. London: Spring Books/Hamlyn Publishing Group, 1969.

McNeill, William H. *Plagues and Peoples.* Garden City, NY: Anchor Press/Doubleday, 1976.

Mencken, August, ed. *By the Neck: A Book of Hangings.* New York: Hastings House, 1942.

Miller, Jonathan. *The Body in Question.* New York: Random House, 1978.

Moenssens, Andre A. "The Origin of Legal Photography." *Fingerprint and Identification Magazine* (The Institute of Applied Science, Chicago), January 1962.

Moenssens, Andre A., and Fred E. Inbau. *Scientific Evidence in Criminal Cases,* 2nd ed. Mineola, NY: Foundation Press, 1978.

Morland, Nigel. *An Outline of Scientific Criminology.* London: Cassell and Company, 1951.

Morris, Richard B. *Fair Trial: Fourteen Who Stood Accused, from Anne Hutchinson to Alger Hiss—Kidd, Burr, Zenger, Spooner, Webster, etc.* New York: Alfred A. Knopf, 1952.

Mortimer, John, ed. *The Oxford Book of Villains.* Oxford: Oxford University Press, 1992.

Murray, Raymond C. *Evidence from the Earth: Forensic Geology and Criminal Investigation.* Missoula, MT: Mountain Press Publishing Company, 2004.

Myers, Eliab. *The Champion Text-Book on Embalming*, 4th ed. Springfield, OH: The Champion Chemical Company, 1902.

Nash, Jay Robert. *Look for the Woman: A Narrative Encyclopedia of Female Poisoners, Kidnappers, Thieves, Extortionists, Terrorists, Swindlers, and Spies from Elizabethan Times to the Present.* New York: M. Evans and Company, 1981.

———. *Murder, America: Homicide in the United States from the Revolution to the Present.* New York: Simon and Schuster, 1980.

Neil, Arthur Fowler. *Man-Hunters of Scotland Yard: The Recollections of Forty Years of a Detective's Life.* Garden City, NY: The Sun Dial Press, 1938.

Newark, Peter. *The Crimson Book of Highwaymen.* London: Jupiter Books, 1979.

Noguchi, Thomas T. *Coroner.* With Joseph DiMona. New York: Simon and Schuster, 1983.

Nohl, Johannes. *The Black Death: A Chronicle of the Plague.* Translated from the German by C. H. Clarke. New York: Harper and Brothers, 1924.

Nordon, Pierre. *Conan Doyle: A Biography.* Translated from the French by Francis Partridge. New York: Holt, Rinehart and Winston, 1967.

O'Brien, Kevin P., and Robert C. Sullivan. *Criminalistics: Theory and Practice.* Boston: Holbrook Press, 1976.

O'Donnell, Bernard. *The Old Bailey and Its Trials.* New York: The Macmillan Company, 1951.

O'Malley, Charles D., and John B. de C. M. Saunders. *Leonardo da Vinci on the Human Body: The Anatomical, Physiological, and Embryological Drawings of Leonardo da Vinci.* New York: Greenwich House, 1982.

Palmer, Thomas. *The Admirable Secrets of Physick and Chyrurgery.* Edited by Thomas Rogers Forbes. New Haven: Yale University Press, 1984.

Parry, Leonard A. *Some Famous Medical Trials*, 1st American ed. New York: Charles Scribner's Sons, 1928.

Parry, Leonard A., ed. *Trial of Dr. Smethurst.* Edinburgh: William Hodge & Company, 1931.

Paul, Philip. *Murder Under the Microscope: The Story of Scotland Yard's Forensic Science Laboratory.* London: Futura Publications, 1990.

Pearsall, Ronald. *Conan Doyle: A Biographical Solution.* New York: St. Martin's Press, 1977.

Pearson, Edmund. *Five Murders: With a Final Note on the Borden Case.* Garden City, NY: Doubleday, Doran & Company, 1928.

————. *Masterpieces of Murder: Together with an Original Essay on the Borden Case*. Edited by Gerald Gross. New York: Bonanza Books, 1963.

————. *More Studies in Murder*. New York: Harrison Smith & Robert Haas, 1936.

————. *Murder at Smutty Nose and Other Murders*. Garden City, NY: The Sun Dial Press, 1938.

————. *Studies in Murder*. New York: Modern Library, 1938.

Pearson, Edmund, ed. *The Trial of Lizzie Borden: An Abridgement of the Original Proceedings Together with Lizzie Borden's Inquest Testimony*. Amherst, MA: University of Massachusetts, 1974.

Pierce, R. V. *The People's Common Sense Medical Advisor; or Medicine Simplified*. Buffalo, NY: World's Dispensary Printing Office and Bindery, 1889.

Pinkerton, Allan. *Thirty Years a Detective: A Thorough and Comprehensive Exposé of Criminal Practices of All Grades and Classes*. Boston: Russell & Henderson, 1884.

Poe, Edgar Allen. *Tales of Mystery and Imagination*. New York: Tudor Publishing Company, 1933.

Polson, Cyril John, and D. J. Gee. *The Essentials of Forensic Medicine*. Oxford: Pergamon Press, 1973.

Porta, Giambattista della. *Natural Magick*. Edited by Derek J. Price. New York: Basic Books, 1959.

Porter, Edwin H. *The Fall River Tragedy: A History of the Borden Murders*. Amherst, MA: University of Massachusetts, 1973.

Potter, John Deane. *The Art of Hanging: The Fatal Gallows Tree in English History*, 1st American ed. South Brunswick, NJ: A. S. Barnes and Company, 1969.

Prendergast, Alan. *The Poison Tree: A True Story of Family Violence and Revenge*. New York: G. P. Putnam's Sons, 1986.

Quain, Richard, ed. *A Dictionary of Medicine: Including General Pathology, General Therapeutics, Hygiene, and Diseases Peculiar to Women and Children*, 12th ed. New York: D. Appleton and Company, 1890.

Radford, Edwin, and Mona A. Radford. *Encyclopaedia of Superstitions*. New York: The Philosophical Library, 1949.

Radin, Edward D. *Lizzie Borden: The Untold Story*. New York: Simon and Schuster, 1961.

————. *12 Against Crime*. New York: Collier Books, 1961.

Rae, Isobel. *Knox the Anatomist*. Edinburgh and London: Oliver & Boyd, 1964.

Rhodes, Henry T. F. *The Criminals We Deserve: A Survey of Some Aspects of Crime in the Modern World*. New York: Oxford University Press, 1937.

Robbins, Rossell Hope. *The Encyclopedia of Witchcraft and Demonology*. New York: Crown Publishers, 1959.

Ross Williamson, Hugh. *Historical Whodunits*. New York: The Macmillan Company, 1956.

Roughead, William. *Bad Companions*. New York: Duffield & Green, 1931.

———. *Enjoyment of Murder*. New York: Sheridan House, 1938.

———. *The Murderer's Companion*. New York: The Press of the Readers Club, 1941.

———. *Nothing But Murder*. New York: Sheridan House, 1946.

———, ed. *Burke and Hare*, 1st American ed. New York: The John Day Company, 1927.

———, ed. *Trial of Dr. Pritchard*. Glasgow: William Hodge & Company, 1906.

———, ed. *Trial of Jessie M'Lachlan*. Edinburgh and London: William Hodge & Company, 1950.

———, ed. *Trial of Oscar Slater*. Edinburgh: William Hodge & Company, 1915.

Rumbelow, Donald. *The Complete Jack the Ripper*. Boston: New York Graphic Society, 1975.

———. *I Spy Blue: The Police and Crime in the City of London from Elizabeth I to Victoria*. New York: St. Martin's Press, 1971.

St. Leger-Gordon, Ruth E. *Witchcraft and Folklore of Dartmoor*. New York: Bell Publishing Company, 1972.

Sandoe, James, ed. *Murder: Plain and Fanciful, with Some Milder Malefactions*. New York: Sheridan House, 1948.

Saunders, J. B. de C. M., and Charles D. O'Malley. *The Anatomical Drawings of Andreas Vesalius: With Annotations and Translations, a Discussion of the Plates and Their Background, Authorship, and Influence, and a Biographical Sketch of Vesalius*. New York: Bonanza Books, 1982.

Schama, Simon. *Dead Certainties: Unwarranted Speculations*. New York: Alfred A. Knopf, 1991.

Scot, Reginald. *The Discoverie of Witchcraft*. New York: Dover Publications, 1972.

Scott, Harold. *Scotland Yard*. New York: Random House, 1955.

Selzer, Richard. *Mortal Lessons: Notes on the Art of Surgery*. New York: Simon and Schuster, 1976.

Semple, Amand. *Essentials of Forensic Medicine: Toxicology and Hygiene*. Philadelphia: W. B. Saunders, n.d., ca. 1892.

Seymour, Jacqueline. *Mushrooms and Toadstools*. New York: Crescent Books, 1978.

Shakespeare, William. *Works of William Shakespeare Gathered into One Volume*, The Shakespeare Head Press ed. New York: Oxford University Press, 1938.

Shew, E. Spencer. *A Second Companion to Murder: A Dictionary of Death by the Knife, the Dagger, the Razor . . . , 1900–1950,* 1st American ed. New York: Alfred A. Knopf, 1962.

Simpson, Keith. *Forty Years of Murder: An Autobiography.* New York: Charles Scribner's Sons, 1979.

———. *Sherlock Holmes on Medicine and Science.* New York: Magico Magazine, 1983.

Singer, Isidore, ed. *The Jewish Encyclopedia,* 12 vols. New York: Funk and Wagnalls Company, 1916.

Singer, Kurt, ed. *My Strangest Case: By Police Chiefs of the World.* Garden City, NY: Doubleday and Company, 1958.

Small, A. E. *Small's Pocket Manual of Homeopathic Practice,* 6th ed. Edited and abridged by Jacob F. Sheek. New York: William Radde, 1864.

Smith, Gene, and Jayne Barry Smith, eds. *The Police Gazette.* New York: Simon and Schuster, 1972.

Smith, Sydney. *Mostly Murder.* New York: David McKay Company, 1959.

Söderman, Harry. *Policeman's Lot: A Criminalist's Gallery of Friends and Felons.* New York: Funk & Wagnalls Company, 1956.

Söderman, Harry, and John J. O'Connell. *Modern Criminal Investigation.* New York: Funk and Wagnalls Company, 1940.

Sparrow, Gerald. *The Great Assassins.* New York: Arco Publishing, 1969.

———. *Vintage Victorian Murder.* New York: Hart Publishing Company, 1972.

Starobinski, Jean. *A History of Medicine.* Translated from the French by Bernard C. Swift. New York: Hawthorn Books, 1964.

Stashower, Daniel. *Teller of Tales: The Life of Arthur Conan Doyle.* New York: Henry Holt and Company, 1999.

Steuart, A. Francis, ed. *Trial of Mary Queen of Scots.* Toronto: Canada Law Book Company, 1923.

Stevens, Serita Deborah. *Deadly Doses: A Writer's Guide to Poison.* With Anne Klarner. Cincinnati: Writer's Digest Books, 1990.

Still, Charles E. *Styles in Crime.* New York: J. B. Lippincott Company, 1938.

Sullivan, Robert. *The Disappearance of Dr. Parkman.* Boston: Little Brown and Company, 1971.

———. *Goodbye Lizzie Borden.* Brattleboro, VT: The Stephen Greene Press, 1974.

Summers, Montague. *The History of Witchcraft and Demonology.* New York: Dorset Press, 1987.

———. *The Vampire in Europe.* New Hyde Park, NY: University Books, 1961.

———. *The Werewolf.* New York: Bell Publishing Company, 1966.

Symons, Julian. *Bloody Murder: From the Detective Story to the Crime Novel.* New York: Mysterious Press, 1992.

———. *Conan Doyle: Portrait of an Artist*. New York: Mysterious Press, 1979.

———. *Crime: A Pictorial History of Crime*. New York: Bonanza Books, 1966.

Taylor, Alfred Swaine. *A Manual of Medical Jurisprudence*, 7th American ed. Philadelphia: Henry C. Lea, 1873.

Thomas, Dylan. *The Doctor and the Devils*. New York: Time Incorporated, 1964.

Thomas, Ronald R. *Detective Fiction and the Rise of Forensic Science*. Cambridge: Cambridge University Press, 1999.

Thompson, C. J. S. *Poison Mysteries in History, Romance and Crime*. London: Scientific Press, 1923.

Thomson, Basil. *The Story of Scotland Yard*. Garden City, NY: Doubleday, Doran, and Company, 1936.

Thomson, Helen. *Murder at Harvard*. Boston: Houghton Mifflin Company, 1971.

Thorwald, Jürgen. *The Century of the Detective*. Translated from the German by Richard Winston and Clara Winston. New York: Harcourt, Brace & World, 1965.

———. *The Century of the Surgeon*. New York: Pantheon Books, 1957.

———. *Crime and Science: The New Frontier in Criminology*. Translated from the German by Richard Winston and Clara Winston. New York: Harcourt, Brace & World, 1967.

———. *Science and Secrets of Early Medicine: Egypt, Mesopotamia, India, China, Mexico, Peru*. Translated from the German by Richard Winston and Clara Winston. New York: Harcourt, Brace & World, 1963.

———. *The Triumph of Surgery*. Translated from the German by Richard Winston and Clara Winston. New York: Pantheon Books, 1960.

Tidy, Charles Meymott. *Legal Medicine*, 2 vols. New York: William Wood & Company, 1882.

Tilton, Eleanor M. *Amiable Autocrat: A Biography of Dr. Oliver Wendell Holmes*. New York: Henry Schuman, 1947.

Toobin, Jeffrey. *The Run of His Life: The People v. O. J. Simpson*. New York: Random House, 1996.

Topinard, Paul. *Anthropology*. Translated from the French by Robert T. H. Bartley. London: Chapman and Hall, 1890.

Tracy, Patricia, ed. "The Borden Family of Fall River: 1638–1900, A Documentary History." Reference material reproduced for History 186. Amherst, MA: University of Massachusetts, 1973.

———. "Fall River Massachusetts: A Documentary History, Part One." Reference material reproduced for History 186. Amherst, MA: University of Massachusetts, 1973.

Train, Arthur. *Courts and Criminals.* New York: Charles Scribner's Sons, 1925.

Trall, R. T. *The Hydropathic Encyclopedia: A System of Hydropathy and Hygiene.* New York: Fowler and Wells, 1855.

Tullett, Tom. *Clues to Murder: Famous Forensic Murder Cases of Professor J. M. Cameron.* London: The Bodley Head, 1986.

———. *Murder Squad: Famous Cases of Scotland Yard's Murder Squad.* London: Granada Publishing, 1981.

Turner, E. S. *Call the Doctor: A Social History of Medical Men.* New York: St. Martin's Press, 1959.

———. *May It Please Your Lordship.* London: The Quality Book Club, 1972.

Tussaud, John Theodore. *The Romance of Madame Tussaud's.* New York: George H. Doran Company, 1920.

Ubelaker, Douglas, and Henry Scammell. *Bones: A Forensic Detective's Casebook.* New York: Harper Collins, 1992.

Underwood, Peter. *Jack the Ripper: One Hundred Years of Mystery.* London: Javelin Books, 1988.

van der Meulen, Louis J. "False Fingerprints: A New Aspect." *Journal of Criminal Law, Criminology, and Police Science* 40 (May–June 1955).

Vaughan, Victor C. *A Doctor's Memories.* Indianapolis: The Bobbs-Merrill Company, 1926.

Vidocq, Eugène François. *Memoirs of Vidocq: As a Convict, Spy, and Agent of the French Police.* London: 1859.

Wagner, E. J. "History, Homicide, and the Healing Hand," in "Medicine, Crime, and Punishment." Special Issue, *The Lancet* 364 (2004): 2–3.

Warren, Ira, and A. E. Small. *Warren's Household Physician: For Physicians, Families, Mariners, Miners; Being a Brief Description, in Plain Language of Diseases of Men, Women and Children.* Revised by William Thorndike and J. Heber Smith. Boston: Bradley & Woodruff, 1891.

Webster, John White, ed. *A Manual of Chemistry on the Basis of Professor Brande's: Containing the Principal Facts of the Science, Arranged in the Order in Which They Are Discussed and Illustrated in the Lectures at Harvard University, N.E.,* 2nd ed. Boston: Richardson and Lord, 1829.

Wells, Gary L., and Elizabeth Loftus, eds. *Eyewitness Testimony: Psychological Perspectives.* Cambridge: Cambridge University Press, 1984.

Wells, Samuel R. *How to Read Character: A New Illustrated Hand-Book of Phrenology and Physiognomy for Students and Examiners with a Descriptive Chart.* New York: Samuel R. Wells, 1873.

Wensley, Frederick Porter. *Forty Years of Scotland Yard: The Record of a Lifetime's Service in the Criminal Investigation Department.* Garden City, NY: Garden City Publishing Company, 1931.

Whibley, Charles. *A Book of Scoundrels*. New York: The Macmillan Company, 1897.

Wilbur, C. Keith. *Revolutionary Medicine, 1700–1800*. Chester, CT: The Globe Pequot Press, 1983.

Willemse, Cornelius W. *Behind the Green Lights*. In collaboration with George J. Lemmer and Jack Kofoed. New York: Alfred A. Knopf, 1931.

Williams, John. *Suddenly at the Priory*. London: William Heinemann, 1957.

Wilson, Colin, and Donald Seaman. *The Encyclopedia of Modern Murder, 1962–1982*, 1st American ed. New York: G. P. Putnam's Sons, 1985.

Wilson, Colin, and Patricia Pitman. *Encyclopedia of Murder*, 1st American ed. New York: G. P. Putnam's Sons, 1962.

Wilson, Keith D. *Cause of Death: A Writer's Guide to Death, Murder, and Forensic Medicine*. Cincinnati: Writer's Digest Book, 1992.

Winn, Dilys. *Murder Ink: The Mystery Reader's Companion*. New York: Workman Publishing, 1977.

Winslow, Jacques-Bénigne. *Exposition Anatomique de la Structure du Corps Humain*, vol. 1. Amsterdam: chez Emanuel Tourneisen, 1754.

Wood, George B. *A Treatise on Therapeutics and Pharmacology or Materia Medica*, 2nd ed., 2 vols. Philadelphia: J. B. Lippincott & Co., 1860.

Woodruff, Douglas. *The Tichborne Claimant: A Victorian Mystery*. New York: Farrar, Straus, and Cudahy, 1957.

Zigrosser, Carl. *Medicine and the Artist: 137 Great Prints, Selected with Commentary*. New York: Dover Publications, 1970.

Zilboorg, Gregory. *The Medical Man and the Witch During the Renaissance: The Hideyo Noguchi Lectures*. Baltimore, MD: The Johns Hopkins Press, 1935.

INTERVIEWS

Dal Cortivo, Leo, Ph.D. (head of toxicology, director of laboratories, Suffolk County Office of the Medical Examiner). Interviewed by the author, 1983.

Davis, Joseph, M.D. (chief emeritus, Miami-Dade County Medical Examiner Department). Interviewed by the author, 1993.

Ehrenreich, Theodore, M.D. (late, head of clinical pathology and laboratories, Lutheran Medical Center; consultant to New York City Office of the Medical Examiner). Discussions with the author, 1973–1980.

Helpern, Milton, M.D. (late, chief medical examiner, New York City). Interviewed by the author, 1972 and 1973.

Menchel, Sigmund, M.D. (former chief medical examiner, Suffolk County Office of the Medical Examiner). Interview and discussions with the author, 1983–1990.

Internet Resources (Web sites listed by site name)

Casebook: Jack the Ripper. Produced by Stephen P. Ryder and Johnno. http://www.casebook.org/

Center for History of Medicine, Harvard University Countway Library of Medicine. http://www.countway.harvard.edu/rarebooks/

Forensic-Evidence.com. Andre A. Moenssens, editor. http://www .forensic-evidence.com/

Forensic Medicine Archives Project. University of Glasgow. http:// www.fmap.archives.gla.ac.uk/

Hypertext Scholarship in American Studies. Center for History & New Media (CHNM) at George Mason University. http://chnm.gmu .edu/aq/—including "Hearsay of the Sun: Photography, Identity, and the Law of Evidence in Nineteenth-Century American Courts" by Thomas Thurston (including footnotes with many links to other related online resources) at http://chnm.gmu.edu/aq/photos/

The Old Operating Theatre Museum and Herb Garret (London). Cultural Heritage Resources. http://www.thegarret.org.uk/

The Victorian Dictionary: The Social History of Victorian London. Compiled by Lee Jackson. http://www.victorianlondon.org/

Zeno's Forensic Site. Zeno Geradts. http://forensic.to/

Index

"Adventure of Black Peter, The," 151
"Adventure of Shoscombe Old Place,
  The," 27, 149–150
"Adventure of the Blue Carbuncle,
  The," 191
"Adventure of the Bruce Partington
  Plans, The," 174
"Adventure of the Cardboard Box,
  The," 198
"Adventure of the Copper Beeches,
  The," 198
"Adventure of the Creeping Man, The,"
  27, 108
"Adventure of the Dancing Men, The,"
  58, 119
"Adventure of the Devil's Foot, The,"
  41–42, 201
"Adventure of the Empty House, The,"
  119, 212
"Adventure of the Golden Pince-Nez,
  The," 88, 89
"Adventure of the Lion's Mane, The,"
  31, 39
"Adventure of the Missing Three
  Quarter, The," 26
"Adventure of the Norwood Builder,
  The," 88, 89, 91, 104, 155
"Adventure of the Red Circle, The,"
  155–156
"Adventure of the Six Napoleons, The,"
  167
"Adventure of the Speckled Band, The,"
  31, 41–42, 43–44, 51, 87
"Adventure of the Sussex Vampire,
  The," 153–154, 201–202, 203, 204,
  206
"Adventure of the Three Gables, The,"
  109
anatomical studies, 4–6, 11, 16
animals, 18–29, 31, 37, 89–90, 194
  blood analysis and, 185–187, 189
  as crime accomplices, 87, 108–109
  as forensic aids, 28–29
  mutilations of, 75, 84–86, 189
  poisonous substances from, 43, 45

superstitions about, 25
  See also insects
anonymous letters, 164–165, 166
anthropometry, 98–99, 103, 105, 106,
  163
antidotes, ineffective, 46
anti-Semitism, 12–15, 83, 162, 194
Anubis (Egyptian god), 25, 29
Aqua Tofana, 47–48
Armstrong, Neil, 144
arsenic, 43, 45–46, 213
  tests for, 48–49, 51, 52–53, 55–56
autopsy, 11–16, 37
  anatomical dissection vs., 7
  description of, 11
  at home, 179, 189–190
  pathologist's hazards from, 15–16
  tools for, 16, 190

Bahamas, 156
Baker, Cecil, 76
Baker Street, 61, 75
Ballets Russes, 150
ballistics, 16, 119–132, 145, 210–211
  three specialized areas, 131
Balthazard, Victor, 124
Balzac, Honoré de, 65, 66
Bankes, Isabella, 51, 52–54
Barlow, Elizabeth and Kenneth, 44–45
Barry, James, 74–75
Bartholin, Caspar, 11
Bartlett, Adelaide, 42
Baskervilles, 18–19, 193
Bay Shore, Long Island, 88–89
Beers, Katie, 88–89
bees, 39
beetles, 37, 38
Belki, Johannes, 14
Bell, John, 4
Bell, Joseph, 54, 55–56
Belper, Lord, 106
Bemis, George, 160
Bergeret, M., 36
Bernhardt, Sarah, 62
Bertillon, Alphonse, 97–98, 103,
  104–105, 106, 109
  Dreyfus case and, 162–163, 164, 212
Bertillon, Louis Adolphe, 97, 98
bertillonage, 99, 103, 105, 106